TURNER'S SKETCHES AND DRAWINGS

THE PASS OF FAÏDO, ST. GOTHARD

TURNER'S SKETCHES AND DRAWINGS

A. J. FINBERG

Introduction by Lawrence Gowing

SCHOCKEN BOOKS · NEW YORK

First published 1910

First SCHOCKEN edition 1968

Copyright © 1968 by Schocken Books Inc.

Library of Congress Catalog Card No. 67-26986

Manufactured in the United States of America

CONTENTS

PAGE

LIST OF PLATES, ... ix

Introduction to the 1968 Edition, ... xvii

INTRODUCTORY, ... 1

The nature of our subject-matter, ... 1
The raw material of art, ... 2
The character of our subject-matter, as embryonic forms of artistic
    expression, prescribes our method of study, . . . 2
Our difficulties of description and analysis, ... 3
The separation of Art-criticism from Aesthetic, . . . 3
Eight aspects of Turner's genius, ... 4

CHAPTER

I. SEVEN YEARS' APPRENTICESHIP—1787-1793, . . . 6

Turner's first drawings, ... 6
'St. Vincent's Tower,' 6
Copies and imitations, ... 8
His debt to art, ... 10
Work with Mr. Hardwick, ... 10
Oxford sketches, ... 11
'Radley Hall,' 12
Working from the Antique, ... 14
The Bristol sketch-book, ... 14
End of the apprenticeship, ... 16

II. THE TOPOGRAPHICAL DRAUGHTSMAN—1793-1796, . . 17

Welsh tour of 1793, ... 17
'St. Anselm's Chapel,' 18
Turner's topographical rivals, ... 18
Midland tour of 1794, ... 20
Limitations of topographical and antiquarian art, . . . 22
'Interior of a Cottage,' 23
Light and Shade as a means of expression, ... 24
The sketch-books of 1795 and their contents, . . . 25
'High Force of Tees' or 'Fall of Melincourt'? . . . 27

TURNER'S SKETCHES AND DRAWINGS

CHAPTER   PAGE

III. THE SUBLIME—1797-1802, ... 29

  Change from pure outline to light and shade, . . . 29
  'Ewenny Priory,' 30
  Contrast between 'Ewenny' (1797) and 'Llandaff Cathedral' (1796), 30
  Transition from Objectivity to Subjectivity, . . . 31
  Growth of taste for the Sublime, ... 31
  There are no sublime objects, but only objects of sublime feeling, 32
  Therefore no guidance but from Art, ... 32
  The Wilson tradition, ... 33
  The two currents in Turner's work at this period—
    (a) Study of Nature ;
    (b) Study of the Wilson tradition, ... 33
  In the 1797 sketches these two currents are kept distinct, . 34
  The North of England tour (1797) and its record, . . 34
  'Studies for Pictures : Copies of Wilson,' . . . 36
  The two currents begin to coalesce, . . . 37
  The origin of 'Jason,' 38
  Scotch tour (1801), ... 38
  Swiss tour (1802), ... 39

IV. THE SEA PAINTER—1802-1809, ... 41

  Contrast between Marine painting and the Sublime, . . 41
  Turner's first sea-pieces, ... 42
  The 'Bridgewater Sea-piece,' 42
  'Meeting of the Thames and Medway,' 46
  'Our landing at Calais—nearly swampt,' 48
  'Fishermen upon a Lee Shore,' 48
  The Dunbar and Guisborough Shore sketch-book, . . 48
  'The Shipwreck,' 49
  The mouth of the Thames, ... 51
  'Sheerness' and the 'Death of Nelson,' 53

V. 'SIMPLE NATURE'—1808-1813, ... 55

  The works of this period an important yet generally neglected
    aspect of Turner's art, ... 55
  Turner's classification of 'Pastoral' as distinguished from 'Elegant
    Pastoral,' 56
  The Arcadian idyll of the mid-eighteenth century, . . 57
  The first 'Pastoral' subjects in 'Liber,' 57
  The 'Windmill and Lock,' 57

CONTENTS

CHAPTER   PAGE

Events connected with the development of Turner's deeper and
more solemn conception of the poetry of rural life, .   .   58
An attempt to define the mood of pictures like the ' Frosty
Morning,'   64
The work of art is nothing less than its full significance, .   .   67
Distinction between mood and character, ...   68

VI. THE ' LIBER STUDIORUM,'   72

Object of this chapter, ...   72
The first ' Liber' drawings were made at W. F. Wells's cottage
at Knockholt, Kent, ...   73
' Bridge and Cows,'   73
Development of the so-called ' Flint Castle,'   .   .   75
' Basle,'   78
' Little Devil's Bridge,'   80
' London from Greenwich,'   80
' Kirkstall Crypt,'   81
Etchings of the so-called ' Raglan Castle ' and ' Source of the
Arveron,'   82
Suggestion for the better exhibition of the ' Liber Studiorum '
drawings, ...   83

VII. THE SPLENDOUR OF SUCCESS, OR 'WHAT YOU WILL'—
1813-1830, ...   84

Survey of the ground we have covered,   .   .   .   84
The training of Turner's sympathies by the Poets,   .   .   85
The limits of artistic beauty, ...   86
The predominantly sensuous bent of Turner's genius,   .   86
The parting of the ways, ...   87
The influence of the Academy and society   .   .   .   88
Turner's first visit to Italy, ...   89
The Naturalistic fallacy, ...   95
Turner's work for the engraver, ...   97

VIII. MENTAL AND PHYSICAL DECAY, AND THE ORIGIN OF
IMPRESSIONISM—1830-1845,   .   .   .   116

Mental Characteristics of the 1815-1830 period, .   .   116
Their influence on form and colour,   .   .   .   117
Colour enrichment a general characteristic of Romantic art,   .   118
What further development is required to give the transition to
Impressionism ?   118
Turner's first Impressionistic work,   .   .   .   119
Vagueness as a means of expression,   .   .   .   119

TURNER'S SKETCHES AND DRAWINGS

CHAPTER   PAGE

Two ways of painting one's impressions.   Turner's earlier way
    contrasted with the modern Impressionistic way,   .   .   119
The change after 1830 is it a change in terms of sight or of
    thought—visual or mental?   120
The content of Turner's later work, ...   120
Relation of Turner's later work to Impressionism defined, .   .   121
The historical development of Turner's later manner,   .   .   126
The Petworth sketches, ...   126
Discovery of the artistic value of the Indeterminate,   .   .   128
'Rivers of France,'   129
Venetian sketches, ...   131
Swiss and Rhine sketches, ...   134
The end, ...   135

IX. CONCLUSION, ...   136

The distinction between Art-criticism and Aesthetic,   .   .   136
The aim of this chapter, ...   137
Art and physical fact, ...   137
The 'common-sense' conception of landscape art as evidence of fact,   137
Mr. Ruskin's treatment of the relation of Art and Nature, .   .   138
His confusion of Nature and Mind, ...   140
Art as a form of communication implies that the dualism of Nature
    and Mind is overcome, ...   143
What does Art represent?   144
An individualised psychical content present to the mind of the artist,   145
Classification of Turner's sketches and studies from the point of
    view of their logical content, ...   146
The assertions in a work of art do not directly qualify the
    ordinary real world, but an imaginary world specially con-
    structed for the artist's purpose, ...   150
The ideal of complete definition, ...   151
Yet the content must determine the form, ...   151
Plea for a dynamic study of Artistic form,   .   .   .   153

INDEX, ...   155

LIST OF PLATES

All the Drawings are in the National Gallery, unless otherwise specified.
(The numbers, etc., in brackets refer to the position of the Drawings in the Official Inventory.)

The Pass of Faïdo, St. Gothard, . . . *Frontispiece*
Water-Colour. 1844. (CCCLXIV. 209.)

PLATE   PAGES

I. St. Vincent's Tower, Naples, ... *Between* 6-7
Water-Colour. About 1787. (I.E.)

II. Central Portion of an Aquatint by Paul Sandby, after Fabris,
entitled 'Part of Naples, with the Ruin'd Tower of
St. Vincent.' Published 1st Jan. 1778, . . *Between* 6-7

III. Radley Hall: South Front, ... *Facing* 11
Water-Colour. About 1789. (III. D.)

IV. View on the Avon, from Cook's Folly, ... *Facing* 14
Water-Colour and Ink. About 1791. (VI. 24)

V. Lincoln Cathedral, ... *Between* 20-21
Water-Colour, exhibited at Royal Academy, 1795.
In Print Room, British Museum.

VI. Lincoln Cathedral, from the South-west, . . *Between* 20-21
Pencil. 1794. (XXI. 0.)

VII. Pony and Wheelbarrow, ... *Facing* 23
Pencil. 1794. (XXI. 27a)

VIII. Melincourt Fall, Vale of Neath, ... *Facing* 26
Pencil, part in Water-Colour. 1795. (XXVI. 8)

IX. Interior of Ripon Cathedral: North Transept, . . *Facing* 28
Pencil. 1797. (XXXV. 6)

X. Conway Falls, near Bettws-y-Coed, ... *Facing* 30
Water-Colour. About 1798. (XXXVIII. 71.)

XI. Conway Castle, ... *Facing* 32
Pencil. About 1798. (XXXVIII. 50a)

XII. Ruined Castle on Hill, ... *Facing* 34
Water-Colour. About 1798. (L. K.)

ix

TURNER'S SKETCHES AND DRAWINGS

PLATE   PAGES

XIII. Study of Fallen Trees, ... *Facing* 36
    Water-Colour. About 1798. (XLII. 18-19.)

XIV. Caernarvon Castle, ... *Facing* 37
    Pencil. 1799. (XLVI. 51.)

XV. Cassiobury : North-west View, ... *Facing* 38
    Pencil. About 1800. (XLVII. 41.)

XVI. Blair's Hut on the Montanvert and Mer de Glace.
    Sketch for the Water-Colour in the Farnley Collection, *Facing* 39
    Water-Colour. 1802. (LXXV. 22.)

XVII. Study for the ' Bridgewater Sea-piece,'   .   .   . *Facing* 42
    Pen and ink, wash, and white chalk on blue paper. About 1801.
    (LXXXI. 122-123.)

XVIII. Study of a Barge with Sails Set, ... *Facing* 43
    Pen and ink, wash, and white chalk on blue paper. About 1802.
    (LXXXI. 138-139.)

XIX. Fishermen launching Boat in a rough Sea,   .   . *Facing* 44
    Pen and ink and wash. About 1802. (LXVIII. 3.)

XX. Study for ' Sun rising through Vapour,'   .   .   . *Facing* 45
    Black and white chalk on blue paper. About 1804. (LXXXI. 40.)

XXI. Study for ' The Shipwreck,'   .   .   .   . *Facing* 47
    Pen and ink and wash. About 1805. (LXXXVII. 16.)

XXII. Men-of-War's Boats fetching Provisions (1),   .   . *Facing* 49
    Pencil. About 1808. (XCIX. 18.)

XXIII. Men-of-War's Boats fetching Provisions (2),   .   . *Facing* 50
    Pencil. About 1808. (XCIX. 22.)

XXIV. ' The Inscrutable,' .   .   .   .   .   . *Facing* 52
    Pencil. About 1808. (CI. 18.)

XXV. Sketch for ' Hedging and Ditching,'   .   .   *Between* 56-57
    Pencil. About 1807. (C. 47.)

XXVI. ' Hedging and Ditching,' .   .   .   .   *Between* 56-57
    Wash drawing in Sepia for ' Liber Studiorum.' About
    1808. (CXVII. W.)

XXVII. (*a*) Mill on the Grand Junction Canal, near Hanwell,
    Pencil. About 1809. (CXIV. 72a-73.)

    (*b*) ' Windmill and Lock,'   .   .   .   *Facing* 61
    Engraving published in ' Liber Studiorum,' 1st June, 1811
    (R. 27.)

LIST OF PLATES

PLATE

PAGES

XXVIII. Whalley Bridge and Village, ... *Facing* 62
Pencil. About 1808. (CIII. 8.)

XXIX. Whalley Bridge. Sketch for the Picture exhibited at the
Royal Academy. 1811. (Now in Lady Wantage's
Collection), ... *Facing* 63
Pencil. About 1808. (CIII. 6.)

XXX. London, from Greenwich Park, ... *Facing* 64
Pencil. About 1809. (CXX. H.)

XXXI. Petworth House, from the Lake, ... *Facing* 65
Pencil. About 1809. (CIX. 4.)

XXXII. Petworth House, from the Park, ... *Facing* 66
Pencil. About 1809. (CIX. 5.)

XXXIII. Cockermouth Castle, ... *Facing* 67
Pencil. About 1809. (CIX. 15.)

XXXIV. Landscape near Plymouth, ... *Facing* 68
Pencil. About 1812. (CXXXI. 96.)

XXXV. (a) Sandycombe Lodge and Grounds. .
Pen and Ink. About 1811. (CXIV. 73a-74.)
Facing 69
(b) Plan of Garden : Sandycombe Lodge, .
Pen and Ink. About 1812. (CXXVII. 21a.)

XXXVI. Scene on the French Coast, . . . *Between* 74-75
Sepia. About 1806. (CXVI. C.)

XXXVII. Scene on the French Coast. Generally known as 'Flint
Castle : Smugglers,' . . . *Between* 74-75
Print of etching, washed with Sepia. About 1807. (CXVI. D.)

XXXVIII. Juvenile Tricks, ... *Facing* 78
Sepia. About 1808. (CXVI. Z.)

XXXIX. Berry Pomeroy Castle. Generally known as 'Raglan
Castle,' . . . . . . *Facing* 79
Sepia. About 1813. (CXVIII. E.)

XL. The Alcove, Isleworth. Generally known as 'Twickenham—Pope's Villa,' etc., ... *Facing* 80
Sepia. About 1816. (CXVIII. I.)

XLI. Sheep-Washing, Windsor, ... *Facing* 81
Sepia. About 1818. (CXVIII. Q.)

XLII. View of a River, from a Terrace. Sometimes called
'Macon,' . . . . . . *Facing* 82
Sepia. About 1818. (CXVIII. Y.)

xi

TURNER'S SKETCHES AND DRAWINGS

PLATE

PAGES

XLIII. Crowhurst, Sussex, ... *Facing* 83
Sepia. About 1818. (CXVIII. R.)

XLIV. Kirkby Lonsdale Bridge, ... *Facing* 84
Pencil. About 1816. (CXLVIII. 4c-5.)

XLV. Raby Castle, ... *Facing* 85
Pencil. About 1817. (CLVI. 16a-17.)

XLVI. Raby Castle, ... *Facing* 86
Pencil. About 1817. (CLVI. 19a-20.)

XLVII. Raby Castle, ... *Facing* 87
Pencil. About 1817. (CLVI. 18a-19.)

XLVIII. Looking up the Grand Canal, Venice, from near the
Accademia di Belle Arti, ... *Facing* 90
Pencil. 1819. (CLXXV. 70a-71.)

XLIX. St. Mark's, Venice, with part of the Ducal Palace, . *Facing* 91
Pencil. 1819. (CLXXV. 45.)

L. The Piazzetta, Venice, looking towards Isola di S. Giorgio
Maggiore, ... *Facing* 92
Pencil. 1819. (CLXXV. 46a.)

LI. Rome, from Monte Mario, ... *Facing* 93
Pencil and Water-Colour. 1819. (CLXXXIX. 33.)

LII. Rome, from the Vatican, ... *Facing* 94
Pen and ink and Chinese white on grey. 1819. (CLXXXIX. 41.)

LIII. Trajan's Column, in the Forum of Trajan, . . *Facing* 95
Pencil. 1819. (CLXXXVIII. 48.)

LIV. Study of Plants, Weeds, etc., ... *Facing* 96
Pencil. About 1823. (CCV. 1a.)

LV. (*a*) Watchet, Somersetshire, ...
Pencil. About 1811. (CXXIII. 170a.)

(*b*) Watchet, Somersetshire, ... *Facing* 100
Engraving published in 'The Southern Coast,', 1st April,
1820.

LVI. (*a*) Boscastle, Cornwall, ...
Pencil. About 1811. (CXXIII. 182.)

(*b*) Boscastle, Cornwall, ... *Facing* 101
Engraving published in 'The Southern Coast,' 10th March,
1825.

LVII. Hornby Castle, from Tatham Church, . . *Between* 102-103
Pencil. About 1816. (CXLVII. 41a-42.)

xii

PLATE   PAGES

LVIII. Hornby Castle, from Tatham Church,   .   .   *Between* 102-103
        Engraving, from the Water-Colour in the Victoria and Albert
        Museum, published in Whitaker's 'Richmondshire,'
        June, 1822.

LIX. (*a*) Heysham, with Black Combe, Coniston Old Man,
        Helvellyn, etc., in the distance, .   .
        Pencil. About 1816. (CXLVII. 40a-41.)
                                       Facing 104
  (*b*) Heysham and Cumberland Mountains,   .
        Engraving published in Whitaker's 'Richmondshire,' 22nd
        August, 1822.

LX. (*a*) Edinburgh, from Calton Hill,   .   .   .
        Pencil. 1818. (CLXVII. 39a.)

  (*b*) Edinburgh, from Calton Hill,   .   .   .
        Engraving published in Scott's 'Provincial Antiquities
        of Scotland,' 1st November, 1820.   *Between*
                                          106-107
  (*c*) Edinburgh, from Calton Hill,   .   .   .
        Pencil. 1818. (CLXVII. 40.)

  (*d*) Figures on Calton Hill, ...
        Pencil. 1818. (CLXVII. 40a.)

LXI. (*a*) Borthwick Castle, ...
        Pencil. 1818. (CLXVII. 76.)
                                       Facing 107
  (*b*) Borthwick Castle, ...
        Engraving published in Scott's 'Provincial Antiquities of
        Scotland,' 2nd April, 1819.

LXII. (*a*) Rochester, ...
        Pencil. About 1821. (CXCIX. 18.)
                                     Between
  (*b*) Rochester, ...   108-109
        Pencil. About 1821. (CXCIX. 21.)

LXIII. Rochester on the River Medway,   .   .   *Between* 108-109
        Water-Colour. About 1822. (CCVIII. w.)

LXIV. Bolton Abbey, ...   *Between* 110-111
        Pencil. About 1815. (CXXXIV. 81-82.)

LXV. Bolton Abbey, ...   *Between* 110-111
        Engraving published in 'Picturesque Views in England and
        Wales,' 1827.

LXVI. (*a*) Colchester, ...
        Pencil. About 1824. (CCIX. 6a.)
                                     Between
  (*b*) Colchester, ...   110-111
        Pencil. About 1824. (CCIX. 7a.)

xiii

PLATE   PAGES

LXVII. Colchester, Essex, ... *Between* 110-111
    Engraving, published in ' Picturesque Views in England and
    Wales,' 1827.

LXVIII. Stamford, Lincolnshire, ... *Between* 112-113
    Pencil. 1797. (XXXIV. 86.)

LXIX. Stamford, Lincolnshire, ... *Between* 112-113
    Engraving published in ' Picturesque Views in England and
    Wales,' 1830.

LXX. (*a*) Tynemouth Priory, ...
    Pencil, with part in Water-Colour, 1797. (XXXIV. 35.)

    (*b*) Tynemouth, Northumberland,   .   . *Facing* 113
    Engraving, published in ' Picturesque Views in Eng-
    land and Wales,' 1831.

LXXI. Bemerside Tower, ... *Between* 118-119
    Pencil. About 1831. (CCLXVII. 82a.)

LXXII. Bemerside Tower, ... *Between* 118-119
    Engraving published in Scott's ' Poetical Works ' (Cadell),
    1834.

LXXIII. Men chatting round Fireplace : Petworth House,   *Between* 122-123
    Water-Colour. About 1830. (CCXLIV. 82.)

LXXIV. Teasing the Donkey : Petworth,   .   .   . *Between* 122-123
    Water-Colour. About 1830. (CCXLIV. 97.)

LXXV. Honfleur, ... *Facing* 126
    Water-Colour. About 1830. (CCLIX. 15.)

LXXVI. Country Town on Stream, ... *Facing* 127
    Water-Colour. About 1830. (CCLIX. 16.)

LXXVII. Sheep in the Trench, ... *Facing* 128
    Water-Colour. About 1830. (CCLIX. 17.)

LXXVIII. Shipping on the Riva degli Schiavone,   .   . *Facing* 129
    Water-Colour. About 1839. (CCCXVI. 20.)

LXXIX. The Approach to Venice : Sunset,   .   . *Facing* 132
    Water-Colour. About 1839. (CCCXVI. 16.)

LXXX. Riva degli Schiavone, from near the Public Gardens,   *Facing* 133
    Water-Colour. About 1839. (CCCXVI. 21.)

LXXXI. Freiburg : The Descent from the Hotel de Ville, .   *Facing* 134
    Water-Colour. About 1841. (CCCXXXV. 14.)

LIST OF PLATES

PLATE   PAGES

LXXXII. Ruined Castle on Rock, ...   *Facing* 135
              Water-Colour. About 1841. (CCCXXXIX. 5.)

LXXXIII. Village and Castle on the Rhine, . . .   *Facing* 140
              Water-Colour. About 1844. (CCCXLIX. 22.)

LXXXIV. The Via Mala, ...   *Facing* 141
              Water-Colour. About 1844. (CCCLXIV. 362.)

LXXXV. On the Rhine, ...   *Facing* 148
              Water-Colour. 1844. (CCCXLIX. 20.)

LXXXVI. Baden, looking North, ...   *Facing* 149
              Water-Colour. 1844. (CCCXLIX. 14.)

LXXXVII. Lucerne : Evening, ...   *Facing* 152
              Water-Colour. 1844. (CCCXLIV. 324.)

XV

Introduction to the 1968 Edition

WHATEVER it is that criticism does for art, the service is rarely as direct or as informative as critics hope. It is far easier to see what criticism owes to a painter like Turner than to discern any debt of his to the multitude of critics. Turner cut so grand a figure in the imaginative landscape of his time that hardly a writer could remain unaffected. The unremitting brilliance, the continuous and dazzling performance of the career, the infectious touch of rhetoric—everything about Turner excited people to measure themselves incongruously against him. The effect on painters was disastrous, but writers were on the whole more fortunate. Even hostility found itself oddly inspired with insight. Earnestness developed a streak of poetry. Enthusiasm was infused with genius.

Thackeray must have intended to receive 'The Fighting Téméraire' with indulgent irony. What emerged on the page, in response to the excitement, 'which, I am sure, when the art of translating colours into music or poetry shall be discovered, will be found to be a magnificent national ode or piece of music,' was sensitive anticipation of the theory of correspondences. More than twenty years earlier, Hazlitt's attack turned in spite of him into a subtle and acute account of a whole new order of painting. A lesser journalist like Robert Hunt gained from the water-colours of the 1820's intimations of enveloping unity and 'bland communion,' uncovering meanings that we are still exploring.

Not even Delacroix was the occasion of more surprising critical insights than was Turner, amid the vituperation he suffered through his long career. Above all, his art and his opponents between them inspired the greatest masterpiece of criticism. But the caution with which he received the appearance of *Modern Painters* was surely justified. Whatever literature and social morality have owed to Ruskin, Turner was hardly his debtor. The study of Turner's achievement languished for more than half a century in the shadow of the book. The first biography, by Thornbury, was by contrast popular and gossipy; it is now consequently somewhat underrated. It remained the chief and highly unreliable source of information until after the end of the century. The level of critical appreciation was in general pious and commonplace; the imaginative response to Turner's genius had been pre-empted by Ruskin. His hand fell equally heavily on the collection of Turner's work bequeathed to the British nation, not entirely to the artist's benefit. It was not until five years after Ruskin's death, and fifty-four years after Turner's, that the Trustees of the National Gallery in London, custodians of about 19,000 water-colours and drawings which had formed part of Turner's bequest, commissioned a complete catalogue of them.

Alexander J. Finberg, whom they invited to undertake it, was an artist, then about thirty-nine years old, who worked as an illustrator and art-critic on a newspaper, *The Morning Leader*. Many years later Finberg described how the Keeper of the National Gallery had first allowed him 'to explore the contents of the eleven large deed-boxes in which what had come to be regarded as "the waste-paper basket" of Turner's workshop had been preserved from the eyes of the profane for nearly fifty years. This mass of material consisted of practically the complete series of sketch-books and notebooks Turner had used between his fourteenth and seventy-first years; also of a large number of sketches and studies for many of his completed works. Unfortunately, the whole collection was in a state of appalling disorder.' Finberg's rearrangement and his *Complete Inventory of the Drawings of the Turner Bequest*, published in 1909, placed the study of Turner on a systematic basis for the first time. Soon after he had finished them, his exasperation with

Ruskin's muddle still upon him, he must have begun the present book.

Turner's Sketches and Drawings stands at a turning point in the study not merely of Turner but of British art as a whole. In the years that followed, often in the annual volumes of the Walpole Society, which Finberg set about organising after the book was published in 1910, a widening circle of historians and connoisseurs began giving the most neglected of the national schools the detailed attention that was overdue. Finberg's own study of the Turner Bequest, which includes an unbroken series of sketch-books that are almost in the nature of diaries, gave his voluminous later work on the artist a new and reliable skeleton of fact. His researches culminated in the *Life*—in fact more like a compendious source-book—which was published shortly after his own death in 1939. But in the *Sketches and Drawings*, almost alone among his publications, Finberg was concerned less with history than with criticism. It is the only one of his books that is primarily interpretive, and thus by far the most subjective, personal, and polemical, and the least likely to be replaced.

Nevertheless, it has a sense of historical perspective that was at the time rare in any field and quite new in the criticism of British painting. It is difficult now to realise how original the early chapters were, at a time when little was known about the British water-colourists. In his third chapter, prompted by a remark of Farington, Finberg provided a pioneer essay on Turner's relation to landscape tradition and made his first moves toward the eradication of Ruskin's traces. Finberg's own aesthetic disposition is apparent early in the book. Turner's 'more or less accurate realisation of an actual scene' forms a subject rather for philosophic debate than for the precise investigation of the image-type that Turner used. Finberg's comparative closeness to the sentiment of the nineteenth century enables him to deal with issues that are now receding, as in his amusing comparison of the Romantic vocabulary of 1830 with that of 1797, and his limitations are those of his time. The plan of the book is rather like that of the almost contemporary Duveen galleries at the Tate, in which one of the grandest halls in any museum was provided for Turner's early pictures, succeeded by progressively smaller and less obtrusive rooms for the increasingly embarrassing products of his later life.

But whatever the original usefulness of the early chapters, the book is no longer read primarily as a source of information about Turner. Its value is rather different. It is the chief monument of a phase of criticism that is itself historic. It records a stage in the awareness not only of Turner but of an order of artistic meaning that had emerged during the nineteenth century, and one which sheds light on the evolution of attitudes that have left their mark. Like all criticism that speaks truly for its time, it is not only more limited and contingent than a critic cares to think, but on occasion more indicative and revealing than he is likely to have known.

The nature of Finberg's subject, the sketches and drawings, posed from the start an issue that would have presented itself rather differently to an earlier or a later critic. The sketches with which he was dealing were, of course, those on paper only; the oil sketches were not (with insignificant exceptions) so much as listed, still less restored or exhibited when he began work on the Bequest. Possibly Finberg hardly knew of them. There is no sign that he noticed the links between the sketches on paper and Turner's explorations in oil paint; he writes as if the latter did not exist, and for Finberg's time they did not. It now seems curious that the drawings were recorded *in toto*, while up to 1905 the Gallery took account of only 100 oils by Turner out of the total of 285 in the Bequest, the last of which came to light forty years later.

There is no harm in a drawing; it is possible to regard a sheet that is too unconventional for easy acceptance as preparatory, tentative, fragmentary, careless, or merely accidental, hardly existing in its own right at all. Finberg indeed begins the book by relegating the sketches and drawings in their entirety to this lower, more pardonable status. An oil on canvas, by contrast, is, or used to be, another thing altogether. There the same eccentricities amount at least to indiscretion, if not to outright defiance or madness. So nearly two-thirds of the oils in the Bequest were for half a century passed over in embarrassment.

INTRODUCTION TO THE 1968 EDITION

Approaching the sketches and drawings, Finberg made a sharp distinction 'between the raw material of the painter's art and its fully articulated products.' To us the division looks at some points a good deal less clear. Our own frame of aesthetic reference is permissive to the point of chaos, and in consequence some part of the intention of nineteenth-century artists may escape us. But Finberg's strait-jacket strains the evidence; there is no reason to think that 'from Turner's point of view the properly finished pictures were all that the public had a right to see and possess; the notes and studies were meant only for his own eye.' A small number of works of the utmost freedom, in both water-colour and oil, were allowed to leave his hands, and nearly all his life Turner was in open and notorious revolt against 'proper finish.' However, the distinction was essential to Finberg's theory, and ultimately he concluded that 'a study as such is not a work of art.' The proposition now appears positively to invite the question: what else can we suppose it to be the work of? It is not the least virtue of Finberg's polemical standpoint that it provokes the reader to argue, and the argument in this case is a profound one. It appears that Finberg's aesthetic system was devised precisely to resist the present definition of art, which we are inclined to widen to include virtually the whole activity of artists. Basically we think of art as a kind of behaviour, a way of life, and we trace the idea back to the Romantic masters, Turner among them. It is no accident that virtually all of them left behind significant bodies of unexhibited work that raise precisely this issue. Finberg's attempt to refute any suggestion that Turner might have preserved his sketches because he prized them now appears a little lame. Paradoxically, his aesthetics required him to devalue the aspect of Turner's art on which his own study was founded.

Finberg's inclination was philosophical. For enjoyment he would retire to bed with a volume of Hegel, and he appreciated an intellectual grandeur in Turner that is commonly overlooked. It is odd that he paid so little attention to Turner's own artistic teaching. Instead, using the sketches as basis, he erected for Turner a full-scale theory of expression on the linguistic model. The studies, in this view, are concerned merely with the me-

chanics of representation, and representation in itself supplies
no more than the terms, the words, for an artistic language. 'It
is of course always possible for the spectator to stop short at the
bare recognition of the pictorial signs, in the same way that it
is possible for the reader of a poem to recognise the meaning of
a few prominent words and ignore the context in which they
occur. . . . We must not merely look at such pictures as these
. . . we must translate the artist's signs into their appropriate
ideas and feelings.'

Finberg's argument in his chapter on 'Simple Nature' is
eloquent, indeed impassioned. The theory appears to stipulate
that there is a quasi-semantic force inherent in the conjunction
of figurative elements—in themselves almost neutral, 'accurate,'
but also, as the critic explains later, 'endlessly supple and fluid'—
which accounts for the expression of a picture like the 'Frosty
Morning.' It is unfair to read Finberg's own rhetoric too literally, but half a century afterwards his suggestion as formulated
seems far from accounting for the profound quality that is felt—
possibly in more of Turner's work than Finberg felt it—to be
akin to poetry. It evokes rather the quality that we like least
in Turner, a certain synthetic or composite tendency that has
an occasional suggestion of fabrication and superficiality. The
theory of expression, like the comparison with Wordsworth,
was evidently suggested by the short phase in which Turner's
landscape style took on at times the deceptive appearance of
pastoral realism—a style that is in fact by no means what it
seems. Finberg's warmest approval was reserved for Turner's
least characteristic aspect, and the terms in which he com-
mended the pictures—'among the truest and highest that Christianity has yet produced . . . impressed with the quietness and
beauty of the best part of the artist's own nature'—seem to
betray a distaste for some other part, perhaps that gaudy,
splendid part of Turner's constitution, for which quietness is
the least felicitous of words. Perhaps it was akin to the aspect
of him that related to his mistress and her children, whom Finberg overlooked or concealed when he came to write the *Life*.

Since Ruskin there had been no more closely argued contribution to the criticism of Turner; like much in the book, it was

intended to act as a corrective. But other elements in the critical situation that Finberg faced were at least as pressing as the Sage of Brantwood's muddles. It is worth looking at this situation closely. The question of whether Finberg's aesthetic thesis holds water at the moment is indeed a good deal less important than the place his book takes, without doubt a considerable one, in the continuous process that leads from Turner to ourselves.

A complicated critical structure is normally intended, among other things, as a fortification against some potential opponent, and Finberg is quite specific. The first opponent is what he calls Naturalism, and if we enquire what the term is intended to mean, the answer is evidently the whole institution of art in Britain in his time. 'So far as the system of art education in this country has any rational foundation, it is based upon this doctrine of naturalism.' In case we should miss the point, there is a footnote reference to Ruskin, and it might have been thought that, if insight into Turner had been the object, Finberg could have made it with a good deal less laying about him. Much of Ruskin's vast expatiation on the subject of Turner and natural knowledge now seems inappropriate; it is interesting to know that it had already begun to seem so in 1910. It is possible, after retrieving the nuggets of biography, to regard the hero of *Modern Painters* as largely and increasingly imaginary, and put the book where it belongs, near to Proust. Yet this fictitious, impossible figure was in a sense Turner's creation. Many of his qualities—his ability to ally himself with the power of nature; his unending concern with the idea of the great artist, and his infatuation with the glory of literature as well; his identification with the new power of society in his time and with some of its morality, and his feeling for the tragic significance of both—all these, when they had animated his vast achievement, still left unexpended a certain mythopoeic force. The genius that enabled Ruskin to sense it and respond like a medium to its dictation left the sober facts about Turner to lesser men.

In 1910 Ruskin's legacy of confusion was still formidable, and both historical and philosophical weapons had to be called in aid. The historical argument deployed in Chapter VII is frankly unfortunate. It involves among other things the display of a total incomprehension of the significance that the crucial visit to Italy in 1819 held for Turner. This is not the place to rectify the record in the light of a later view, which further research may show to be equally partial. But those who read for the first time in Finberg's survey of the 1820's of 'a weak and empty "Forum Romanum" for Mr. Soane's Museum' may wish to know that this is in fact the canvas in the Tate Gallery, in which new-found conceptions of the greatness of art and antiquity and the brightness of reflected southern light were fused into a bold and radiant picture.

The other argument against Ruskin continues, gathering force, throughout the book. Idealist philosophy is held to show that the doctrine of Naturalism contains a fatal defect of logic; Naturalism, in fact, is impossible. 'If we take it to mean that art does or can or ought to give us a copy of the given actual world as it exists apart from what Mr. Ruskin calls the meddling action of man's intelligence, then it is obvious that we have fallen into very serious error. . . . Even if we suppose . . . the copy of base, unadulterated reality fixed on the canvas, nobody could possibly recognise it or know that it was there.' Finberg in fact reasoned himself into a position not unlike that which E. H. Gombrich has derived from a later psychology of perception. Gombrich was led to an illuminating analysis of the historical mechanics of representation, which incidentally put the perversities of twentieth-century figuration somewhat in their place. Finberg's conclusions were a good deal more limited. His argument seems a long way round to sort out the confusion between Ruskinian stipping and the obviously far from 'Naturalistic' work of Turner. Finberg had been trained as a painter in France as well as in England, and perhaps there were scores to settle. Moreover, he had another issue to deal with that required all his philosophical weaponry: he too was uneasy about modern art. For him the bogey was Impressionism, and he linked it with another, while protesting that they were distinct—the spectre of what he regarded, with virtually all serious critics, as Turner's lamentable degeneration in the last twenty years of his life.

This is the point at which most present readers will finally part company with the author, yet it is in a sense the most revealing and significant part of the book. It is certainly puzzling; for a start, it is not certain what Finberg meant by Impressionism. If he had in mind the French painters whom we think of, his attack, which was once more founded on his philosophy of perception, seems misconceived. 'Now . . . Impressionism aims at getting rid of all the cognitive elements in concrete perception.' Of course, it did no such thing. It appears rather that the Impressionists were distinguished precisely by their understanding of the concrete reality of painting and of the kind of conceptual formulation that belongs appropriately to it. There is an incidental puzzle in Finberg's discussion. It would be interesting to know who were the 'later Impressionists' who are said to have 'devised a mechanical instrument which they hold in front of their eyes, and which operates very much like a shutter used for taking instantaneous photographs.'

In Finberg's scheme of things, the seemingly photographic image that gave the 'data of sense in their least organised condition' was evidently the most menacing bogey of all. In fact the threat was by no means imaginary. He had seen a whole staff of fine black-and-white artists, himself among them, dismissed from a newspaper and replaced by the camera, with only one, the least capable of them as he remembered, retained to touch up the photographer's work. The traumatic experience gave him a better reason than any critic before or since for mistrusting the tonal image, but it introduced a quite irrelevant confusion into his view of Turner. To us it appears that the later watercolours, even in their 'bedazzlement of sunlight,' were, so far from momentary, as powerfully and profoundly organised as anything in early nineteenth-century art.

Finberg sweeps back and forth from past to present across the wastes of indistinctness, the vagueness of execution, the poverty of context that he finds and the mistakes of criticism from Ruskin onward, correcting error and reproving vice with a magisterial breadth that recalls his old antagonist. Turner's 'vagueness of execution,' beginning, as Finberg acutely noticed, in 1830 with 'Calais Sands' (which hangs rather out of the way of critics at Bury in Lancashire)— 'his distinctively Impressionist manner'—was bad. But critics who had lately 'hailed him as the father of Impressionism' were worse, and the Impressionists themselves were worst of all.

The whole chapter is a transparent demonstration of a fact that is not altogether easy to accept. Whatever the ostensible subject, art-criticism is necessarily about something else as well: the use of art in the critic's own society and time. On the face of the matter there was no particular reason to draw Impressionism into the discussion. Finberg himself showed that it had no connection with Turner's later achievement. Yet on a deeper level there was every reason: attitudes to current art are never irrelevant to an attempt to interpret the cognate art of the past. The only guide to the tracks through history is the awareness that they have destinations, at which a critic, whether he knows it or not, is either happy or unwilling to arrive. Finberg was surely right in thinking that Turner's later style was quite different in kind from that of any of the painters known as Impressionists. But the real virtue of this chapter is that he betrays so clearly a family resemblance between his reasons for disliking each.

Finberg's aesthetic philosophy and the logical impasse that he built out of it for the miserable followers of Ruskin—Naturalism and Impressionism—were sometimes at odds with his attitude to the actual works of art. His conclusion was enlightened: 'Strictly speaking, a work of art is a symbol, and a symbol is not a copy or imitation of the meaning it stands for.' Yet it appears to have forbidden him to value the late works of Turner —images whose application would seem to be very plainly symbolic. The philosophic term is exclusively technical; it is never allowed to connote the visible symbols that we know. Finberg's account of the actual symbolism of the pictures is in fact strangely impoverished. In Turner's Venice, for example, he can see no more than 'the imagination of the ordinary Englishman— the unconscious crystallisation of the desires of the middle-class tourist for southern warmth, freedom, colour, variety and bodily pleasure.' This is a sad way below Turner's image of the city that was the 'birthplace and the theatre of colour.' Even the verse Turner attached to 'The Sun of Venice putting to Sea' was better:

> Fair shines the morn and soft the zephyrs blow,
> Venezia's fisher spreads his painted sail,
> Nor heeds the demon that in grim repose
> Expects his evening prey.

The ominous lines (a reminiscence of The Bard) might have provided an epigraph for Odilon Redon, and the comparison is not altogether inappropriate. Turner's vision was more comprehensive than Redon's, yet there is a certain relationship in the way the 'Sun of Venice' materializes out of rosy colour in the centre of the canvas like a visionary vignette. One cannot risk speculating: what might have happened if a critic with Finberg's devotion to Turner had possessed the sense of fate and of colour that current symbolist art and thought could teach? Would not the response to Turner have been quickened? The antagonism to Impressionism would have fallen into place. But there was no such critic. Finberg's reference to the French symbolist poets was at least half sardonic. His place was firmly in the chain of English thought, supplying the antithesis to Ruskin's sprawling thesis, and already aware, as it seems, of the purely visual criteria that were soon to supervene. It was perhaps in rear-guard defence against the purism that was to be associated with the English post-Impressionist critics that he fired the truest shot in the whole of his aesthetic armory: 'But the point which I cannot hesitate to press home—because I see clearly that the whole question of the value and place of art in modern civilisation depends upon it—is this, that the work of art is nothing less than its full significance.' For the rest, his theory meant most when he was theorising on the historical method that he had pioneered and demonstrated in the early chapters. He held out a 'new ideal for criticism . . . a synthetic view of function and form, the interpretation of function in relation to structure.' The ideal remains a worthy one. In practice, criticism as such ceased to concern him. He turned to an aspect of art more open to verbal resolution—the biographical research to which, in combination with art dealership, he devoted the rest of his life.

We must admit that the significance of the book as a prime link in the chain of criticism in England from Ruskin onward is in part a melancholy one; it is indicative of the mental climate in which Britain turned its back on modern art and on the British contribution to it with the rest. The grace of the book, which surely saves it from being no more than a document, lies in the fact that, over and over again, Finberg's original reaction to the works themselves (and, no doubt, his brilliant pen) got the better of his restrictive theory. At the height of his condemnation of Turner's late work and especially of the poverty of content that he thought he detected in it, he wrote thus about a water-colour of Freiburg: 'His eye seems now to classify and arrange what he sees in terms of space and motion, much as we should imagine an eagle to look down upon the welter and turmoil of our lives.' We could ask for no better evocation. The interesting thing about this passage, with its alertness to the spatial and kinetic intimations that now appear so meaningful in Turner, is that it is evidently the reaction of 1910. Something was in the air, and impatience with the immobility of the post-Impressionist formulations, which Finberg surely shared, went some way to account for it. It was the year in which Boccioni and Balla, in images of space and motion that Finberg would have loathed, began to soar like eagles. Good critics are occasionally more up to date than they know.

LAWRENCE GOWING

Leeds
March, 1968

TURNER'S SKETCHES AND DRAWINGS

TURNER'S SKETCHES AND DRAWINGS

INTRODUCTORY

The nature of our subject-matter—The difference between sketches and
finished works—The character of our subject-matter, as embryonic forms
of artistic expression, prescribes the method of study we must adopt—
Our method is broadly chronological—But to follow Turner's work year
by year in detail would carry us beyond the limits of our present undertaking—I have, therefore, broken up Turner's career into eight stages or
phases of development.

THE object of the following pages is to re-study the
character of Turner's art in the light of his sketch-
books and drawings from nature.

During Turner's lifetime his rooted objection to part with any
of his sketches, studies, or notes often formed the subject of ill-
natured comment. Yet we owe it to this peculiarity that the
drawings and sketches included in the Turner Bequest at the
National Gallery comprise practically the whole of the great
landscape painter's work done direct from nature. The collection
is, therefore, of very great psychological interest. It shows
clearly upon what basis of immediately presentative elements the
airy splendour of Turner's richly imaginative art was built : and
amongst the twenty odd thousand sheets of drawings in all stages
of elaboration, the embryonic forms of most of the painter's
masterpieces can be easily traced.

A careful examination of the drawings shows that Turner's
objection to part with his sketches and notes was not the outcome
of a blind and deeply ingrained passion for accumulation, but

1

that it was the necessary result of the painter's clearly defined conception of the radical difference between the raw material of the painter's art, and its fully articulated products—the difference between mere sketches and studies and fugitive memoranda, and the fully elaborated works of art to which such preliminaries are subservient, but with which they should never be confused. From Turner's point of view the properly finished pictures were all that the public had a right to see or possess; the notes and studies were meant only for his own eye. Even in his later years, when he consented to exhibit what he expressly called a 'record' of a scene he had witnessed, he grumbled when it was admired and treated as a picture, although in this case the 'record' was not a hurried memorandum, but a fully elaborated attempt 'to show what such a scene was like.'[1]

The method of our study must be determined by the general character of our subject-matter. Our main business is with fragmentary records, hurried memoranda, half-formed thoughts, and tentative designs. We must not and cannot treat these dependent and embryonic fragments as independent entities; we cannot pick and choose amongst them, or love or dislike them entirely for their own sakes, as we can with complete works of art which contain within themselves the grounds of their own justification or insufficiency. To grasp the significance of our sketches and studies we must study the goal towards which they are striving. We must not be content to admire even the most beautiful of these sketches entirely for its own sake, but must study them for the sake of their connection with the works which they were instrumental in producing.

These considerations have also weighed with me in the selection of the numerous illustrations with which the publishers have generously enriched this volume. On the whole I have chosen the illustrations rather for the light they throw on Turner's conception of art and methods of work than for their own individual attractiveness; but the glamour of execution is so invariably present in all that came from Turner's hand, that few of these drawings will be found which do not possess a very powerful aesthetic appeal of their own.

---

[1] See *Modern Painters*, vol. v, p. 342 *note*.

INTRODUCTORY

In dealing with Turner's work from the point of view I have indicated, we are forced to touch upon problems which the prudent art-critic is apt to avoid. In studying the relation between the preliminary sketches and studies and the finished works into which they were developed, we find ourselves plunged into the midst of some of the most baffling difficulties of psychology and aesthetic. In attempting even to describe the relation between the more rudimentary and the more fully articulated processes of artistic expression, we are forced, whether we like it or not, to face the problems of the relation between form and content, between treatment and subject, between portrayal and portrayed; and we cannot go far without finding ourselves obliged to reconsider the common-sense ideas of Truth, Nature, and Art. We cannot avoid such problems if we would. If I face them, therefore, instead of emulating the discretion of my elders, it is, I am sure, from no ingrained love of abstractions, but rather from an overpowering interest in all the concrete forms of pictorial art.

The separation of aesthetic from art-criticism which is so much favoured at present, though it eases the labour of thought both to the art-critic and to his readers, seems to me otherwise inexcusable and fraught with serious artistic and intellectual dangers. Art-criticism cut adrift from general principles cannot help degenerating into a blatant form of self-assertion or an immoral form of practical casuistry—a finding of good reasons for anything you have a mind to; and aesthetic, divorced from all living contact with the concrete phenomena of art, is one of the dullest as well as the most useless of studies. But this is not the place to set forth in detail or defend my conception of the function and methods of art-criticism. I will merely say that I regard it as a form of rational investigation of the phenomena of pictorial art; it has no immediate practical aim; and it does not propose to prolong or intensify the enjoyment which works of art provide.

We find then that we cannot study Turner's sketches in isolation from his finished works. But to follow his completed work year by year in detail would obviously carry us beyond the limits of our present undertaking. I have, therefore, broken up Turner's career into eight facets or aspects. In the first chapter I deal

3

with his seven years' apprenticeship, from 1787 to 1793, using his sketches to throw light on his youthful aims and methods. The second chapter, covering the years 1793 to 1797, deals with the work of the topographical draughtsman. I then study the gloomy and romantic side of Turner's art, when he was mainly under the influence of Richard Wilson and of the churchyard and charnel-house sentiment of Edward Young and Joseph Warton. The fourth chapter is devoted to Turner's early sea-pieces, and the next to his work as a painter of what his contemporaries called 'Simple Nature.' This phase of Turner's art is difficult to describe in a few words. One way would be to call it a phase of Wordsworthian naturalism, but it must be remembered that it was not an echo or a by-product of Wordsworth's poetry, but an independent and simultaneous embodiment in another form of art of sentiments common both to Wordsworth and to Turner. Pictures like Turner's 'Frosty Morning' and 'Windsor' were as new, as unprecedented, as Wordsworth's most characteristic poems. This side of Turner's art shows him as the founder of a genuinely national school of homely realism, as the head of the Norwich school and the master of David Cox, De Wint, Callcott, and the rest.

The sixth chapter deals with the designs engraved in the *Liber Studiorum*, and the sketches on which they were based. The seventh is devoted mainly to the work engraved in the *Southern Coast*, *Richmondshire*, Scott's *Antiquities*, the *Rivers* and *Ports*, and the *England and Wales* series, the work by which the artist is perhaps best known. My eighth chapter treats of the period when signs of mental decay began to be apparent. These years saw the production of what have been called the first Impressionistic pictures. Then, by way of bringing to a head some of the observations on the nature of artistic expression which our investigations have forced upon our notice, I have added a final chapter dealing mainly with the relation between Art and Nature. The subject-matter of this chapter is not so attractive as that of the others, but I do not think it right to omit it.

This selection of the facets of Turner's dazzling and complex genius is necessarily arbitrary and incomplete. The aspects I have chosen to throw into relief can make no pretence to be exhaustive. They must be taken as a poor but necessary device for the introduction of a kind of superficial order into our present task —as a concession to the weakness and limitations of the powers of the student, rather than as a successful summary of the multifarious forms into which one of the most prolific and many-sided creative activities of modern art has poured itself. And the threads of this living activity which I have sought to isolate, never existed in isolation. Turner was not at one period of his life a romantic and at another a pseudo-classic or Academic painter, a sea-painter at one time, and a painter of 'simple Nature' at another. Turner was always a sea-painter and a topographer, a romantic, a pseudo-classic, and an impressionist, as well as a master of homely realism. While he was painting 'Hannibal Crossing the Alps' he had the 'View of High Street, Oxford' on his easel ; the 'Abingdon' and the 'Apollo' were painted at the same time as were the 'Frosty Morning' and the 'Dido and Aeneas.' He could paint a huge dull empty canvas like 'Thomson's Lyre' when his muse was putting forth its lustiest and most vigorous shoots ; he could give us 'The Fighting Téméraire' when his powers seemed stifled amid the fumes of early Victorian sentimentality. His genius is hot and cold like Love itself, a fine and subtle spirit that eludes the snares of our plodding faculties. But unless we desire merely to bedazzle and intoxicate our senses, we cannot afford to dispense with the poor crutches upon which our pedestrian intellect must stumble.

CHAPTER I

SEVEN YEARS' APPRENTICESHIP—1787-1793

Turner's first drawings — 'St. Vincent's Tower' — Turner's copies and imitations—His debt to Art—Work with Mr. Hardwick—Oxford sketches —'Radley Hall'—Drawings from the Antique—The Bristol sketch-book —End of the apprenticeship.

THE legend runs that Turner's first drawings were exhibited in his father's shop-window, ticketed for sale at prices ranging from one to three shillings.

There is nothing improbable in this story, though the drawings referred to by Thornbury,[1] as having been bought by a Mr. Crowle under these conditions, do not happen to have been made by Turner. I have not, indeed, been able to discover any drawing which can confidently be said to have been purchased from the barber's shop in Maiden Lane, but there are some in the National Gallery which show us exactly what kind of work Turner was capable of producing at the time when he might have resorted to this rough and ready method of attracting patronage.

A typical drawing of this kind is the brightly-coloured view of St. Vincent's Tower, Naples, reproduced on Plate i. of the present volume. It is oval in shape, measuring about 8 × 10 inches, and has evidently been cut out without mechanical assistance, as the curves of the oval are somewhat erratic. As the youthful artist had not visited Italy at this period, I thought it probable that this drawing was based upon the work of some other artist, and I was fortunate enough to be able to trace it to

---

[1] *The Life of Turner*, by Walter Thornbury, 1897 edition, p. 27. The drawings referred to are now in the Print Room, British Museum.

PLATE I

ST. VINCENTS TOWER, NAPLES

PLATE II

CENTRAL PORTION OF AN AQUATINT BY PAUL SANDBY, AFTER FABRIS
PUBLISHED 1 JAN., 1778

its source. It is copied and adapted from an aquatint by Paul Sandby, after Fabris, published on 1st January 1778, entitled ' Part of Naples, with the Ruin'd Tower of St. Vincent.' Sandby's engraving is a large one (about $13\frac{1}{4} \times 20$ inches), and comprises an extensive view of the harbour and bay of Naples, with the Castel dell' Uovo in the middle distance, and St. Elmo crowning the buildings on the right. Turner has picked out as it were the pictorial plum of this mass of topographical information. He has set the ruined tower boldly in the centre of his design, and has used only just so much of the surrounding buildings and scenery as was necessary to make an appropriate background or setting for it. He has reduced the Castle of the Egg to insignificance, and closed up his distance with appropriate but imaginary mountains. In the engraving a passing boat with figures divides our interest with the tower. Turner has suppressed it. He has also reduced the size of the quay upon which the tower stands, thus increasing the apparent height of the tower. The few meagre weeds clinging to the battlements in the engraving have developed luxuriantly in Turner's drawing, thus adding considerably to its picturesqueness. The foreground figures seem to have been adapted from those in the engraving.

It is probable that these slight differences between the engraving and the water-colour were made involuntarily, for it is evident that Turner did not have the engraving under his eyes while he was making the drawing. He had probably seen the engraving in some shop-window, and had made a hasty pencil sketch of the part that interested him. That he was working from a somewhat perfunctory sketch and not direct from the original is proved by the fact that he has introduced three arches into the building on the quay immediately at the foot of the tower, instead of the two in Sandby's engraving. But in the engraving there is a small rounded turret on the battlements of the quay which comes just in front of the place where Turner has introduced his third arch. It is clear that he mistook the indication of this turret in his rough sketch for a third arch in the building beyond.

It would, of course, be imprudent to suppose that Turner chose to work in this way partly from memory, with the deliberate

7

intention of giving his imagination freer play; he was probably forced to do so by the material exigencies of his position. But certainly this way of working was admirably calculated to strengthen his memory and call into play his innate powers of arrangement and adaptation.

The colour scheme, which is probably the artist's own invention, is light and pleasing. The golden rays of the setting (? rising) sun are painted with evident enjoyment. The warm yellow light of the sun is transfused over the whole of the sky, turning the distant clouds into crimson. The keynote of the colour is thus orange yellow, passing through pink to burnt sienna. In spite of the lightness of the colour the drawing was worked over a black and white foundation, light washes of Indian ink having been used to establish the broad divisions of light and shade in the design. These washes afterwards formed the groundwork of the greys and cooler colours, being warmed in parts (as in the tower) with washes or touches of pink and burnt sienna, or worked up into more positive hues by subsequent washes of blue and yellow.

The handling of the drawing—the sharp decided touches, the neatness and dexterity of its washes, and the rapid march of the whole work—shows what a hold the idea of a unified work of art had already obtained over Turner's mind. The clear, determined workmanship shows that he must have been thinking of the whole from the beginning, and not of the representation of a number of separate natural objects.

This childish effort seems to me of great interest as marking with extraordinary clearness the point of departure of Turner's art. From the beginning he sees things pictorially, as elements in a conceptual whole, not as isolated and independent objects. His sense of design—both as the faculty of expression as well as of formal arrangement—is thus developed, while the merely representative qualities of art are ignored or at least subordinated. This early grasp of the idea of pictorial unity is obviously the result of Turner's study of works of art, and not of his study of nature. Since Mr. Ruskin's labours it will not be possible for any student to overlook the enormous profit which Turner derived in his subsequent work from his unwearied observation of the phenomena of nature; it is well, therefore, to be careful not to overlook the prior debt which Turner had contracted to art, and the extraordinary advantage his early grasp of pictorial unity gave him in appropriating the multifarious variety of natural shapes and colours.

The other drawings of this period in the National Gallery only serve to emphasise Turner's indebtedness to art. Some of these are plain straightforward copies. The most elaborate of these is the copy of ' Folly Bridge and Bacon's Tower ' which has long been exhibited in the Turner Water-Colour rooms (No. 613 N.G.). This is copied from an engraving by J. Basire published in the *Oxford Almanack* for the year 1780. The colouring, however, is original. This copy is signed and dated, ' W. Turner, 1787.' Among the other copies is a pencil outline of the Old Kitchen, Stanton Harcourt, from the engraving in Grose's *Antiquities*. There is also a coloured drawing, somewhat similar in size and shape to that of St. Vincent's Tower, of Dacre Castle, Cumberland. I am unable to say from what engraving this is copied or adapted.[1] It may have been a slightly earlier effort than the Neapolitan subject, as the Indian ink underpainting is less skilfully done and the general effect is heavier and more monotonous.

These drawings, made, I believe, between Turner's twelfth and fourteenth years, show the youthful artist in the act of acquiring the rudiments of that pictorial language which he was to use in after years with such mastery and ease. We see him acquiring this language by intercourse with his fellows who use it, not, as is the modern way, through the course of a random study of nature. He is learning from tradition, and the thought of the artistic community as expressed in the current pictorial language is gradually forming and moulding his ideas. He is imitating those around him, as a child imitates the words of its nurse and mother.

On the present occasion, I need do no more than call attention in passing to the immense advantage Turner enjoyed in being initiated thus early and in this easy and natural way into the

[1] Since these lines were written I have been lucky enough to discover its source. It is based on an engraving in Gilpin's *Northern Tour*, vol. ii., facing p. 85. Turner has followed the engraving fairly carefully, but has introduced two figures of his own in the foreground.

sphere of art. He was thus saved from those years of futile and heart-breaking experiment to which the modern system of nature study dooms all those students whose native powers are not entirely deadened by its influence. The habit thus early forced upon him of regarding himself as an actual producer, *i.e.* as a maker of articles with a definite market value, must also have been beneficial to him. The existence of a class of real patrons, whose tastes had to be consulted and whose pockets contained actually exchangeable coin of the realm, must have placed some insistence upon the social aspect of art, and have helped to prevent the boy from making the mistake which so many subsequent artists have made, of considering their work merely as a means of self-expression, instead of as a means of super-individual or universal communication. Another important result of these early employments was the facility and mastery in the use of his material which they gave him. Between the water-colours of different periods of Turner's career there are the most astonishing contrasts of subject-matter and sentiment, but in all of them one finds the same inimitable grace, strength, and dexterity of workmanship, the same unequalled technical mastery over the medium ; and this purely executive address—this 'genius of mechanical excellence,' to use Reynolds's expression—could have been attained only as the result of an early familiarity with this particular form of artistic expression.

About his fourteenth year (1789) Turner was placed with an architect, Mr. P. Hardwick. It seems to me doubtful whether he was regularly apprenticed, or was intended to take up the study of architecture from a practical point of view. The evidence upon this point is extremely limited, but what little there is points to his employment upon purely pictorial tasks, such as the dressing out of projects or views of buildings with a plausible arrangement of light and shade and a pleasing setting of landscape background. We know that Mr. Hardwick built the New Church at Wanstead,[1] and that Turner made for his master a water-colour drawing both of the old church which was pulled down and the new one that took its place. I have not been fortunate enough to trace the

---

[1] It was finished in 1790 and consecrated on the 24th June. See Lysons's *Environs of London*, vol. ii, p. 237.

PLATE III

present owner of these drawings, but the water-colour of the old church was exhibited at the Old Masters (R.A.) in 1887. There is, however, in the National Gallery a pencil outline of the new church, squared for enlargement, which shows no signs of training in the practical work of the architect's profession.

The earliest of Turner's sketch-books now in the National Gallery was in use during the period of this connection with Mr. Hardwick. A pencil sketch of a church by the river, easily recognisable as Isleworth Old Church, with barges moored beside the bank, is probably the note from which the water-colour was made which Mr. Hardwick's grandson lent to the Old Masters in 1887. Most of the other drawings, however, appear to have been made during a stay near Oxford. There are sketches of Clifton Nuneham (then Nuneham Courtenay), near Abingdon; of Radley Hall, between Abingdon and Oxford; of a distant view of Oxford; a sketch of a ruined tower which may represent Pope's Tower in the ruins of the Harcourts' house at Stanton Harcourt, and two drawings of Sunningwell Church, a village about two miles from Radley and three from Abingdon. As Turner's uncle, Joseph Mallord William Marshall, his mother's elder brother, after whom he was named, was then living at Sunningwell, it is probable that these drawings were the result of a summer holiday spent with his relative.

These drawings represent Turner's first attempts to draw from nature. They are characterised by an absence of blundering and a sense of pictorial logic and requirements which could only belong to a beginner whose eye and hand had already been disciplined in the production of works of art. One cannot but feel that the mould into which the immediate experiences of the artist were to be cast had already been firmly set before his pencil was placed upon the paper, nay, before the particular sights in question were actually seen. In other words, the pictorial formula into which the material gathered from nature was to be worked up had been clearly determined before the artist set out to gather such material for himself. Turner's confidence in the unbounded felicity of immediate contact with nature was not commensurate with that of modern artistic theorists. He does indeed entrust himself to the open fields, but it is not until he

11

has armed himself with a stout though flexible panoply of artistic convention.

But though the draughtsmanship is conventional, I do not think it can fairly be called mannered. The actual statements made are made with the utmost simplicity and directness. In the drawings of Sunningwell Church (on p. 12 of the sketch-book), of Radley Hall (pp. 9 and 14), and of Isleworth Old Church (p. 22), the general proportions and main facts of the buildings are noted with deliberate and methodical care. The artist knows what facts he will want when he comes to make his finished water-colours, and he takes those facts and calmly ignores all the particular effects of light and shade, colour and accident which his experience of other artists' work had shown him would not be useful to him. Thus there is a strongly marked selective activity at work, which gives what I think can be more correctly described as style than as manner. Yet I should not be surprised to find the term mannerism applied to the curiously monotonous calligraphic scribbles which stand for trees and clouds in these drawings. That they are conventional and singularly indefinite I readily admit, yet they are not deliberately learnt 'ways of doing trees' like those, for instance, which a student of J. D. Harding's teaching might adopt. They are as they are because their immediate function is clearly determined by their ultimate purpose. In making his finished water-colour drawing at home the trees and clouds, as well as the whole system of light and shade, were merely the docile instruments of pictorial effectiveness. The exact shape of each tree and cloud in his drawing, and even their exact positions, were determined as the work progressed by purely pictorial requirements. A detailed statement of the exact shape of any particular tree or cloud in the actual scene from which the sketch was made would therefore have been not only of no use to the artist, but a positive hindrance, as it would have complicated the problem of formal arrangement before the artist, even if it did not actively hinder its solution. In these sketches from nature Turner therefore takes his skies and foliage for granted as much as possible, merely hinting at their general existence in a loose and tentative way.

But if the charge of mannerism cannot be fairly brought

against the sketches made face to face with nature, it is otherwise with the water-colours which were afterwards elaborated from them. Drawings like the view of 'Radley Hall,' reproduced on Plate III., and the 'View of the City of Oxford' might almost be said to consist of little else than mannerisms. The manner of doing trees and skies and of arranging the planes of the scene is taken over directly from Paul Sandby, as are also the method of working in transparent washes and the gamut of colours used. The 'View of Oxford' is indeed nothing but a feeble echo of some of Sandby's fine drawings; it tells us little of Turner himself, beyond an indication of a certain liking for scenes of this kind. Perhaps the most noteworthy point in the drawing is the demonstration it affords of the superior development of his sense of tone to his sense of form; the buildings sway to and fro in the wind, the foliage is childish and ridiculous, but the difference between the broad expanses of ground and sky is clearly marked, and the limpid sky gives an undeniable charm to it all.

There is perhaps a little more of himself in the view of 'Radley Hall.' The way the tree-trunks seem to blow themselves out, and toss themselves this way and that, while their branches explode in the wildest and most fantastic contortions,—all this is given with such keen and frank enjoyment, that it points to something more than a mere passive reproduction of a purely technical recipe. The trees in those drawings of Sandby which Turner had studied do indeed behave in this way, but Turner identifies himself so closely with the inner meaning of these forms that they become his own legitimate property. The sense of exuberant freedom in the trees is intensified by contrast with the rigid restraint of the building in the middle distance. It is as though the boy's imagination was glad to get away from the realm of necessity and disport itself in aimless gambols through space, free from the encumbrance of inert matter and of the laws of gravitation. It is this habit of getting at the inner emotional content of the pictorial conventions he adopts, that stamps Turner's whole career of imitation and appropriation with its peculiar character, making him invariably richer for all his borrowings, and more original for all his imitations.

These two drawings were made in 1789, during the artist's

13

TURNER'S SKETCHES AND DRAWINGS

fourteenth year. About the beginning of 1790 he joined the schools of the Royal Academy, acting, it is said, upon the advice of Mr. Hardwick. During part of 1790 and for the next two or three years he worked in what was then called the 'Plaister Academy,' *i.e.* from casts taken from the antique. Laborious chalk and stump drawings of the Apollo and Antinoüs of the Belvedere, the Venus de' Medici, and the Vatican Meleager, as well as of the more robust forms of the Diskobolos and Dying Gaul, are still in existence to demonstrate the diligence with which he pursued these uncongenial studies. Such work must have given his masters a singularly poor and misleading opinion of his talents. In June, 1792, he was admitted to the Life Class, while still continuing to attend the Antique. This academic training, however, must have been useful as an antidote, or at least as a supplement, to the topographical work to which all his spare time was devoted.

He seems to have spent his holidays in 1791 partly with his uncle at Sunningwell and partly with some friends of the family, the Narraways, at Bristol. The sketch-book in use at this time is now in the National Gallery. The volume was never a handsome one,—it was probably stitched and bound by the artist himself—but its present appearance is deplorable; the cardboard covers are broken, the rough and ready backing is almost undone, a number of the leaves have been cut or torn out, and the remainder are in a generally dirty and dilapidated condition. In spite of these disadvantages it gives us a valuable glimpse of Turner's interests and acquirements at the age of sixteen.

Our first impression is that his year's work drawing from the cast has produced hardly any perceptible effect. The drawings of buildings are in some cases even more perfunctory than those in the 'Oxford' Sketch-Book. The sketch of Bath Abbey Church (on page 14 of the book), for example, is not a very creditable performance for an ambitious Royal Academy student. Its carelessness, however, may have been due to limited oppor-tunities, but we must remember that this hasty scrawl, with the assistance of a few written notes and diagrams, was sufficient to enable the artist to produce afterwards an elaborate water-colour of the subject. A still more elaborately wrought and

14

PLATE IV

VIEW ON THE AVON, FROM COOK'S FOLLY
WATER COLOUR AND INK. ABOUT 1791

carefully considered water-colour was the result of another sketch (on the reverse of page 16) in this book, a view of 'Stoke, near Bristol, the seat of Sir H. Lippencote,' now in the possession of Mrs. Thomas. This pencil sketch is quite as perfunctory as that of Bath Abbey. It is evident that nature 'put him out' or that the artist's youthful impatience induced him to hurry over the first stages of his work. These sketches from nature were merely means to an end, and so long as they contained sufficient hints to set his subsequent work going he was perfectly satisfied. However, in some of the drawings where the first sketch from nature has been worked over subsequently (as in the water-colour of Captain Fowler's seat on Durdham Downs [on pp. 17a and 18]), we can trace an increased delicacy of hand, an added capacity for dealing with complex and irregular forms, and greater knowledge of the natural forms of trees.

But it is evident that the wild and romantic scenery of the Avon gorge made a deeper impression on the young artist's imagination than the spick and span seats of the gentry. The ruins of Malmesbury Abbey are sketched from every available point of view, and there are hurried and clumsy sketches of 'The Ruins of a Chapel standing on an Island in the Severn,' 'A View of the Welsh Coast from Cook's Folly,' and others of 'Blaze Castle and the Deney and Welsh Coast,'[1] and the 'Old Passage.' The drawing described as a 'View from Cook's Folley (*sic*), looking up the River Avon with Wallis Wall and the Hot Wells' (reproduced on Plate IV.), shows clearly the bent of Turner's mind towards the wildness and freedom of nature, as well as his strong love of ships.

If it were our intention to follow Turner's work year by year, we should have to study in detail the drawings of Oxford, Windsor, Hereford and Worcester, and especially the Welsh and Monmouthshire sketches which belong to the years 1792 and 1793. As it is, it is sufficient for our purpose to notice that the work of these two years shows a gradual increase of power in making sketches from nature. The young artist slowly gathers confidence in himself. Nature ceases to 'put him out,' to fluster

---

[1] These titles are written on the backs of the drawings by the artist himself—an excellent practice which he very soon abandoned.

him with her multitudinous details and ever-varying effects. He begins to treat nature as a conquered enemy, and there is just a suspicion of youthful impertinence in the cool and methodical way in which he gathers up the kind of facts he wants, and ignores everything that does not come within the scope of his pictorial formulas. But by this time it is evident that his period of apprenticeship is at an end, and that we must turn our attention to the work of the brilliant young topographical draughtsman.

CHAPTER II

THE TOPOGRAPHICAL DRAUGHTSMAN—1793-1796

Welsh tour of 1793 — 'St. Anselm's Chapel' — Turner's topographical rivals—Midland tour of 1794—Topographical and antiquarian draughtsmanship—Its main interest is not embodied in the work—The marvellous *petit-maître*—The 'Cottage Interior'—Light and shade as a means of expression—The sketch-books of 1795 and their contents—'High Force of Tees' or 'Fall of Melincourt'?

AMONG the five drawings by which Turner was represented in the exhibition of the Royal Academy in 1794, one was a view of the Devil's Bridge, Cardiganshire. This was doubtless one of the first results of the sketching tour in Wales made in 1793. We can readily believe that Turner's imagination was powerfully impressed by the wild and gloomy scenery of the country and its romantic ruins, but his efforts to embody his impressions were not at first very successful. For the moment his powers as an architectural draughtsman were more in evidence than his powers of expressing grand and gloomy ideas. The romantic turn of his mind had to be more fully developed before it could command public support, and for the time being this phase of his art seemed swamped in the flood of topographical employment which the immediate success of his less ambitious drawings in the 1794 exhibition brought him.

In a contemporary press notice, preserved among the Anderdon collection of catalogues in the Print Room of the British Museum, Turner's drawings of 'Christchurch Gate, Canterbury,' and the 'Porch of Great Malvern Abbey, Worcestershire,' are said to be 'amongst the best in the present exhibition. They are the productions,' the writer continues, 'of a very young artist, and give strong indications of first-rate ability ; the character of Gothic

17

architecture is most happily preserved, and its profusion of minute parts massed with judgment and tinctured with truth and fidelity. This young artist should beware of contemporary imitations. His present effort evinces an eye for nature, which should scorn to look to any other source.'

The first of the drawings which called forth this praise is now in the Fitzwilliam Museum, Cambridge (Ruskin Bequest), the other is probably the 'Malvern' now in the Manchester Whitworth Institute (No. 73). The critic's remark about the danger of 'contemporary imitations,' which I take to mean the danger of Turner imitating the works of contemporary artists, may probably account for his neglect to mention another drawing exhibited at the same time, which strikes the present-day observer as a more accomplished and remarkable effort than either the 'Malvern' or 'Christchurch Gate.' I allude to the drawing described in the R.A. catalogue as 'St. Anselm's Chapel with part of Thomas à Becket's Crown—Canterbury Cathedral,' which I take to be the drawing now in the Manchester Whitworth Institute (No. 272). This is a work of infinite patience and wary skill, a remarkable combination of far-sighted knowledge of ultimate effects united with the utmost delicacy, firmness, and patience of execution. These qualities do not seem to me so clearly marked either in the Christchurch Gate or Malvern drawings, but very likely to the contemporary observer, especially to one avid of originality, the drawing of 'St. Anselm's Chapel' may have appeared more ordinary or conventional.[1]

The success of these drawings established Turner's position as one of the foremost architectural and topographical draughtsmen of the day. But we must not make the mistake of supposing that Turner's success was the result of an absence of serious rivals. De Loutherbourg, Dayes, Hearne, Wheatley, Sandby and Rooker were by no means unworthy rivals. Nor must we jump to the conclusion that Turner, at the age of nineteen, had outstripped such competitors in any but the purely topographical branches of their profession. The best of the older men were artists of wide

[1] The fourth architectural subject in the exhibition is described as a view of the 'Inside of Tintern Abbey.' If this was the drawing now in the Victoria and Albert Museum, as the evidence seems to indicate, the critic's preferences seem even more incomprehensible. On the whole this is, I think, a finer work even than the 'St. Anselm's Chapel.'

18

sympathies and ambitions, who could not rest satisfied within the narrow limits of purely topographical work. They looked upon such work as a kind of necessary drudgery, useful from a pecuniary point of view, but not calling for the whole-hearted exercise of all their talents and enthusiasm. Dayes, to whom Girtin was apprenticed, and from whom Turner had learnt a great deal, seems to have detested topographical work, in spite of the skill and delicate charm with which he treated it. All his enthusiasm was reserved for figure subjects in the grand manner, for which there was no market. In this 1794 exhibition he had four illustrations for Dr. Aitken's *Environs of Manchester*, which have the perfunctory look of work done against the grain, and a 'View of Keswick Lake,' which may possibly have been the slight and charming drawing of this subject now in the Victoria and Albert Museum, too small and fragile a thing to attract much attention. The versatile and brilliant De Loutherbourg did not exhibit this year; Hearne also was absent. Rooker had five of his delicately-accomplished but rather prosaic drawings. Paul Sandby had two views of Rochester Castle, and 'A View of Vintners at Boxley, Kent, with Mr. Whatman's Turkey Paper Mills,' where the excellent paper upon which almost all Turner's drawings were made was manufactured. Wheatley sent no landscapes this year, and Girtin, Turner's senior and rival, had a single exhibit, a 'View of Ely Minster,' the first drawing he had had accepted by the Academy. The result of this state of things was that Turner's architectural and topographical work was pitted against only the perfunctory or tired work of his older rivals. For the moment all his indefatigable patience and amazing energy and skill were concentrated on this one point of attack, with immediately decisive results.

Turner had now achieved an honourable footing in his profession. Dr. Monro bought his 'Anselm's Chapel' and gave him commissions for many other drawings. Booksellers found his name an attraction. With publishers ready to buy his drawings, though at prices that would merely excite the derision of a modern artist, and with patrons like Dr. Monro ready to encourage his more ambitious efforts, his opportunities of travel were greatly enlarged.

TURNER'S SKETCHES AND DRAWINGS

Turner spent the summer of 1794 making a tour of the midland counties of England. Northampton, Birmingham, Lichfield, Shrewsbury, Wrexham, Chester, Matlock, Derby, Nottingham, Lincoln, Peterborough, Cambridge and Waltham were among the places he visited. The views published in the *Copper Plate Magazine* during the next three years of Nottingham, Bridgenorth, Matlock, Birmingham, Chester, Peterborough and Flint were made from sketches taken on this journey, as were also those of King's College, Cambridge, Flint, and Northampton, published in the *Pocket Magazine* during 1795. But these were the least important results of the tour. The work into which Turner threw all his enthusiasm and ambition was sent to the exhibition of the Royal Academy of 1795, which contained no less than eight of his important and highly finished drawings. The best known of these are the 'Peterborough Cathedral; West Entrance,' which was included in Messrs. Agnews' 1908 annual exhibition of water-colours—it had suffered somewhat from the light and had been restored, but was still an impressive work; the 'Welsh Bridge, Shrewsbury,' now No. 276 in the Manchester Whitworth Institute, a carefully wrought and exquisitely accomplished drawing; and the 'Cathedral Church at Lincoln' (Plate v.) now in the Print Room. This elaborately finished drawing, I am inclined to think, played an important part in Turner's development. It is almost the only drawing I know from his hand which has a papery and unconvincing general effect, which is monotonous and insensitive in its textures, and hard and metallic in its details. For once in a way Turner seems to have deferred to the ideals of elaboration of the ordinary connoisseur, who likes to see every detail in every part of a work pushed to its highest point of finish. For these reasons the drawing must have been very generally admired when it was first exhibited, but Turner could not have been satisfied at all with his own work, for he promptly abandoned the style. This is the most 'mappy' of all Turner's drawings, and we know that for the rest of his life he had the greatest horror of this quality.

When we examine the pencil drawings made from nature on this tour we find them all severely governed by the ends they were intended to serve. The sketches for the publishers' work

PLATE V

LINCOLN CATHEDRAL
WATER COLOUR EXHIBITED AT ROYAL ACADEMY, 1795
(Print Room, British Museum)

PLATE VI

LINCOLN CATHEDRAL, FROM THE SOUTH-WEST

PENCIL. 1794

are generally made in a small note-book (about $4\frac{1}{2} \times 6\frac{3}{4}$ inches in size). They are invariably in pure outline, without the slightest suggestion of light and shade—nothing but the scaffolding of the more important shapes upon which the final designs were to be elaborated. On such a small scale the ease and grace of Turner's touch are not much in evidence. The sketches are severely business-like, and done as quickly and with as little effort as possible. There is more effort and feeling in the casual studies with which the leaves of this sketch-book are interspersed. The accompanying sketch (Plate VII.) of a pony standing ready saddled gives a good idea of the mature wisdom of Turner's style of sketching at this period, its determination to grasp the larger truths of form and structure, as well as the quickness, readiness, and versatility of his powers of perception.

The drawings for the more ambitious subjects are generally made on larger and separate pieces of paper about $8 \times 10\frac{1}{2}$ inches in size. On this scale the delicate play of the artist's wrist becomes appreciable. The dominant impression left by a glance through these drawings is one of excessive orderliness and methodical neatness. There is no hurry, no scamped or perfunctory work, still less are there any signs of dilatoriness or even slowness. The artist's respect for relevant fact is equalled by his appreciation of the value of time. His calm objective outlook, his steady, unwavering grasp of general principles enable him at every point to economise his labours, to store up the record of the greatest possible amount of material facts (*i.e.* of facts material to his purpose) with the utmost celerity, clearness, and the least possible expenditure of manual effort. This is particularly noticeable in the treatment of the towers in the Lincoln Cathedral drawing (Plate VI.), where every advantage has been taken of the repetition of forms. A possible, though not a very satisfactory, way of doing justice to the predominance of conceptual over purely visual elements in this work, would be to say that the artist has here drawn with his head rather than his eye, that he puts down not so much what he sees as what he understands.

I am tempted to linger for a moment over the placid and self-contained air of this phase of Turner's work, because we shall so soon get into an altogether different atmosphere, and because we shall understand Turner's after work all the better the more clearly we grasp the character of the work we are now examining. The self-contained air to which I allude is connected in my mind with the character and limitations of topographical work. Now the essential character of topographical and purely antiquarian work is that it does not aim primarily at expressing the imaginative or emotional effects of the objects it represents. It takes these imaginative or emotional interests for granted, relying indeed on them for the ultimate justification of its work; but the work, as topographical and antiquarian, aims directly only at an adequate representation of the particular scenes or buildings with which it is concerned. There is, as it were, a tacit division of labour; the artist being called upon to record accurately and vividly a certain scene or building, merely as a scene or building, while the spectator is expected to supply the requisite mental associations and emotional colouring. The artist draws a castle, we will say, as a mere object of sight, while the spectator is supposed to remember that the castle was built by such and such a king, and that certain moving events took place in it or near it. This division of labour simplifies the work of the topographical artist, reducing his business to a clear-cut affair of definite visual facts. Hence the Oriental stolidity of Turner's topographical work, its Oriental patience, neatness, and precision. In a drawing like the 'Lincoln Cathedral' Turner is as wholly immersed in the succession of particular material facts as a Japanese or Chinese artist. As with the Japanese and Chinese artists the material facts are not there entirely for their own sakes; in Turner's case they imply an antiquarian interest, as the Eastern artists' work implies an added religious or poetical significance. But the point to which I desire to draw attention is, that this added significance is not embodied in the work itself. It is something extraneous and fortuitous, and the work itself falls apart into something dependent. It is in fact an accessory, a work of mere illustration, not an independent work of art.

We shall have to return to this subject in our next chapter, when we find Turner wrenching himself free from the trammels of topography and antiquarianism to soar into the regions of

22

PLATE VII

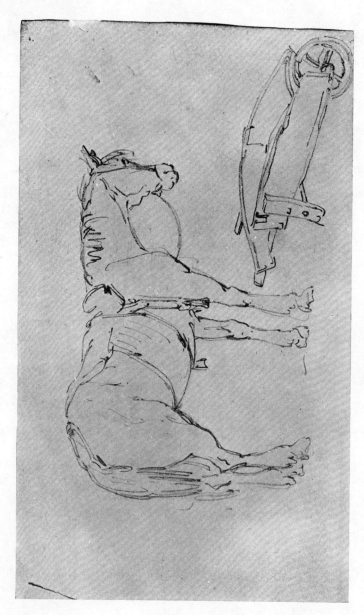

PONY AND WHEELBARROW

PENCIL. 1794

artistic freedom. In the meantime we will turn our attention to the topographical drawings which Turner sent to the exhibition of 1796.

Of the eleven drawings by which Turner was represented at the Royal Academy this year, nine were apparently of a topographical character. I have only been able to examine two of these recently—the 'Transept and Choir of Ely Minster,' in the late Mr. R. F. Holt's collection, and the 'Llandaff Cathedral,' in the National Gallery (Exhibited Drawings No. 795). If we may judge from the rather cold impression these two drawings make upon us, it is probable that they owe their existence rather to the artist's professional diligence than to any overmastering impulse towards artistic expression. But the work, if not particularly enthusiastic, is distinguished by its thoroughness and workmanlike spirit. Every mechanical difficulty is fairly faced and mastered with imperturbable coolness, patience, and dexterity. So palpably is the artist's attention fixed upon the executive side of his art, especially in the 'Llandaff Cathedral,' that a contemporary prophet might well have been excused if he had seen in it only the promise of the making of a marvellous *petit-maître*, and had declared that its author could not be possessed of a spark of native genius.

Perhaps if we could see either of the two other drawings which, to judge from their titles, were neither topographical nor antiquarian in subject, we might find evidence which would induce us to modify this dominant impression of intellectual coldness and unruffled placidity. In particular, the title 'Fishermen at Sea' seems to suggest possibilities of romantic expressiveness, especially when we know that the subject was treated by the same hand that was to give us in a few years' time the 'Calais Pier,' Lord Iveagh's 'Fishermen on a Lee-Shore,' and the 'Shipwreck.' But this drawing has not been traced, and the second drawing, the 'Internal (or interior) of a Cottage,' has apparently shared the same fate.

There is, however, a slight possibility that the latter subject may be correctly identified with the small drawing in the National Gallery, exhibited under the title of 'Cottage Interior' (406 N.G.). This drawing has been, somewhat rashly, supposed to represent the underground kitchen beneath the barber's shop in Maiden Lane. There are absolutely no grounds for such an assumption, and a moderately careful examination of the drawing shows that it does not represent an underground kitchen or room of any kind. It is clearly a room on the ground-floor, but the lower part of the window has been curtained off, with the object of getting a picturesque arrangement of light and shade, and this fact may have lent some plausibility to the suggestion that the light was falling through a grating above. If I am right in identifying this drawing with the 1796 exhibit the study was made at Ely, as the catalogue informs us.

But whether this drawing was exhibited at the Academy or not, it clearly belongs from internal evidence to the latter part of 1795 or the beginning of 1796. It therefore offers us an interesting connecting link in the development of Turner's art, showing the line of study which turned the youthful topographer into the romantic artist.

Yet there is little of the romantic spirit on the face of this drawing. A poor interior bathed in gloom, with a narrow stream of light falling on an old woman sitting beside a copper and surrounded by an array of pots and pans. But it is significant, because it bears witness to the direction of Turner's mind to the study of light and shade as a separate vehicle of expression. In the topographical drawings proper, light and shade is not used for its emotional effect, but simply as a means of representation, that is to say, to bring out the shapes and details. In the ' Interior ' we see Turner beginning to isolate the system of light and shade, to study and grasp its possibilities as a separate factor of artistic expressiveness.

But if we turn to the sketch-books containing the record of Turner's summer wanderings in 1795, we find no lack of evidence of the essentially artistic cast of his mind, and of his wide sympathies with nature. His journeys this year were mainly confined to portions of the coast-line, to the Isle of Wight, and the south coast of Wales from Chepstow to Pembroke Bay. It was not by any means the first time he had seen the sea, but he was then able to study it more closely than before, and under its wilder aspects and conditions.

THE TOPOGRAPHICAL DRAUGHTSMAN

The outward appearance of the two principal sketch-books used this year bears clear indication of bright professional prospects. These handsome calf-bound volumes, each with four brass clasps, put forward solid claims to respect—claims which a young artist standing alone without a backing of influential patrons would shrink from advancing. Opening the book devoted to the Isle of Wight subjects, we find the first page headed in ink with the words 'Order'd Drawings,' and underneath a record of subjects and sizes of drawings to be made for Sir Richard Colt Hoare and Mr. Charles Landseer, the engraver. In the South Wales book we find the record of further commissions from these two patrons, and others from Viscount Malden, Dr. Mathews, Mr. Laurie, Mr. Lambert, Mr. Mitchell and Mr. Kershaw. These indications suggest that the drawings in these volumes were not made entirely for the artist's own use and enjoyment. They are certainly for use, as their neat and careful array of details proves, but they were also destined to bear the scrutiny of possible patrons, and excite, if possible, a desire in their breasts to see them carried out in a more elaborate medium. This may account for a certain smugness or primness in much of the work itself, for its faint suggestion of youthful conceit and a priggish air of conscious rectitude.

The sketching tour opens at Winchester, and we can follow the artist to Salisbury and Southampton. We then find him suddenly at Newport, in the Isle of Wight. The remainder of the book is devoted to this island. At Newport Turner was chiefly interested in Carisbrook Castle. We can then trace his footsteps southward to Ventnor and along the South-West coast to the Needles; thence back to Newport, with a visit to Brading, where he made a delightful drawing, partly finished in water-colour, of Bembridge Mill.

The workmanship throughout is admirably deft, graceful and accomplished. It is not, however, till the artist gets to the open sea round the Needles that his imagination seems stirred at all. In the centre of the drawing on page 39 stands the blunt face of the chalk cliffs; on the left, the incoming waves play round a few broken stumps of rock. Between the cliffs and the spectator there is a small bay in which some fishermen's boats ride on the rising tide. The waves play prettily with the boats, but these are carefully tethered fore and aft, thus showing that their owners have learnt to mistrust the gracefully advancing waters. In the distance the cold dark volume of sea seems to justify these suspicions. Gradually a sense of the sternness of the eternal conflict between the sea and the dry land impresses itself on our minds. The whole coast seems in the clutch of a ruthless and never-resting foe. In some scenes the high cliffs seem to stand proudly and defiantly in the water; here they are in full retreat, the havoc of the foreground proving that the soft chalk is crumbling at the touch of its pitiless enemy.

And now we can see the usefulness of the discipline and training of topographical draughtsmanship. Confronted with a scene like this, which powerfully stirs his emotions, the artist is not forced to remain dumb; he has an organ of expression ready to his hand. The supple pencil-point hurries its suggestive outlines over the paper. There is yet time to add some record of the more delicate passages of modelling, and to suggest something of the colour of the water and cliffs. The artist's brush is as docile as his pencil. There is no experimental blotting and splashing; every touch is expressive, and the pressure of haste only adds greater certainty to the swift touches. The artist has to stop before he has tinted half his paper, but he has torn out the heart of his subject.

Leaving the Isle of Wight, Turner made his way to South Wales, passing through Wells. The scenery of South Wales is of a wilder description than that of the Isle of Wight, and it must have touched his imagination profoundly. But thanks to his ready science, his hand never falters; all the ruined castles and abbeys, the water-mills and water-falls, the details of the rocky coast-line, the white-crested waves and tangled forests, are bundled with celerity into neat little outlines and stored ready for future use. Among the subjects are the castles of Kidwelly, Carew, Laugharne, Llanstephen and Goodrich, and they are drawn as they had never before been drawn or will be again. One of the views of Carew Castle will serve the artist thirty years later when he comes to treat this subject for his 'England and Wales' series. But to me the most significant drawing in

26

PLATE VIII

MELINCOURT FALL, VALE OF NEATH

PENCIL, PART IN WATER COLOUR. 1795

the book is the waterfall on page 8. The whole subject is drawn in with the pencil as usual, and then just the most important part is finished in water-colour. This piece of water-colour work is an admirable example of Turner's sensitiveness to impressions, his quickness and readiness, and the adaptability of his methods. The rocks and the crystalline facets of the water at the top of the fall are painted in with sharp staccato touches, while the skilful dragging of the dry brush suggests the dissolving of the water into spray with extraordinary vivacity.

This drawing forms our eighth illustration, though no reproduction can do justice to it. Mr. Ruskin admired the work warmly, and it formed part of the selection he made for the Oxford Loan Collection. He named the drawing the 'High Force of Tees,' but I believe this description to be incorrect. In the sketch-book the leaf on which the drawing is made follows immediately a drawing of the water-mill at Aberdulâs, and a note made on the fly-leaf of the book, written by Turner for his own guidance on the tour, mentions that the 'Rocks and Waterfall' near Aberdulâs were 'well worth attention.' The nearest waterfall to Aberdulâs is the cascade formed by the river Clydach, known as the Fall of Melincourt. I have therefore ventured to substitute this title for Mr. Ruskin's 'High Force of Tees.'

An artist so sensitive to the subtlety and mystery of natural scenery, as these sketch-books show Turner to have been, and one so unusually gifted to express these qualities, could not long be confined within the prosaic limits of topographical and antiquarian work.

CHAPTER III

THE SUBLIME—1797-1802

Change from pure form to light and shade—'Millbank' and 'Ewenny Priory'—Contrast between 'Ewenny' and 'Llandaff'—The transition from objectivity to subjectivity—The growth of taste for the Sublime—There are no sublime objects, but only objects of sublime feeling—No guidance but from art—The Wilson tradition—The two elements in the sketches and studies of this period, (1) The study of Nature, and (2) The assimilation of the Wilson tradition — In the 1797 sketches these two operations are kept distinct—The North of England tour and its record—'Studies for Pictures: Copies of Wilson'—The two operations begin to coalesce in the 1798 and 1799 sketches—The origin of 'Jason'—The Scotch (1801) and Swiss (1802) tours.

THERE is an evident connection between such a study of light and shade as the 'Interior of a Cottage' (406 National Gallery) and at least two of the exhibits in the exhibition of 1797. One of these, the 'Moonlight, a study at Millbank,' was probably Turner's first exhibited oil painting; the other, 'Transept of Ewenny Priory, Glamorganshire,' I am inclined to regard as the first drawing in which the budding genius of the young artist was authoritatively announced. It is impossible to be sure whether the direction of Turner's attention to the subtler problems of light and shade led him to turn to oil painting as a more suitable medium for the expression of such effects, or whether his resolution to explore the resources of the more complex medium had the effect of directing his attention to the expressional qualities of light and shade. The 'Millbank' bears on its face the evidence of Dutch influence (Van der Neer, van Goyen, etc.) as well as of inexperience of the technical requirements of the new medium. This inexperience renders the work

28

PLATE IX

INTERIOR OF RIPON CATHEDRAL: NORTH TRANSEPT

PENCIL. 1797

THE SUBLIME

insignificant with regard to the development of the artist's personality, but the bent of his mind towards the mystery and expressiveness of darkness is notable.

In the water-colour of 'Ewenny Priory'—now one of the chief treasures of the Cardiff Art Gallery (Pyke-Thompson Bequest)—Turner's genius is less hampered by technical difficulties. If this be indeed the drawing that was exhibited in 1797 [1] it shows an amazingly rapid development in the artist's powers, especially when we compare it with the 'Llandaff Cathedral' (790 National Gallery), which was exhibited only twelve months earlier. The 'Llandaff' is merely the work of a clever and skilful topo-graphical draughtsman, the 'Ewenny' is the work of a powerful imaginative artist. The gloomy interior of the Norman ruin is no longer an object to be measured, dated, classified and labelled. It is no longer an 'interesting specimen' that we have set before us. The artist has now broken with the ordinary, every-day world of sense-experience, and we plunge with him into the world of the imagination, where objects are no longer separated from and held over against the self; they now throb and tingle with our own emotional life.

This change of aim—we may speak of it for the sake of brevity as the change from objectivity to subjectivity—is accompanied by a change of method in the workmanship of the two drawings. In the 'Llandaff' (as in the 'Lincoln') the forms of all the objects are made out with the greatest possible clearness. When the artist has told us as clearly and precisely as possible the exact shape of every object from his chosen point of view, we feel that he has done all that he set out to do, and all that we can reason-ably demand from him. Then these objects are left standing side by side in relative independence of each other and of us; they have no necessary connection one with the other, like the parts of a piece of music, or the points of an argument. Their only bond of union is the abstract one of space. The whole effect is of some-thing severed from direct experience; the objects represented

[1] For it appears that there is some doubt about the matter. The Rev. E. S. Dewick possesses another version of this subject, similar in size and design, but very inferior in workmanship. The clumsiness and woodenness of the workmanship have been taken as evidence that the drawing was an earlier one than that at Cardiff. But it may also indicate that it is merely the work of an unskilful copyist.

have an unreal air of permanence and immutability, with something of the intellectual coldness and aloofness of a diagram or mathematical symbol.

In the 'Ewenny' drawing we are brought into contact with objects which have not yet been severed from the emotional colouring of immediate experience. Instead of a series of abstract spatial determinations, appealing only to the abstract understanding, we now have a presentation fraught with the infinite suggestiveness of living, sensible experience. Each object represented is now no longer held over against the self as something alien, something indifferent to and independent of humanity, like the laws of the physical sciences; each object has now become merely a moment in the affective life of an individual. It therefore touches our own feelings, challenges our hopes and fears, appeals intimately to our sympathies with the contagion of the emotions of an actual companion. We cannot remain indifferent to such an appeal if we would. Unless our nerves tingle as the eye plunges from the familiar objects of the foreground into the gloom beyond, the picture has not begun to exist for us. But immediately it touches our inner life into responsive activity the picture becomes transformed from so much indifferent paper and pigment into an aspect of our own affective life. We have caught the contagion of the artist's emotional experience, in which the objects of his representation were submerged.

I am far from wishing to suggest that the distinction between the two kinds of art which I have endeavoured to indicate is either very obvious or easy to grasp. But it is, I am convinced, a very real and a very weighty distinction, and as such is worthy of the most careful study. But, however carefully we study the matter, and however profoundly convinced we may be that the distinction is firmly grounded in the essential nature of art itself, yet we can never hope to describe it in the precise terms of the exact sciences. We can never hope to understand the exact nature of the ties which bind the expressive symbols of Romantic art to the echoes they awaken with mathematical certainty in the breast of each individual. The problem of the relation between thought and feeling still agitates the rival schools of philosophy, and this is not the place to discuss such matters. What is immediately important

PLATE X

CONWAY FALLS, NEAR BETTWYS-Y-COED
WATER COLOUR.   ABOUT 1798

for us is to see that Turner's art has passed from one stage of growth to another, and to realise for ourselves as best we can the nature of this progression. To me it seems clear that the line of Turner's personal development is following roughly the line upon which the artistic faculty of mankind has developed; that the transition from topography to the stage we have now entered upon coincides in part with the movement from Classic to Romantic art, from the art which is in bondage to the world of external reality, to the art which moves and has its being in the inner world of our ideas and feelings. The 'Llandaff' and 'Lincoln' belong to the classic (or the pseudo-classic, if you will) art of the eighteenth century, while the 'Ewenny' inaugurates the Romantic art of the nineteenth century. On its technical side the change is from form to tone, from a system of predominantly unemotional space-determinations to a medium which is more immediately in contact with the inward feeling of all self-conscious beings.

In moving from the Augustan point of view towards the Romantic, Turner was but walking in an already well-beaten track. During the last half-century the influence of Milton had been growing, the taste for the gloomy, the mysterious and the picturesque had found expression in Young's *Night Thoughts*, in Gray's *Elegy*, in Walpole's *Castle of Otranto*, and had found critical exponents in Warton's *History of English Poetry*, and in Burke's Essay *On the Sublime and Beautiful* (1756). Dr. Percy's *Reliques* had found many readers and admirers, and Macpherson's *Ossian* had stirred the enthusiasm of Europe. In painting Richard Wilson and De Loutherbourg had struck the same note of gloomy grandeur.

Now the essence of this kind of art—the Sublime—is not merely to strike the spectator dumb with amazement or terror, but also to make him feel that man's moral freedom is superior to the most terrible forces of Nature.[1] The mere representation of the fearful and terrible sights of inorganic nature is therefore not by itself enough to evoke a feeling of the sublime; before he can do this the artist must also excite in the spectator the consciousness of his power to overcome or resist such objects. It is

---

[1] Cf. Bosanquet's *History of Æsthetic*, p. 277; also Kant's *Kritik of Judgment*, sections 28 and 29.

therefore a purely subjective feeling that the artist has to represent, though this feeling is directed towards or centred round a certain definite series of objects. But these objects as coloured with the strength and resolution of the heroic mood—the mood of Kant's *animi strenui* [1]—cannot properly be said to exist as natural objects. The real subject of the artist's work is therefore, strictly speaking, the invisible and the intangible, a mere mood of the soul, an attitude of our own mind towards certain objects of thought.

Of course we should all have been justified before the feat had been accomplished, in declaring that it was impossible for pictorial art to paint the invisible, but now that it has been accomplished we have no alternative but to recognise the fact. Common-sense says the thing is impossible, and experience proves to us that common-sense is wrong. The careful student of modern criticism will know how splendidly Mr. Ruskin fought against experience in this matter and how he was worsted. I am really sorry for common-sense. To paint the invisible and intangible—it is a hard nut to crack. But I protest we have no choice in the matter. The thing is there before us. It is a pity it is not quite so simple and easy as we should like it to be, but it is best, I think, to face the difficulties honestly.

Turner's problem, then, as a painter of the sublime, was one in which the mere study of natural objects could not help him. He might search out the most fearful sights in nature, watch the loftiest waterfall of the mightiest river, volcanoes in all their violence of destruction, hurricanes, lightning flashes and storms, but these objects alone, though they might stimulate his feeling of moral freedom, could not show him how to express this faculty of moral resistance which 'gives us,' as Kant says, 'the courage to measure ourselves against the apparent almightiness of nature.' [2] There was no help for Turner in this task but in the works of those artists who had succeeded in expressing such emotions, and it was to Wilson and De Loutherbourg that Turner went, not to learn how to represent natural objects as such, but to learn how to use such objects as the media of inward perceptions and ideas. De Loutherbourg's influence was mainly in the direction of rhodomontade and melodrama, but Wilson's, though not

---

[1] *Op. cit.* (Dr. Bernard's translation), p. 141.   [2] *Op. cit.,* p. 125.

PLATE XI

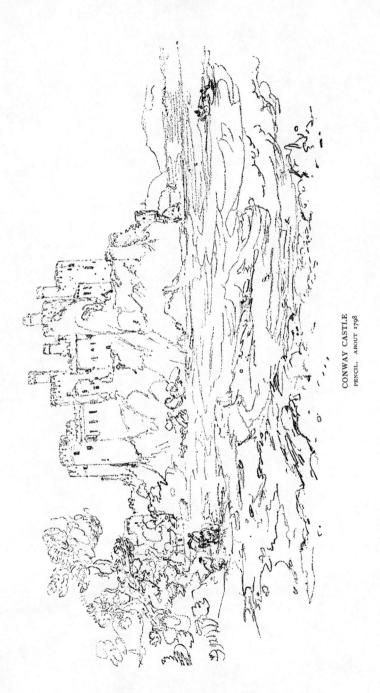

CONWAY CASTLE

PENCIL. ABOUT 1798

THE SUBLIME

devoid of danger, led Turner safely into the enchanted regions of romance.

The three chief expressive—as distinguished from representative—factors in Wilson's work are darkness of tone, the scheme of colour, and the quality of the paint. I am inclined to think that the general darkness of Wilson's pictures is the necessary result of the kind of subjects he treated. The darkness is necessary to tune the mind of the spectator to gloomy and tragic thoughts, —to spread over his mind what Johnson calls ' a general obscurity of sacred horror, that oppresses distinction, and disdains expression.' In his worst pictures this darkness of key readily passes into emptiness and blackness; but in his best pictures this darkness ranges through a gamut of subdued and glowing colour, which relieves the gloom and comforts us as it were in our distress. The tone and colour are thus to some extent determined by the character of the objects represented; the tone by their general emotional effect, and the colour scheme as conditioned by the tone, though controlled within rather wide limits by the natural colours of the objects represented. But the third element, the quality of the paint, seems altogether independent of the objects represented. It seems to reveal only the artist's attitude towards these objects. It is as thoroughly subjective as the emotional vibration in the voice of an excited speaker. Under this term, the quality of the paint, I include all the immediate presentative elements of painting, the thickness or thinness of the impasto, the way the paint is put on, the signs of the brushwork, everything, in short, that tells us how the artist felt towards the objects he was representing.

The main object of Turner's study during the period we are dealing with was the assimilation of the Wilson tradition, his study of the facts of Nature, simply as facts, falling into the second place. For a time the two lines of study are kept distinct. On the one hand, the work of neat and systematic note-taking face to face with nature is continued, and on the other hand, a number of studies aiming at the embodiment of the artist's subjective attitude make their appearance. The final synthesis of the two factors, the without and the within, is of course only arrived at in the finished work of art, but the contents of the sketch-books

33

of this period fall easily apart, according as they lean either in the direction of the particular facts or in the direction of the emotional synthesis.

The drawings made during the tour in the north of England, which Turner made in the summer of 1797, belong almost entirely to the first kind. In one sketch-book we find most of the more important ruined abbeys and castles of Yorkshire, Durham, and Northumberland drawn with the most delightful ease, accuracy, and charm. Here we have Kirkstall Abbey drawn from every available point of view, Ripon Cathedral, studied both without and within, Barnard and Richmond Castles, Dunstanborough, Bamborough, Durham Castle and Cathedral, Warkworth, Lindisfarne and Norham. The drawing of the interior of Ripon Cathedral, reproduced as Plate ix., is merely an average example of the kind of work that Turner now seemed to produce without the slightest effort. The most complicated structure and detail now presented no difficulties to his well-trained eye and hand. The ease with which he mastered all the material forms that met his eye may have left his mind at leisure to enjoy the moral atmosphere of the buildings, may have left his imagination free to range backward over its past history; but there is no trace of emotion or imagination in the graceful play of these clear-cut, accurate, and methodical outlines.

Melrose Abbey formed the highest point north in this journey. Leaving Melrose, Turner struck across to Cumberland, no doubt passing through Carlisle to Keswick. After the bustle and noise of much of the northward half of his journey, the peace and quiet of the English lakes must have been noticeable. In looking through the hundred or more pencil sketches made at Keswick, Buttermere, Ullswater, Patterdale, Windermere, Coniston, etc., one is struck by the absence of the conventional note of Romantic horror. There is no trace of what used to be called the bold and appalling singularities of nature.[1] There is indeed a marked absence of human activity in these drawings. We are alone with

[1] The conventional eighteenth-century attitude towards these scenes seems well expressed by a description in Paterson's *Road Book*. 'To the south of the Derwent-water,' the passage runs, 'is the rocky chasm of Borrowdale, a tremendous pass, at the entrance of which dark caverns yawn terrific as the wildness of a maniac, etc.,' page 435.

PLATE XII

RUINED CASTLE ON HILL
WATER COLOUR. ABOUT 1798

nature, but nature's aspect is generally peaceful and friendly. The mountains are high, but we enjoy climbing them and the fine views we get there. Their shapes above all interest us immensely. They do not strike us at all as appalling singularities, but as replete with an infinite grace and variety, under which we feel a fundamental reasonableness, an intuitive sense of intelligible design. And then there are not only the bare shapes, but their wonderful clothing of light and shade; the play of the gleams of sunlight and the long shadows across the deep bosoms of the hills, and the games the wreaths of mist and cloud play with the distant mountain-tops, and the wild races of the mountain-torrents over their favourite tracks. Occasionally there is time for more than the regulation pencil outline. Then the brush and a few colours come out, and a stretch of the distance wakes from its cold abstraction into life. Such sketches as 'The Head of Derwentwater, with Lodore Falls and the entrance to Borrowdale,' the ' Hills of Glaramara,' and ' Buttermere Lake ' (Exhibited Drawings No. 696), were produced in this way. In these we see beautiful effects of mist, with the sun playing through them, noted with subtle sympathy and accuracy, but the general effect is not at all gloomy; it is rather one of peace, serenity, and gladness.

This is the raw material out of which Turner set to work in the autumn and winter of 1797 to manufacture some important oil pictures full of gloom and wrath. The young artist reminds me of Johnson's acquaintance who had resolved to be a philosopher, but found his native cheerfulness always breaking through. Turner's unaffected delight in Nature·certainly stood in the way of his aspiration towards the sublime. But he was not a man to be easily thwarted. We can trace in the pictures exhibited in 1798 the conflict between the elements given in perception and the subjective requirements of the artist, but by sheer diligence and strength of will he succeeded in moulding his cheerful perceptions into concepts full of gloom and horror. The picture of ' Buttermere' (N.G., at present on loan to the Albert Memorial Museum, Exeter) is based on a pale and delicately charming water-colour drawing (696 N.G.), but little of the charm or delicacy of the original sketch survives in the oil painting, which is ruthlessly swamped in more than Wilsonian blackness. He succeeded best where the record of his perceptions was slightest. There are several sketches of Norham Castle, but they are all in pencil and very slight. For some reason or other the artist was evidently in a hurry. Perhaps partly because of this insufficient note-taking, here was a favourable subject round which his imagination was free to play, unhampered by any very clearly determined immediate perceptions. The picture of Norham Castle, exhibited at Somerset House in 1798, was Turner's first distinct success in this kind of work, and he repeated the subject several times.

A small green-covered pocket-book, which still bears Turner's label, 'Studies for Pictures: Copies of Wilson,' gives us a glimpse of the processes by which the sights of nature were converted into works of art. Here we see the subjective impulses of the artist struggling into expression; the artist's love of gorgeous colour and dramatic effect nourishing itself and forging a material form for its own support. Among the designs in this interesting little book are several marine and coast subjects, a shipwreck, an interior of a forge with men busy casting an anchor, some river scenes, a rainbow standing over a dark city, several church interiors, and some studies of turbulent skies. It is difficult to distinguish Turner's studies for his own pictures from his copies of Wilson, but one of the drawings is probably a copy of Wilson's 'Morning,' and another, of his 'Bridge of Augustus at Rimini.' I have not been able to see either of these original pictures, so as to compare them with Turner's copy, but a comparison of the copy with the engraving by Joseph Farington, published by Boydell, shows some important discrepancies in the arrangement of the light and shade. The character of these discrepancies leads one to suppose that they were not made intentionally by Turner, but were the result of his attempt to reproduce the general effect of the picture from memory. He may have made a slight pencil sketch of the picture in some gallery, and washed in the general effect afterwards from memory.

This is, of course, only a supposition, but it is somewhat strengthened by examination of a larger and more elaborate copy of Wilson's 'Landscape with Figures,' a picture now in the National Gallery (No. 1290). That Turner's water-colour is intended to be a copy is proved by the endorsement on its back—

PLATE XIII

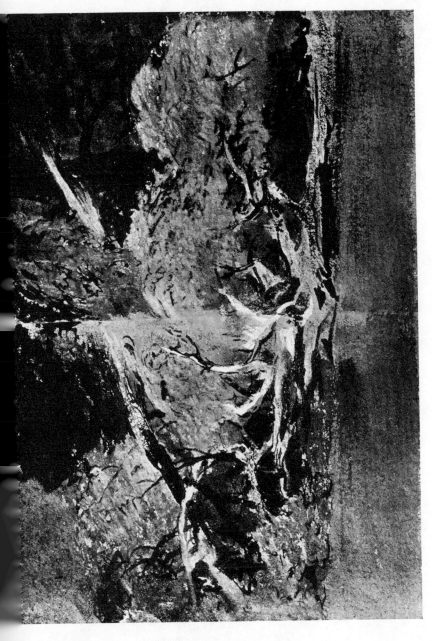

STUDY OF FALLEN TREES
WATER COLOUR. ABOUT 1798

PLATE XIV

CAERNARVON CASTLE
PENCIL. 1799

THE SUBLIME

'Study from Wilson,' but when we compare it with the original
we find that the various discrepancies in the copy can only be
accounted for by supposing that Turner was working to a considerable extent from memory. I admit the evidence is not con-
clusive, but I do not think we shall be far wrong if we take it
that Turner did not at this time make any elaborate copies of
Wilson's pictures, but that he studied them closely and enthusiastically, and relied more upon his memory than his notes.

In the sketches made during the following years we find that
these two separate operations show a tendency to coalesce.
Turner has evidently taken a dislike to his earlier map-making
style, and tries hard to see nature like Wilson. His sketches
from nature become slighter and more hurried. In his efforts
towards breadth he comes very near emptiness, and in his attempts
to get away from his neat bit-by-bit style of work he often comes
near downright clumsiness and carelessness.

The summers of 1798 and 1799 were largely spent in North
Wales. Here he found exactly the material that chimed in with
the mood of sternness and gloom he wished to express: steep,
convulsive mountains, wild valleys and broken passes, the bare
skeletonlike ribs of broken ships aground on lonely estuaries,
massive ruins of huge castles perched on inaccessible crags,
gnawed to the bone as it were by the wind and rain and
remorseless Time.

His mental grasp has clearly broadened. He no longer sees
buildings as isolated objects, but they now fall into their places as
incidents in the wide panorama of the country. Nothing is now
drawn for itself; the trees are emanations from the ground, the
dry land and the waters are kinsmen, the stones in the foreground
are parts of the distant mountains, and the mountains huge elder
brothers of the pebbles by the river-side. The bubbling waters
are but clouds made captive, the clouds the freed souls of the
brooks, the trees the organ of their transformation; and castles
like Conway, standing with their roots plunged deep into their
rocky foundations, seem but rocks raised to a higher power. The
distinction between human art and physical nature is everywhere
broken down. The spirit of life in nature is identified with the
volitions and passions of the artist's own soul: he has become

37

sensible 'to the moods of time and season, to the moral power, the affections and the spirit of the place.'[1]

This state of mind is closely akin to the mood in which the myths of the Old World had taken shape. Small wonder, then, if the broken and withered branches of a stricken tree writhing among vigorously shooting brushwood should suggest to Turner's mobile fancy the idea of snakes and dragons. The sketch here reproduced (Plate xiii.) strikes me as probably the origin of the picture of 'Jason' which was exhibited in 1802.

In 1800 or 1801 Turner made a tour through the Highlands of Scotland. The immediate results were slightly disappointing, but the experience gained undoubtedly contributed to the effectiveness of the work done during the first visit to Switzerland, made in 1802. In the Scotch sketches Turner had hit upon a method of working that enabled him to cover a great deal of ground in a short space of time, and which had the additional advantage of exercising his memory, and of making his sketches from nature more like the first draughts of his finished pictures than like so many unfused notes or memoranda. All the more promising scenes he met with were sketched slightly in chalk upon large sheets of paper prepared with a wash of light brown. These sketches were seldom carried far before the actual scenes, but as soon after as was convenient—possibly at the inn in the evening—these skeletons were filled up from the artist's retentive memory and ever-ready invention. In this way he was able to fortify himself against the multiplicity of nature's irrelevant facts, and to find a ready form of expression for the reaction of his own mind upon the sights of nature.

Colour was very little used in the Scotch sketches, all the larger drawings—numbering, I think, between forty and fifty—being worked entirely in black and white. But a considerable number of the Swiss drawings are coloured, though, I believe, none of them directly from nature. Turner's procedure in the case of these drawings appears to have been practically the same as with the Scotch series, but after the skeleton sketch from nature had been elaborated with pencil and white and black chalk, colour was sometimes resorted to, less as a record of facts

[1] Wordsworth, *Prelude*, Bk. xii, 118-120.

PLATE XV

CASSIOBURY : NORTH WEST VIEW

PENCIL. ABOUT 1800

PLATE XVI

of local colour, than as an additional instrument of expression of the subjective mood. Among the drawings elaborated in this way are the sketches upon which several of the Farnley drawings (the large 'Mer de Glace, Chamounix,' 'Falls of the Reichenbach,' 'Pass of St. Gothard,' 'Blair's Hut, Mer de Glace,'[1] etc.), were based. In some cases the finished works are less impressive than the first sketches, which are almost overpowering in their concentrated vehemence and gloomy majesty. But we must beware of regarding these as simple sketches from nature. They are more strictly studies for pictures than sketches from nature, and it is hardly too much to say that they owe more of their energetic emotional appeal to the Wilson tradition, which Turner had by this time thoroughly assimilated, than to the immediate inspiration of nature.

[1] See Plate XVI. for the study for the Farnley picture.

CHAPTER IV

THE SEA-PAINTER—1802-1809

Connection between marine painting and the sublime—Turner's first marine subjects—The 'Bridgewater Sea-piece'—'Meeting of the Thames and Medway'—'Our landing at Calais' and 'Calais Pier'—'Fishermen upon a Lee Shore'—'Guisborough Shore' and 'Dunbar' sketch-books—'The Shipwreck'—At the Mouth of the Thames'—'The Nore,' 'Sheerness,' etc.—'Death of Nelson.'

WE have studied in the preceding chapter the first phase of Turner's genuinely creative work. We have seen the artist tear himself free from the trammels of the prosaic understanding, with its clear-cut distinctions between external nature and subjective thought and feeling, and plunge whole-heartedly into the concrete world of the poetic imagination. The accomplished draughtsman of the visible has developed into the perfervid poet of the invisible. Objective reality, as such, is shattered and trampled ruthlessly underfoot.

'Woe! woe!
Thou hast destroy'd
The beautiful world
With violent blow
'Tis shiver'd! 'tis shatter'd!
The fragments abroad by a demigod scatter'd!
Now we sweep
The wrecks into nothingness!
Fondly we weep
The beauty that's gone!
Thou, 'mongst the sons of earth,
Lofty and mighty one,
Build it once more!
In thine own bosom the lost world restore!'

The distinction between percipient and object is brushed aside, and the external world becomes the medium and the means

40

of manifestation of inward perceptions and ideas. How far the external world can be built up again in the bosom of the self-conscious subject depends largely upon the opportunities and genius of the individual.

In pictures like the 'Kilgarran Castle,' 'Norham Castle,' and 'The Trossachs'—to take perhaps the three most successful works of the kind of art we have been studying—the mind only partially coalesces with its objects. Such art only deals with a limited range of subject-matter, and it treats its objects rather as foils to the contemplative mind than as having significance and worth in themselves. The terrors of inorganic nature are not represented for their own sake, but are paraded to mark the triumph of the moral freedom that rises superior to them. The artist is therefore forced to do violence to external nature, to subdue it and degrade it into a symbol of what is antagonistic in his own conscious experience. Yet by sheer force of artistic treatment all this hostile and negative matter is brought within the realm of art, and made into an object in which the self-scrutinising spirit of man finds itself mirrored.

But the sublime lies only on the threshold of beauty. It succeeds, in so far as it does attain its effect, only by making extreme demands upon the acquired culture and reasoning powers of the spectator. The sublime cannot be adequately represented by any sensuous object, but the very inadequacy of these objects can stir up and evoke this feeling in the properly prepared spectator.

There are ampler possibilities of beauty in the realm of the sea painter. At first sight it may seem that the change is merely a change from one region of inorganic nature to another, from rocks, torrents and glaciers, to the stormy and impetuous sea. But if we examine the substance of Turner's marine pictures carefully, we find that they contain elements which lend themselves more readily to a systematic unity in sensuous form. In his mountainous pieces Turner found room for very little immediate human interest. Man and his everyday occupations are banished from the steep and rocky places he chooses to represent, as incompatible with the gloomy, awe-struck feeling he wishes to evoke. The only immediate link with the feelings and interests of those for whom he worked which these pictures contained, was the shattered masonry of a castle built in the recesses of the past by men long since dead, but whose purposes and fate still awoke echoes in the historical imagination of the present. In his marine subjects Turner entered more closely into relation with the substantive interests of his time. During the Napoleonic wars the sea had come to be recognised as the chief safeguard of the nation. The dangers of the sea, the courage and skill of her sailors, were England's only bulwarks against the invincible legions of Napoleon. The gathering of the French armies of invasion along the shores of Brittany, the flotillas of gun-boats and flat-bottomed boats safely moored at Boulogne and Ambleteuse, focussed the attention of the nation upon a point outside the limited and varying interests of the individual citizen, and united them all in the same community of hopes and fears. The existence and welfare of the nation were at stake, the need of self-sacrifice was felt, and the individual became animated with the common sentiments of the nation. The stress of circumstance woke up what I may call the merely physical and material nation into a self-conscious spiritual unity, thinking the same thoughts and throbbing with the same emotions.

At such a moment the poet's and the artist's task is made comparatively easy. Their individual experiences are charged with a universal import; their art rises to the dignity of a public function. They have only to be true to their own impulses to realise the absolute beauty of eternal life. And it was happily at such a moment in the life of the English nation that Turner wearied of his ruined castles and terrifying mountains—of the picturesque in general—and devoted himself to marine painting.

The list of Turner's exhibited works shows that he was early drawn to the sea and sailors. In 1796 he exhibited a drawing called ' Fishermen at Sea,' the next year another entitled ' Fishermen coming Ashore at Sunset, previous to a Gale,' and in 1799 there were two oil pictures, one of ' The Battle of the Nile,' and the other of ' Fishermen Becalmed previous to a Storm—Twilight.' I have not, unfortunately, been able to see any of these works, but some studies and drawings in the National Gallery made about 1796 show that Turner began his career as a marine painter under

PLATE XVII

STUDY FOR THE "BRIDGEWATER SEA PIECE"

PEN AND INK, WASH, AND WHITE CHALK ON BLUE PAPER. ABOUT 1801

PLATE XVIII

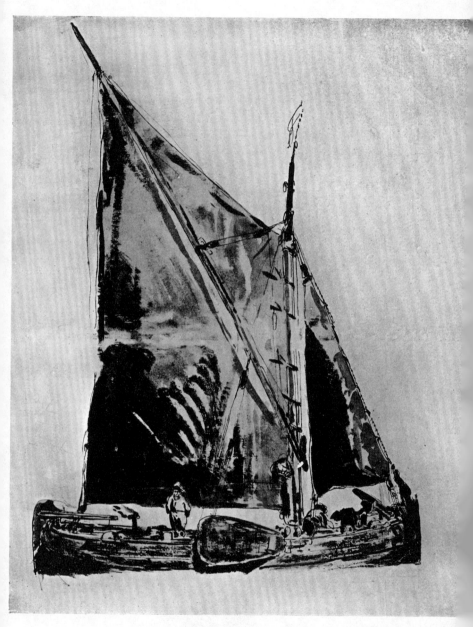

STUDY OF A BARGE WITH SAILS SET

PEN AND INK, WASH, AND WHITE CHALK ON BLUE PAPER. ABOUT 1802

THE SEA-PAINTER

the marked influence of Rowlandson, George Morland and De Loutherbourg. There is one animated little drawing with brown ink outlines of sailors getting some obstreperous pigs on board a small coasting vessel in a strong gale of wind. Apparently the cart has been driven into the sea beside the vessel, an impossible feat in such a sea; the sea must also be too deep for the wheels of the cart to rest on the ground, and if the wheels touch the bottom there is not enough water for the two boats. But in spite of these minor defects the subject provides scope for a fine animated group of men in the cart struggling with the pigs, who have determined to precipitate themselves into the water rather than go where they are wanted.

That Turner was not altogether satisfied with his design is proved by the existence of two other versions of the same subject. In one of these the motive of the cart in the sea has been abandoned. The cart is now placed in the foreground on the beach, and the rearing horses and struggling and shouting men are clearly inspired by Rowlandson's and De Loutherbourg's treatment of similar themes. These drawings are in pencil outline only, but there is also a rather elaborate water-colour of a shipwrecked sailor clinging to the rocks, with huge glassy-coloured waves in the manner of De Loutherbourg.

Turner's unfamiliarity with the sea no doubt accounted to some extent for its attraction. His imagination was here free to disport itself untrammelled by the bonds of experience, and safe from the irksome yoke of the familiar. When we come to study Turner's first important sea-piece, the fine picture in the Bridgewater House collection of 'Dutch Boats in a Gale: Fishermen endeavouring to put their Fish on Board'—first exhibited in 1801, we can see how little art is bound to depend upon the individual artist's personal experience. Turner had painted landscapes before he knew the country, and buildings before he had seen them, so now he paints sea-pieces before he has been to sea. There is no evidence to show that he had ventured out of sight of land before 1802, and then it was only to cross the Channel from Dover to Calais. But before this he had exhibited not only the Bridgewater picture to which I have referred, but a large 'Battle of the Nile' (1799), Lord Iveagh's superb 'Fishermen upon a Lee

43

Shore' (1802), and the almost equally fine 'Ships bearing up for Anchorage' (1802), in the Petworth gallery.

It is true that he had used to the uttermost the few opportunities which had fallen in his way of observing the sea from the shore, and that he had some little experience of ships and sailors in rivers and on the coast. (See, for example, the series of sketches of boats' crews towing men-of-war in the River Usk, in the 'Cyfarthfa' Sketch-Book of 1798.) What direct knowledge of this kind he possessed he naturally used, but there can be no doubt that the main body of his knowledge as well as inspiration was derived not at first-hand, but indirectly, at first, through the pictures of English painters like De Loutherbourg, and later, through the pictures and drawings of the Dutch sea-painters. The point is worth the attention of those who treat the close connection between art and nature which happens to exist just at present as an inherent characteristic of pictorial art, and make much of this supposed characteristic in opposition to the freedom of music. When we cease to keep our attention riveted on the naturalistic art of the present, we soon find indications that the essential forms of pictorial art are as much independent constructions of the creative mind as the forms of music.

In the group of studies for pictures of the sea which are related to the Duke of Bridgewater's picture, we see Turner playing with pictorial forms with as much freedom as a musician plays with his notes. The horizontal line of the sea, the heaving waves, the masses of light and dark in the sky, the stolid forms of the big ships, the instability of the smaller boats,—these are notes which Turner never seems wearied of evoking, and weaving into ever fresh combinations. The demands of mere representation count for almost nothing in these entrancing drawings. The artist draws simply because he loves his artistic symbols, loves weaving them into designs, and because his gift of melodic invention is inexhaustible.

The group of drawings to which I refer seems to have been made originally in a small book, solidly bound in calf. On one of the covers Turner has printed boldly in ink 'Studies P,' and 'Shipping,' which means, doubtless, Studies for Pictures of Shipping. The paper is blue with a coarse surface, similar to

PLATE XIX

FISHERMEN LAUNCHING A BOAT IN A ROUGH SEA

PEN AND INK AND WASH. ABOUT 1802

PLATE XX

STUDY FOR "SUN RISING THROUGH VAPOUR"

BLACK AND WHITE CHALK ON BLUE PAPER, ABOUT 1804

that commonly used by students in the French ateliers, and known as Michallet paper.   The designs were generally roughly pencilled in, and were then carried further in pen and ink, with bold washes of Indian ink.   White chalk was also freely used.   The book was in use before 1799, as it contains a number of studies for the painter's diploma picture of Dolbadarn Castle.   These studies are made in coloured chalks, most of them still very effective, although they have wasted a good deal of their force upon the pages that have been pressed down over them.   This is, I believe, one of the few occasions on which Turner has been known to work in pastel.   Doubtless many of the shipping designs were never carried out, but among them there are studies for the large water-colour of Carnarvon Castle exhibited in 1800, and for the two water-colours of Pembroke Castle, one (now belonging to Mrs. Pitt Miller) exhibited in 1801, and the other (the glorious one now belonging to Mr. Ralph Brocklebank) exhibited in 1806.

But the actual studies for the ' Bridgewater Sea-piece ' were made in a much larger book, a book which seems to have been devoted at first to the purpose of making life studies at the Academy classes.   But it contains only about half a dozen drawings of this kind, while about sixty pages are devoted to studies of pictures, some historical, like the ' Deluge,' etc., but most of them sea-pieces.   The paper is coarse blue, like the smaller book, the size of the leaves being $17 \times 10\frac{1}{2}$ inches, and most of the studies are continued over the two open pages.   Throughout the book one recognises a certain sense of pride and exaltation in the mere size of the paper, and in the unchecked freedom with which the artist's hand and imagination could disport themselves.

One of the earliest studies for the 'Bridgewater Sea-piece ' represents simply a straight line of sea with two ships on it in the distance, one foreshortened, the other in profile.   In the extreme distance is a line of white chalk suggesting a strip of sunlight on a distant coast.   The idea is so bald and empty and so unlike the final result that one would not connect the study with the picture did it not bear Turner's inscription, ' Duke's Picture,' in the margin.

The next study shows that Turner's mind is occupied with the

idea of filling up the emptiness of the middle distance and foreground. On the left we have two fishing-boats pitching to the
right in shadow, while the two frigates ride at anchor in the distance, very much as in the first sketch. The two groups are
united simply by the cast shadow on the water thrown by the
fishing-boats in the direction of the frigates (Plate XVII.).

The next study shows the artist trying to find a more interesting way of uniting the two groups. Here the two motives are
tied together as it were by a small rowing-boat with men in it half
hidden in the trough of the waves. The group of fishing-boats is
also slightly altered, their sails accentuating their common sway-
ing motion. In this drawing the various objects are no longer
juxtaposed in a seemingly casual or arbitrary way. A subtle bond
of union has sprung up between them. The rowing-boat rocks
the reverse way to that of the large group of sailing vessels. The
two rocking motions reinforce and explain one another. The
movement of each gains in vividness, and they both increase the
intensity of our perception of the steadiness and weight of the boat
riding at anchor out there on the right. In this way the sea comes
to life in its effects, and the design is ready to be transferred to
the canvas and for further elaboration.

This playing with our feelings of equilibrium and movement
constitutes one of the prime factors of Turner's enjoyment in his
earlier sea-pieces. He is taking possession of his new realm,
getting his sea-legs as it were. We see this plainly in the beautiful
little picture of 'The Meeting of the Thames and Medway' in the
National Gallery. (This is a small version of the larger picture now
in America. There is also another equally fine small version in the
University Galleries, Oxford.) The strong heaving wave on which
the buoy dances in the foreground sets the main motive of the
picture—the play of wind and waves—clearly forward. The
small boat with the four men in it is flung sideways and upward.
We feel it as the light plaything of the heavy waves. In the
middle distance there are two groups of heavier craft with sails
set, one group, on the left, coming straight towards us, the other
group scudding straight across the picture plane, just about to
disappear out of the frame on the right. The dancing buoy and
the light rowing-boat in the foreground make us feel at once the

PLATE XXI

STUDY FOR "THE SHIPWRECK"

PEN AND INK AND WASH. ABOUT 1805

weight and bulk of these sailing hoys. We feel them settling down in the mettlesome sea, gripping it tight as a rider grips his horse with his knees, while they fling out their sails to the wind. They are like living, panting, quivering animals. In the far distance rides a large frigate at anchor, and the firm base line of the horizon might stand as a symbol of the self-possession, strength of will, and unity of the conscious self, which delights in differences, while never entirely losing itself in the multifarious maze of experience.

In our sketch-book there are some of the undeveloped germs of this picture. In these sketches parts of the design have been firmly grasped, but the whole movement has not yet come to light. In the fine drawing running across pages 90 and 91, for example, the action of the two scurrying hoys on the right, together with the rocking boat in the foreground, is clearly marked. But there is nothing to counterbalance the swift rush of these boats. If we look at this study with the remembrance of the final design in our minds we feel there is something missing. We want the heavy waddling hoys on the left coming towards us, with their hulls jammed deep in the waves ; we want something to give us a sense of solidity, something, as it were, to hold on to, to steady ourselves in the sway and rush.

All these trial sketches, this laborious piecing together of the designs, suggest that Turner was not trying to realise something that he had actually seen. No doubt this was the case, yet we must not hastily conclude that he was simply making it all up out of his head, as the common saying runs. His smaller sketch-books show that he had constantly watched such scenes. The object of his trial sketches was therefore to find an adequately expressive form which would do justice to the wealth of his experience. He was not trying simply to make an abstractly beautiful composition. His task was rather to knit together into conceptual unity his wide range of experience, and then to body this forth in a carefully selected and articulated sequence of sensuous signs.

But some of the pages of the book in which the sketches referred to above occur, prove that the well-known picture of 'Calais Pier' is in the main an attempt to realise a scene that Turner had actually witnessed. On pages 58 and 59 there is a vigorous drawing in black and white chalk inscribed ' Our landing at Calais—nearly swampt.' The packet boat had evidently had a rough crossing, and now the passengers are being landed in boats with considerable difficulty. In this sketch the boat seems to have stuck on the harbour bar, and, beyond, the packet which the passengers have just left is lowering its mainsail. Another sketch shows the small boat flung finally on the shore with the passengers struggling among the surf. The picture is no doubt an attempt to realise the scene which presented itself immediately on the arrival of the packet boat, before the passengers began to land. This was Turner's general idea, but the composition had to be invented and appropriate details found to sustain and reinforce the main idea.

This incident occurred in 1802, and we have to go back to the previous year to find what seem to me the materials used in the construction of Lord Iveagh's superb ' Fishermen upon a Lee-Shore in Squally Weather,' a picture that will be fresh in the public mind, as it formed one of the chief attractions at the exhibition of English pictures at the Franco-British Exhibition held in London last year (1908). Two little pocket-books, used during Turner's journey to the Scotch lakes, are filled with drawings of the heavy billows of the North Sea thundering on a lee shore. The first book was used on the Yorkshire coast, the other on the wild coast between Berwick and Edinburgh. The Yorkshire book bears Turner's label, ' Guisborough Shore,' on the back. It consists of a small number of pages of coarse blue paper. These pages are filled with magnificent impressions of waves dashing against rocks, and of dark, heavy fishing-boats silhouetted against the foaming white sea. The ' Liber' design of the ' Coast of Yorkshire near Whitby ' (R. 24) was doubtless suggested on this occasion.

The other book, the ' Dunbar' sketch-book as Turner named it, consists of leaves of stout Whatman coated with washes of a murky pinkish brown. The advantage of using white paper prepared in this way is, that the artist can get his lights by simply using his knife to scratch away the preparation. This book contains sketches of the ruins of Roslin Castle, the Bass Rock, Tantallon and Dunbar Castles. The wild and disconsolate scenes

PLATE XXII

MEN-OF-WAR'S BOATS FETCHING PROVISIONS (1)

PENCIL. ABOUT 1808

between St. Abb's Head and Dunbar seem to have deeply impressed Turner's imagination. As we turn over the leaves of this book we seem to hear 'the sombrous and heavy sound of the billows successively dashing against the rocky beach' that Scott speaks of in his description of Fast Castle in the *Bride of Lammermoor*. The artist seems too excited to draw in his old static fashion. The stretches of sullen sea are sketched again and again, the white crests of the incoming waves being dug out furiously with the knife. But only the large masses of light and dark are indicated. Here we have a stretch of cold light in the sky with the dark sea and cliffs looming against it, the whole vague and fragmentary, but irresistibly impressive. But perhaps the most eloquent pages in the book contain two glorious studies of storm-tossed waves. We are looking out from the shore, with the waves breaking at our feet. Even in his more elaborate work Turner has never suggested the tremendous weight and power of the sea-waves so vividly as in these hurried and tiny sketches. The furious work with the knife on both sides of the paper has reduced it almost to a rag; but the rag is eloquent, and such studies as these help us to understand how it was that Turner could paint the sea so very much better than any artist either before his time or since.

'The Shipwreck,' one of the most successful of Turner's early sea-pieces, was painted in 1805. The picture is doubtless a 'composition' in which Turner has endeavoured to sum up his knowledge of the sea, but, as was usual with him, it contains a nucleus of directly observed fact. These two sides of his art, tireless and the most searching observation, and the subsequent artistic manipulalation of what he had seen and felt, are clearly displayed for us in two little ragged paper-covered note-books labelled by the artist 'Shipwreck' and 'Shipwreck 2.' The first contains the succinct record of an actual shipwreck, the second the series of trial compositions which he made before the final design of the picture was fixed.

Eight of the pages of the first book—it only contains sixteen pages in all—have long been exhibited among the Turner water-colours in the National Gallery. They are framed together, and numbered 535. They represent so many different views of a barque going to pieces on the shore. There can be no doubt of the veracity of these bold, masterly pen sketches; as Mr. Ruskin says of them, ' I believe even those who have not seen a shipwreck, must recognise, by the instinct of awe, the truth of these records of a vessel's ruin' (*Ruskin on Pictures*, p. 221). In the margin of one of the drawings Turner has scribbled 'Pepper (?) bargh Vessel. Hemp. O. Iron bundles like Hoop.' The scenery vaguely suggests the coast of Kent to me —possibly Gravesend.

These sketches are so impressive that one would have thought that Turner would have been satisfied to take any one of them as a basis for a picture. But his mind seemed unsatisfied until he had exalted actuality into something of epic grandeur. The second little book shows how he set to work to make his pictures express a clearer intention and a wider mental outlook than any single incident could.

The first sketch shows us a large ship settling down at the bows, with a single rowing-boat in the foreground. We are far away from the shore. The tragedy is intensified by taking place on the high seas, but the presentment is evidently too bare and matter-of-fact for the artist. In the next sketch the ship is turning over towards us, though slightly to the right, so that we see its decks plainly, with the masts foreshortened towards us. Somewhat nearer to us is a welter of boats and figures, with a fishing-boat with sails set on the right, all placed low down in the trough of the sea. On page 13, the vessel is turned half over towards us, but to the left. The fishing-boat in the foreground sailing into the picture also has its mast and sails sloping violently to the left. This swing in the same direction of the two most prominent objects in the design strikes us as monotonous, and doubtless for this reason excited Turner's disapproval. On page 16, the vessel is brought nearer and made a more prominent object in the design. It is now turned over away from us and slightly to the left. The welter of boats and figures is placed beyond the vessel, instead of in the foreground. In another sketch the ship lies on its side helpless on the right of the design, its masts and rigging in the water stretching right across the picture. Another of the sketches has been reproduced as Plate xxi. This is, perhaps, a little more fully realised than some of the others. It seems to have been drawn straight off in pen and ink, then the stormy sky and waves were indicated with an impetuous wash of

50

PLATE XXIII

MEN-OF-WAR'S BOATS FETCHING PROVISIONS (2)

PENCIL.   ABOUT 1808

Indian ink, which was then thumbed, dabbed, and coaxed to give
the requisite modelling. The sweep of the waves, their vicious
choppy spurts and explosions of spray, are given with a directness
and simplicity of means that I believe would have excited the
admiration of Korin himself.

I need not continue to describe all the pages in detail. The
point of interest is that Turner tried successively every possible
movement in the sinking of a big ship and looked at them from
every possible point of view. Then he finally decided that his
second sketch was the most suggestive and striking, so he took it
up again, and after considerable modification in the details, developed it into the completed work.

Between 1805 and 1809 Turner must have spent a good deal
of his time sailing up and down the lower reaches and the mouth
of the Thames. The contents of several sketch-books prove this.
In one there is a view of the Dutch coast with Flushing in the
distance, evidently drawn from the sea. But the subjects as a
rule are nearer home. In the book labelled ' River and Margate '
the subjects range from the Fishmarket at Hastings to Cobham
and Walton Bridges. These include sketches near London
Bridge, at Purfleet, Greenwich, Gravesend, Southend, Herne Bay,
and Margate. But these are only treated as backgrounds to the
ships and boats. We have pages and pages of wherries and
Thames barges bundling along with all sails set past massive ships
of the line at anchor, all drawn as swiftly as they seem to move.
These are almost too slight for reproduction, but the two
animated scenes of men-of-war's boats victualling, reproduced as
Plates XXII. and XXIII., give an excellent idea of the spirit in which
Turner worked on these occasions. Looking out to sea we see a
number of ships of the line riding at anchor. Round the landing-
stages in the foreground are the ships' boats taking in stores of
bread, hay and straw, sheep and fish. The day is fine, but there
is evidently a wind blowing; the sea is choppy; there is plenty of
spray about, and the pennants stand out taut from the masts of
the big ships in the offing. It is all drawn with a few hurried,
nervous pencil outlines, nothing is described in detail, yet the
whole scene is brought as vividly before us as the most elaborate
oil painting could bring it.

51

TURNER'S SKETCHES AND DRAWINGS

Another little book, labelled ' Boats. Ice,' shows that Turner was no mere fair weather sailor. The sketches were evidently made during a severe winter. The book starts off with several lurid sunsets. On page 9 we see some boatmen on their barges, a church, probably Gravesend Church, in the distance. The sun has disappeared behind a bank of clouds. These have the word ' grey' scribbled over them. Over a few hurried lines of pencil radiating from a centre behind these clouds are the suggestive words ' Fire and Blood.' On page 12, we have a stretch of river with a distant group of trees on the left looming through the fog. The river is strewn with fragments of ice. On the right a single boat is visible, its tall mast and stays standing out boldly against the sky. Above, the upper part of the sun's face is just appearing through the clouds. This slight, sensitive sketch is helped out for the artist—though for the imaginative spectator it hardly needs such help, so eloquent is it—by scribbled notes of colour ; ' Boat . . . yellow,' the water in the foreground, ' Greenish Black in Shadows. Ice white and grey.'

On the next page we find two barges with brittle fragments of ice hanging round them. On page 16, there is a barge moored beside what seems to be a huge iceberg, with two figures on it, though it may only be a rocky shore distorted by snow and ice into its fantastic appearance. But the sketch on the next page looks emphatically like an iceberg. The following sketch is here reproduced (Plate XXIV.), so the reader may judge for himself what it is. To me it looks like floating icebergs, the foremost one containing a wrecked vessel embedded in its surface. This page was cut out by Mr. Ruskin and exhibited at Oxford with the title, ' The Inscrutable.'

Turner has summed up these experiences of his in a group of absolutely unrivalled sea-pieces. Pictures like Mr. F. H. Fawkes's ' Pilot hailing a Whitstable Hoy,' Mr. G. J. Gould's ' The Nore,' Mr. P. A. B. Widener's ' Meeting of the Thames and Medway,' and Lady Wantage's ' Sheerness,' seem to me beyond all question the most glorious pictures of the sea ever painted. The finest Dutch pictures of this kind, with all their admirable qualities, do not seem ever to get beyond a certain prosaic outlook. This matter-of-fact effect is enhanced by—if it is not altogether due to it

PLATE XXIV

THE SEA-PAINTER

—the ruthless display the artists make of their special knowledge
of the construction and rigging of their vessels. I believe Turner's
knowledge of this kind was almost as exhaustive as theirs, but
whether as full or more limited, he made a better use of what he
did know. His objects are never there simply for themselves.
They are always subordinated to a genuinely imaginative conception. His pictures, therefore, are not the work of a man with a
professional speciality. They are real epics of the sea. From
their own imaginative point of view their workmanship is almost
perfect. Their style is sonorous and weighty. They are as solemn
and majestic in conception as they are manly in feeling. They
have something of that 'beauty which,' as Milton sings, 'hath
terror in it.' Together 'they move in perfect phalanx to the
Dorian mood'—the noblest sequence of poems ever dedicated
to the majesty of the sea.

When we compare such pictures as these with a subject like
'The Death of Nelson,' in the National Gallery,—a subject dealing
directly with a particular historical incident—we cannot but feel
that they owe something of their loftiness and grandeur to their
exaltation above all merely limited feelings of patriotism. I
suppose a Frenchman could hardly be expected to look at the
'Nelson' with quite the same feelings as an Englishman; or a
Dane to regard the 'Spithead; Boat's crew recovering an anchor'
—which actually represents the return of the English fleet with
the Danish ships captured at Copenhagen—in the way this event
was hailed in England. The feeling of patriotism is no doubt an
admirable and useful one in real life; but in so far as art is tied
down to the service of a particular kind of patriotism, it is limited
to this definite end, and is not entirely free in and for itself. And
art which is not entirely free from all finite ends cannot rise to the
full height of its own destiny.

Yet in the very greatest art there is no opposition to all that is
essentially noble and heroic in patriotism. A masterpiece like
Lady Wantage's 'Sheerness,' for example, is as full of all the
essential virtues of patriotism as a picture like the 'Death of
Nelson.' The difference is only in the degrees of emphasis placed
on certain aspects of the whole conception. In the 'Sheerness'
the interest is concentrated on the guardship at the Nore, and all

53

that is implied in this aspect of a nation's discipline, hardihood, watchfulness, and self-sacrifice. And on this idea of military (or naval) service for the Fatherland the possibility of actual struggle and, if need be, death at the hands of any national enemy is clearly involved. The 'Death of Nelson,' therefore, only makes explicit a single moment held in solution in the other picture. Hence the question is not between the value of patriotic feeling and a shallow, empty form of cosmopolitanism as artistic motives, but merely under which aspect the virtues of patriotism are to be contemplated. Which aspect does fullest justice to the whole conception of personal devotion and sacrifice to the commonweal? My own feeling is that the point of view which raises itself above the particular interests of one nation, and treats the hardships and dangers of national defence as an inevitable condition of human life, is more in accord with the freedom and universality of the highest art. The question, I repeat, is only one of degree, and these remarks will be entirely misunderstood if they are taken to imply that I should have wished that either the 'Nelson' or the 'Spithead' had not been painted. In the 'Spithead,' as a matter of fact, the connection with the particular historical incident which called it into existence has long dropped out of sight, whilst the 'Nelson' has always caused a certain feeling of dissatisfaction even among the most ardent and exclusive of patriots. This vague feeling is possibly at the root of the adverse technical criticisms to which it has been subjected by sailors and naval experts. These criticisms are generally in themselves entirely wrongheaded and sometimes fatuous, for the picture is certainly a grand and impressive one, and by far the most adequate representation in pictorial art of an event of the greatest national importance. But the intuitive sense of the nation has always thought more highly of such a picture as 'The Fighting Téméraire tugged to her last Berth,' than of the 'Death of Nelson.' In 'The Fighting Téméraire,' as in the earlier masterpieces to which I have referred, there is no touch of chauvinism or vainglory, yet it is generously and passionately patriotic: but it is magnanimous patriotism, which honours its foe and looks beyond and above the present momentary noise and strife.

CHAPTER V

'SIMPLE NATURE'—1808-1813

The works of this period an important yet generally neglected aspect of Turner's art—Turner's classification of 'Pastoral' as opposed to 'Elegant Pastoral'—The Arcadian idyll of the mid-eighteenth century—The first 'Pastoral' subjects in 'Liber'—'Windmill and Lock'—The capture of the Danish Fleet in 1807—Turner's visit to Portsmouth—His return journey —'Hedging and Ditching'—An attempt to define the mood of pictures like 'The Frosty Morning,' 'Windsor,' etc.—Distinction between mood and character.

THE phase of Turner's work which we are now to consider seems to me one to which the critics have hardly done justice. The supreme beauty of two of the pictures of this group has certainly been recognised—I allude to the 'Trout Stream' and Lady Wantage's 'Walton Bridges,' but these works have been treated mainly on their individual merits, instead of in their connection with a clearly-marked and most significant aspect of the artist's genius. Chronologically, this period ranges from about the year 1808 to 1813, and it includes, in addition to the two works just mentioned, the 'Windsor,' 'Abingdon,' 'Kingston Bank,' 'Frosty Morning,' 'Union of the Thames and Isis' and 'Sandbank with Gipsies,' all in the National Gallery, as well as Sir Frederick Cook's 'Windmill and Lock' and Mr. Orrock's 'Walton Bridges.' These works all strike me as characterised by a certain mood or standpoint which possesses the profoundest significance for modern art,—a mood, moreover, which has not yet, to my knowledge, been satisfactorily analysed, and which Turner could never afterwards recall in all its essential beauty, though he frequently made the attempt.

I must confess that in spite of all my efforts I am quite unable to find a term that will adequately characterise this phase of

55

TURNER'S SKETCHES AND DRAWINGS

Turner's art. Turner's own classification of such subjects as those mentioned above is 'Pastoral,' as distinguished from the 'Elegant Pastoral.' But this description is inadequate, because it seems to refer simply to the objects contained in the works, while it is exactly the mood or emotional standpoint from which the subject-matter is treated that seems to me all-important. The contemporary term for this kind of work, and one which Turner sometimes used himself, was 'Simple Nature,' and this description, though inadequate enough, is perhaps as good as any other we might hit upon. It indicated, at least, an antagonism to any artificial way of treating natural scenes, and suggested a certain unsophisticated plainness and directness of approach, and these qualities are certainly contained in the complex and subtle conception we are in search of. It is, then, as a painter of 'Simple Nature' that we have now to consider our subject.

In externals, this phase of Turner's art is occupied with scenes of ordinary rural life; it deals with the country as the home and working place of the peasantry. This gives us the distinction between the 'Pastoral' and the 'Elegant Pastoral' subjects in the 'Liber,' the elegant pastorals dealing with the country as the imaginative home and background of the stock figures of conventionally imaginative art. The elegant pastoral subjects are generally peopled with nymphs, classical shepherds and shepherdesses, goddesses and peacocks, while the pastoral subjects which are not elegant are peopled with real labouring men and women and unideal-looking children.

But the external subject-matter of a work of art tells us very little by itself. The important point is the universal which binds these objects together or organises them into an individual conception. We must think of our group of pictures as falling within the larger class of strictly pastoral subjects, but characterised by a special method of treatment and conception. One way of approaching this special conception will be to mark off a few of the pastoral subjects in the 'Liber' which do not fall within it. And this is all the easier because Turner's first pastoral subject in the 'Liber' is conventional and empty, and he only gradually worked himself into a conception of the full possibilities of the category. That is to say, he first took up this form of art in a

PLATE XXV

SKETCH FOR "HEDGING AND DITCHING"

PENCIL. ABOUT 1807

PLATE XXVI

"HEDGING AND DITCHING"

WASH DRAWING IN SEPIA FOR "LIBER STUDIORUM." ABOUT 1808

casual and external way, and then gradually took possession of it and mastered it.

The first three plates in the ' Liber ' are classified as ' Pastoral,' Elegant Pastoral,' and ' Marine.' When we compare the marine subject (the so-called ' Flint Castle,' which we now know to have been a scene on the French coast [1]) with the two pastoral subjects, we cannot but be struck with the disparity between the two classes of subjects. The marine subject is vigorous and veracious, the pastoral subjects unreal and conventionally poetical. This point of view is in keeping with the conception of the elegant pastoral, but ' The Bridge and Cows ' (R. 2)—the pastoral subject —is as gentle and pretty as a picture in an idyll of Gessner or Thomson. This, indeed, represents Turner's point of departure as a painter of rural subjects—the standpoint of the senti-mental, affected, and unconvincing Arcadian idyll of the middle of the eighteenth century.

The ' Straw-Yard,' the second pastoral subject in the ' Liber,' strikes me as a cross between a Gainsborough and a Teniers. Gainsborough's influence is noticeable in the landscape, while the ungainly horses, the awkward men and clumsy farm implements are in the spirit of Dutch realism. These hints of the plainness and toughness of the marine subjects suggest what Turner will do when he feels equally at home in rural subjects, but at present we have merely two incompatible points of view in arbitrary juxta-position. ' Pembury Mill,' the third pastoral, is rather more homogeneous in intention. It is a scene of cheerful industry and plenty, the noise of the millstone mingling with the cooing of pigeons, and lush leaves growing beside the water-wheel. It is a pretty subject, while no conscious attempts have been made to prettify or blink the actual facts of the case. The ' Farm-Yard with the Cock' (R. 17) still belongs to the eighteenth-century idyll. It is a pleasing combination of Gainsborough and Morland, or perhaps an echo of Wheatley. In the ' Juvenile Tricks ' (R. 22) [2] Turner's bent towards homely realism is clearly marked, but we do not get definitively away from the eighteenth century till we come to the ' Windmill and Lock ' (R. 27). [3] Here we are in an entirely different world from that of Arcadian poetry. We have

---

[1] See Plate XXXVII. [2] Plate XXXVIII. [3] Plate XXVII (b).

now put away childish things, and are face to face with the big real world in which man earns his bread with the sweat of his brow; in which men and women labour and sin, sorrow and repent. It is indeed the real world, the world of common perception and common experience, yet transfigured with the solemn glow of the truest and profoundest poetry.

The engraving of the ' Windmill and Lock ' was published in June, 1811, but the picture and drawing were made some time before this date. In the part of the ' Liber ' published immediately before the one which contained this plate, there was a plate of ' Hind Head Hill ' (R. 25), which bears the date of 1st January, 1811. This subject was sketched in November 1807. It is therefore probable that the two drawings were made soon afterwards, let us say in 1808.

The period of the inception of ' Hind Head Hill,' then, marks the commencement of the era of Turner's deeper and more solemn conception of the poetry of rural life. This subject itself, though classified in the ' Liber ' as 'mountainous,' belongs to all intents and purposes to the phase of art which we are now studying. The bare hills dotted with sheep, with the murderer's corpse creaking upon the distant gibbet, are quite in harmony with the mood of Wordsworth's *Lyrical Ballads*. In the same sketch-book are also the first ideas of no less than three other ' Liber ' subjects, all conceived in the same mood of spiritual exaltation, and all sketched during the same journey from Portsmouth to London.

The events connected with this journey were of a nature calculated to throw Turner's mind out of its ordinary habits and thoughts, to carry him ' out of himself,' and to prepare him for seeing the familiar scenes of everyday life in a fresh light. These events have therefore a special interest for us in this connection.

In May 1807 the Prince Regent of Portugal warned the Prince of Wales that Napoleon was on the point of invading England with the Portuguese and Danish fleets, and that the Emperor of Russia had bound himself by secret articles in the Treaty of Tilsit to support him in this measure. The ministry were informed of the plot, and Canning lost no time in dealing with the situation. An envoy was sent to the Crown Prince of Denmark at Kiel, with the demand that the Danish navy should be delivered over to England, to be taken care of in British ports, and restored at the end of the war. The demand was, of course, indignantly refused. But the situation was so serious that the ministry felt compelled to order the seizing of the Danish fleet, if it was not lent quietly. Denmark held the keys of the Baltic. Napoleon's troops were ready to overrun it at a moment's notice, and seize the fleet and all the naval stores, all that he wanted, in fact, for his attack on England. In securing the Danish fleet, the English then were simply taking it from Napoleon, and were merely acting for the purpose of self-preservation. By the 1st of September the French had occupied Stralsund. Copenhagen was immediately bombarded, and on the 8th the British entered the city, and the navy and arsenal were surrendered.

How this blow affected Napoleon is shown from a passage in Fouché's *Memoirs*, published in 1824. 'About that time it was,' says Fouché, 'that we learned the success of the attack upon Copenhagen by the English, which was the first derangement of the secret stipulations of Tilsit, by virtue of which the Danish fleet was to be placed at the disposal of France. Since the death of Paul I., I never saw Napoleon give himself up to such violent transports of passion. That which astounded him most in that vigorous enterprise was the promptitude with which the English ministry took their resolution.' (Quoted in Miss Martineau's *History of England*, 1800-1815, p. 283). At the time the mind of the public was profoundly stirred by this event. But the victors had almost brought the Danish ships within sight of England before the news of the frustration of Napoleon's plans was made public. Turner must have been as excited as any one, for he set off immediately to Portsmouth, to see the victors sail into the harbour with their prizes and to celebrate the occasion in his own way.

When Turner left London his sketch-books as a rule bear witness of the fact. In the 'Spithead' sketch-book there is no record of the journey down from London. The first thirty pages are taken up with sketches of the movements of vessels in Portsmouth harbour, on one of them being a sketch of a boat's crew recovering an anchor. In the following May, Turner included in his one-man show at his studio in Queen Anne Street

West, an unfinished picture 'of the Danish ships which were seized at Copenhagen, entering Portsmouth Harbour' (*Review of Publications of Art*, No. 2, June 1, 1808, p. 167). In the foreground a 'packet with soldiers on board' is mentioned, and 'two boats toward the left hand corner of the picture, one of which is heaving or letting go an anchor.' The whole description, and these details in particular, prove beyond a doubt that this was the picture which, when finished, was exhibited in the following year (1809), at the Royal Academy, under the title of 'Spithead : Boat's Crew recovering an Anchor,' and which hangs now in the National Gallery under this name. The change of title was most probably due to prudential considerations, as, after the first revulsion of popular feeling, the ministry had to endure considerable obloquy on account of this action, Napoleon's intention of invading the country as well as the existence of the secret articles of the Treaty of Tilsit being stoutly denied, and the government being pledged not to reveal the source of the information on which they had acted.

Our immediate interest in this event is with the effect produced on Turner's mind by the scenes which he had witnessed in and around Portsmouth. The sight of the united English and Danish fleets was one calculated to stir Turner's imagination profoundly. The artist's sensitive nature must also have been deeply affected by contact with the excited and jubilant populace, and with the sailors and fighting men upon whose individual exertions the safety of the country depended.

Such moments of national excitement tend inevitably to dwarf the petty and merely particular interests and prejudices of the individual. The substantive interests of the community, the universal forces that move men and hold them together, then present themselves in all their stark reality and overwhelming importance to every heart and mind. In such a mood, with a mind humbled and humanised, Turner set out to return to London.

As we turn over the leaves of the 'Spithead' sketch-book we can see clearly that the sights of the common round of rural life which greeted the artist after he had left Portsmouth behind, had gained a new interest and significance for him, by contrast with the stirring scenes he had just witnessed. He is no sooner clear

PLATE XXVII

MILL ON THE GRAND JUNCTION CANAL, NEAR HANWELL

PENCIL. ABOUT 1809

"WINDMILL AND LOCK"

ENGRAVING PUBLISHED IN "LIBER STUDIORUM," 1 JUNE, 1811

of the town than the groups of trees and the peaceful stretch of fields make their tranquillising influence felt. Several pages of sketches remind me forcibly of the scenery of 'The Frosty Morning.' Then we find groups of farm hands resting from their labour, some carts and horses, ploughing scenes, a study of horses and pigs, and then the hurried scribble reproduced in Plate xxv., the germ from which the beautiful 'Hedging and Ditching' design in the 'Liber' was developed. Then come several Hind Head sketches, and before the hill is out of sight, comes the original sketch of another 'Liber' subject, the solemn and tender 'Water Mill' (R. 37). After this we stop to watch the blacksmith at work, and peep into some cottages, barns, etc. To eke out his hasty hieroglyphs Turner frequently adds a few explanatory words. On the margin of one sketch we read 'Woman frying. Boy looking. Children at Tub, a girl beating the barrel, etc.'; and on another 'W.' (short for woman) 'cutting Turnips. Interior of a Barn. Cows eating at the Entrance, etc.' And before we get quite to the end of the book come four sketches of St. Catherine's Hill, near Guildford, one of which went to the making of another 'Liber' subject (R. 33).

The two sketches here reproduced, of the 'Windmill and Lock' and 'Hedging and Ditching' subjects (Plates XXVII. and XXV.), illustrate admirably Turner's attitude towards nature at this period. Such sketches are nothing more nor less than memoranda for the artist's own use. Taken by themselves they are all but meaningless. Even to the artist himself their significance, as memoranda of real scenes, must have been of the slightest. The focus or real nucleus of their meaning is rather the subjective feelings which the scenes and their whole context evoked in the artist, than the particular objects or scenes themselves. This sentiment, the total emotional impression, is, of course, not expressed in the sketches themselves, though now that the completed designs have told us what this is we can hardly help reading some of it into the sketches. But to the artist himself these sketches were useful as preliminary statements, as tentative objectifications of his meaning. The work of 'carrying out' these sketches (or 'working them out') was simply the process of the further specification of this meaning. And to describe this work as an attempt to realise or reproduce the actual scenes in nature which Turner had sketched, is only in a very limited sense correct. The point of interest is the complex of subjective feeling aroused on a particular occasion by a chance conjunction of objects and circumstances, and in the final design the artist's aim is to find a particular conjunction of pictorial signs which shall permanently objectify this emotional complex. Hence the actual objects and the particular form of their conjunction in the real scene lose all the importance which they possess as real objects, and become degraded, or at least subordinated, to a purpose which falls entirely outside their own existence. They are now nothing but pawns or counters in the artist's game of pictorial expression, and as such the artist has absolute power over them, altering them, and annihilating them, as best suits his purpose. The artist is also entirely within his rights when he introduces fresh elements from other and different scenes to enforce and make clear his meaning. That Turner used these privileges to the utmost in the case of both these subjects is evident when we compare the sketches with the finished designs. These points seem to me worth insisting upon, because the real nature of artistic idealisation is so little understood and so generally misrepresented, and the opportunities of studying it genetically are of rare occurrence.

But the very fact that during the period of which we are now treating, the stress in Turner's work is nearly always upon the subjective sentiment, and that the objective scenes and objects are relegated to a position of subordination detracts very largely from the immediate interest in the sketches from nature which Turner made during this time. Taken by themselves these sketches are in the highest degree vague and incomplete. They are valuable to us mainly for the purposes of comparison with the completed designs, and as illustrations of Turner's methods of work. And for these purposes I think the two examples we have just studied are sufficient. I have not, therefore, deemed it advisable to illustrate this chapter with any other sketches of the same class. The three further illustrations I have chosen are of a different character. When Turner was called upon to treat subjects of a definite topographical character he was necessarily

PLATE XXVIII

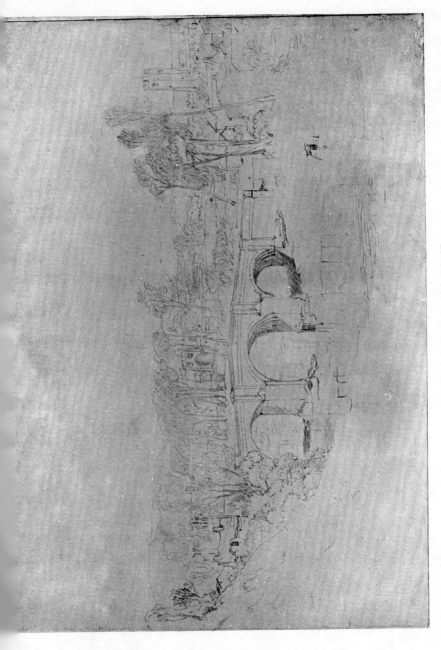

WHALLEY BRIDGE AND VILLAGE

PENCIL. ABOUT 1808

PLATE XXIX

restricted in the liberties he could take. In such cases his field of selection was confined within the possible points of view from which his subject could be regarded. In the two drawings of Whalley Bridge here reproduced (Plates XXVIII. and XXIX.) we see him searching for that aspect of the place which shall fit in or harmonise with the mood which was predominant in his own mind at this time. It is only from the point of view of such a subjective emotional attitude that the first drawing (Plate XXVIII.) could have been rejected in favour of the second (Plate XXIX.). As a representation of the actual place, the first drawing is much more adequate than the second. But it is evidently just this topographical and objective adequacy which constituted the defect of this fine drawing from Turner's point of view. In the other drawing there is far less to occupy the attention. Here the interest is concentrated on a few simple forms. The mind is, therefore, thrown back on itself, and forced as it were to call up its own resources to amplify and fill out the painter's forms. And this is the mood of poetic contemplation or meditation expressed in the beautiful picture of this subject which Turner exhibited in 1811, and which is now in Lady Wantage's collection.

The third drawing to which I referred is the study for the picture of 'London from Greenwich Park,' now in the National Gallery. There is no trace of the emotional setting of the finished picture in the sketch (Plate XXX.). It is merely a record of the facts. But the artist has already grasped in his own mind the significance of these facts with such clearness that the bare facts even in this memorandum have become eloquent.

The full scope of Turner's work at this period, then, can only be gathered from his completed works. And as I have said, I do not think this aspect of Turner's genius has so far had full justice done to it. I will therefore make an attempt to indicate in a few words what I regard as the distinctive qualities of this group of works; and to simplify my task I will centre my remarks round two pictures, both in the National Gallery, and therefore easily accessible to every one, viz., 'A Frosty Morning' and the 'Windsor,' which seem to me to typify the qualities and merits of the whole group.

After what has gone before I do not think I need say much to

TURNER'S SKETCHES AND DRAWINGS

combat the opinion that these pictures are simply reproductions of actual scenes. Their relation to the actual sights of nature is exactly the same as that between the two 'Liber' designs we have just examined and the sketches upon which they were based. In the designs, and in these pictures, there is indeed a wealth of subtle and penetrating observation of natural forms, habits, and colours, but this material is never there simply for its own sake. These colours and forms of natural beauty are the elements of which the artist's language is compounded, the pictorial equivalent of the names of natural objects in the verse of a great poet. To fix one's attention on these factors in the whole complex structure of such works as 'A Frosty Morning' and 'Windsor,' and to say that these fragments of meaning are all that they contain, seems to me as inexcusable as it would be to isolate the nouns in a poem, and to insist that we must ignore that play of thought and feeling around this common basis in which the real value of even the simplest poem consists. We can, of course, always stop short in our understanding of any statement, and the temptation is very great to stop short at some superficial characteristic in such a highly complex individuality as a work of modern art. In the case of the two pictures with which we are now concerned, these characteristics happen to be not only superficial and obvious, but they happen also to be easily nameable, whereas the complete ideational and emotional structure of the whole work is very far from being easily named or described. Yet it is just this particular and special emotional and ideational whole which constitutes the very being of the work of art, and which alone gives it value. It is because modern art-criticism has seized with such avidity upon the primitive sense-factor in pictorial language, and has insisted with so much energy that the art cannot or ought not to attempt any kind of ideational articulation, that it has failed to do justice to this phase of Turner's art.

To call these pictures, then, imitations or reproductions of natural scenes is not altogether inaccurate. They are this, but at the same time they are so much more. The forms and colours of nature are there, but they are superseded and sublimated in exactly the way that the particular events described in Dorothy Wordsworth's journal are superseded and sublimated in the poems

64

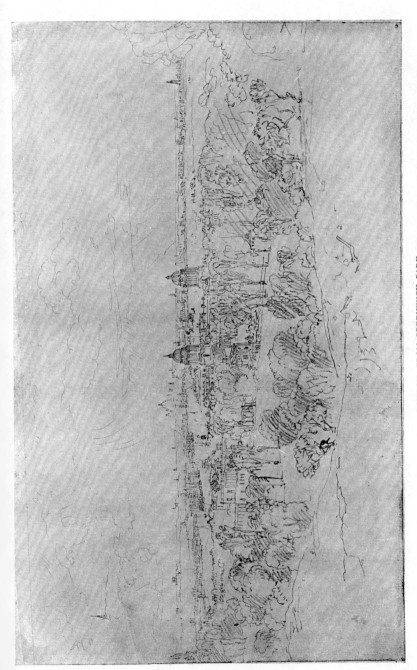

PLATE XXX

LONDON, FROM GREENWICH PARK

PENCIL. ABOUT 1809

PLATE XXXI

PETWORTH HOUSE, FROM THE LAKE

PENCIL.   ABOUT 1809

which her brother founded upon these events. 'The array of act and circumstance, and visible form' becomes exactly what the poet's or artist's 'passion makes them.'[1] In other words, the matter of sense intuition is taken up into the world of intelligence. This matter, which in the first place was something immediate or given, now loses its natural and positive attributes, loses its authority as fact, but gains a wider scope and ampler authority by being taken up into the world of mind and used as a sign. And here again an opportunity presents itself for shallow and wrong-headed criticism. Those who are under the dominion of the theory that art should only represent sensuous facts in their immediacy resent the transformation which the data of sense must undergo before they can take their place in the organised world of meaning. To them, therefore, such pictures as these are defective ; the colouring is not sufficiently natural, not bright enough, nor are the contrasts sufficiently strong. These pictures are not painted in 'the key of nature.' In a word, they are old-fashioned, because the artist has done something more in them than the theories of impressionism can consecrate.

We have then to avoid two mistaken ways of regarding these works. We must not look upon them (1) as attempts to reproduce the actual brilliancy and colour of natural lighting, nor must we treat them (2) as prosaic and literal imitations of actuality devoid of all the higher poetry of art. That these works are open to — nay, have almost invariably fallen victims to — these two opposite forms of depreciation, is a striking proof of the success with which they have avoided those fatal extremes in which so much of the art of the present lies engulfed.

But it is not enough simply to avoid the dangers which modern theorising throws in the way of the interpreter. A really concrete and fruitful criticism will not stop short till it has made the attempt to grasp, however imperfectly, by thought the full and special significance of each work. And again, when we have made it clear to ourselves that

> 'the array
> Of act and circumstance, and visible form,
> Is mainly to the pleasure of the mind
> What passion makes them,'—

---

[1] *The Prelude*, Bk. xiii, l, 287 *sq.*

when we have agreed that Turner has used the sights of nature as a means to express the emotions or the mood which they aroused in him,—when all this is granted we are still merely at the threshold of the works themselves.   A mood, an emotion, a state of feeling, these are all vague and general terms.   There is nothing necessarily admirable or beautiful in a mood or a state of feeling, Feeling and emotion may be pleasant or unpleasant, harmonious or jarring, depressing or invigorating.   And if the main value and beauty of these pictures resides in the particular and definite mood or state of feeling which they induce, this mood must have distinguishable contents, and it is the business of art criticism to do what it can to define these contents.

In Wordsworth's ' Lines, composed a few miles above Tintern Abbey,' he contrasts his present state of feeling towards nature with that of his youthful days.   In the days of his thoughtless youth, he says, the forms and colours of the landscape had haunted him like a passion.   He had loved them for themselves.   But now, he says, Nature is no longer 'all in all' to him.   It has now gained a remoter charm supplied by thought, an interest ' unborrowed from the eye.'   He now hears

> ' the still, sad music of humanity,
> Nor harsh nor grating, though of ample power
> To chasten and subdue.'

Before the sights of nature he now feels the presence of elevated thoughts, a sense of something 'more deeply interfused,' a sense of something discernible only with the inner eye ; a sense of the Divine that animates both nature and humanity, both what the eye sees and what the heart and mind create,—the spirit ' whose dwelling is the light of setting suns,' the spirit

> ' that impels
> All thinking things, all objects of all thought,
> And rolls through all things.'

It is in this mood, it seems to me, that Turner contemplates the scenes and incidents of rural life which he represents in these pictures, and it is this mood which these pictures embody.   The ' Frosty Morning' is therefore very much more than a representation of a country road, with a little hedging and ditching going on

66

PLATE XXXII

PETWORTH HOUSE, FROM THE PARK

PENCIL. ABOUT 1809

PLATE XXXIII

COCKERMOUTH CASTLE

PENCIL   ABOUT 1809

on one side, an ordinary stage-coach in the distance, and a little sparkling hoar-frost on the ground. The 'Windsor' is also much more than a representation of some drovers with their cattle in one of the meadows near Windsor Castle on a summer (or spring) morning. Not only are these bare facts represented, but the mood in which we must contemplate them is also stated. We have not read these pictures aright, we have not really brought them into contact with our own life, until we contemplate the bare external facts in the light of the mood which the artist has prescribed for them. It is, I know, commonly taken for granted that pictorial art is impotent to achieve this kind of determination; that the artist is at the mercy of any chance mood which the spectator may bring to his work; that the artist can only represent objects and spatial relations, and that he can lay no constraint on the spectator to think and feel about these objects in any particular way. And no doubt a large proportion of modern art productions actually do no more than this, and attempt no more. But these are merely the failures of modern art. All the great works of modern art — such as those of Rembrandt and Jean François Millet—not only represent objects and scenes, but lay down the related thoughts and feelings which they are to inspire. Yet it is of course always possible for the spectator to stop short at the bare recognition of the pictorial signs, in the same way that it is possible for the reader of a poem to recognise the meaning of a few prominent words and ignore the context in which they occur.[1] But the point which I cannot hesitate to press home— because I see clearly that the whole question of the value and place of art in modern civilisation depends upon it—is this, that the work of art is nothing less than its full significance. It is only in so far as we master or appropriate this wealth of inner significance that the work of art can be said to exist for us; we must not only read the words of a poem, but we must understand them, and in the same way we must not merely look at such pictures as these of Turner, but we must translate the artist's signs into their appropriate ideas and feelings.

It is only when we succeed in getting clear of that shallow

[1] See, for example, Jeffrey's account of the Sixth Book of the *Excursion,* quoted in Professor Raleigh's *Wordsworth,* pp. 8 and 9.

TURNER'S SKETCHES AND DRAWINGS

materialism which clings to the letter, while it ignores the power
behind it, that the full scope of pictorial art can dawn upon us.
But when we once realise that the mood expressed in such pictures
as the ' Frosty Morning ' and ' Windsor ' is an essential part—nay,
is the very essence of the works themselves, we shall begin to
understand how nearly related great art is to religion; how
insensibly the one passes into the other. In such pictures as
these—and I do not hesitate to rank them among the truest and
highest that Christianity has yet produced—in pictures like these
the ordinary scenes of rural life and labour are impressed with the
quietness and beauty of the best part of the artist's own nature,
and fed with the lofty thoughts that only poets dare utter in
words. Such pictures are indeed in the old monkish sense an act of
worship. The mood they call up and sustain is a blessed mood in
which the mystery and the weight of this unintelligible world are
lightened. Such pictures as these are literally an imitation or
reminiscence of the great moments of life, and possess life and
food for future years.

I will conclude this chapter by answering some objections that
I believe are likely to be made to the interpretation I have offered
of this group of Turner's works. These objections would be based
on arguments drawn from the commonly received idea of Turner's
personal character. The mood expressed in this group of pictures
is, it might be urged, the habitual mood or way of feeling of the
perfectly good man; it is only in the perfectly good and religious
life that we find this reconciliation of inner Freedom and external
Necessity, and Turner, we have reason to suppose, was not a
perfectly good and religious man. This objection I admit has
force, but I think it is fully met by pointing to the distinction
between a mood, a passing state of feeling, and a permanent habit
of mind or settled character. It may not have been Turner's
happiness to mature this mood of reconciliation into the master
light of his whole life, yet the mood itself is one that few, if any,
human hearts are entirely unfamiliar with. It is a mood that
sits about us all in our earlier days. The feelings of love and
reverence may well be one of the primary facts of human nature.
It may be that Turner, if we examine the whole of his life,

PLATE XXXIV

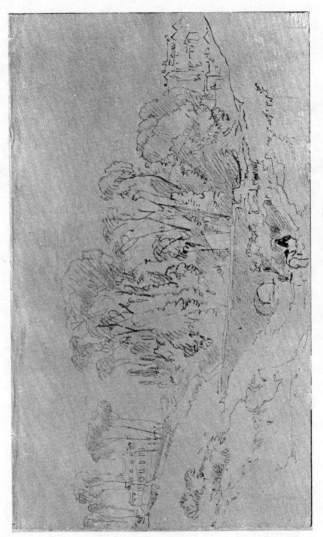

LANDSCAPE NEAR PLYMOUTH

PENCIL. ABOUT 1812

PLATE XXXV

DESIGN FOR SANDYCOMBE LODGE AND GROUNDS

PEN AND INK. ABOUT 1811

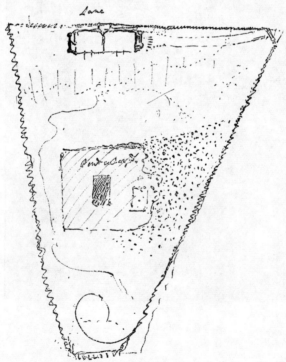

PLAN OF GARDEN: SANDYCOMBE LODGE

PEN AND INK. ABOUT 1812

cannot be regarded as a perfectly good and religious man, yet at this particular period of his life his works prove beyond all shadow of doubt that he was capable of feeling towards nature and man in the way that is habitual with the perfectly good man. As an artist these works of his show that at this time he was able to raise himself in the point of feeling to the level of a good and complete man. But this is a very different thing from the demand that the artist shall himself be at that time and for the remainder of his life the kind of man whose momentary state of feeling he represents. The actual behaviour of the artist as an individual has only an indirect bearing on the question of the moral worth of his work. What is important is, that the content of the moral idea shall be present in the state of feeling expressed in his work. He may not have laid firm hold of the good will; he may not have made it a permanent part of his own life. All that is necessary for his immediate purpose is that he shall have grasped it in idea, —a much easier task, and one that constant reading of the poets is quite sufficient to accomplish.

That Turner was always a great lover and reader of poetry is already well known. After he broke away from strictly topographical work, he seldom exhibited a picture without the accompaniment of some poetical quotation. To judge from these quotations Thomson's *Seasons* was a favourite book with him, and we also find Milton, Ossian, Akenside, Dr. Langhorne, and Mallet laid under contribution. But the clearest evidence of the place poetry occupied in his mind at this time is afforded by his sketch-books, which contain on the whole even more poetry than drawings. On almost every sheet we find transcriptions or reminiscences of verses that had caught his fancy, or attempts of his own to express himself in metre. These attempts, it must be confessed, are seldom far from failure, for the artist's command of words was not instinctive, like his power over pictorial signs. Yet the quantity of these attempts and the patient persistence with which he ground out indifferent verse, prove that the art of poetry was one that held at least as high a place in his affections as his own art.

As Turner's verses were on the whole so unsuccessful, I will only offer the reader one example, and that a short one. It was written in one of his sketch-books about the year 1809. He had gone to Purley on the Thames, near Pangbourne, to indulge himself with a few days' fishing—his sole form of recreation. But the rain had kept him in all day, and to while away the time he betook himself to poetry. He begins by apostrophising the fair leaves of his sketch-book which 'Delusion tempts him to violate with his pen. The rain seems to have continued, for on the next page he begins again :—

> ' Alas, another day is gone
> As useless as it was begun.
> The crimson'd streak of early morn
> Checks the sweet lark that o'er the corn
> Fluttered her wings at twilight grey ;
> Expectant eyed the moving ray,
> Twitter'd her song in saddening mood
> To $\begin{Bmatrix} \text{calm} \\ \text{hush} \end{Bmatrix}$ her clamorous callow brood
> In hope of less inclement skies.
>
> The hapless fisher ——
> No fly can tempt the finny brood
> When the wash'd bank gives up its mud.
> Beneath some tree he takes his stand
> —— in doubtful shelter
> .   .   .   .   .
> Anxious to fancy every streak a ray.
> Not so the cotter's children at the door,
> Rich in content, tho' Nature made them poor,
> Standing on threshold emulous to catch
> The pendant drop from off the dripping latch.
> The daring boy—thus Briton's early race
> $\begin{Bmatrix} \text{To feel the heaviest drop upon his face} \\ \text{Foremost, must feel the drops upon his face,} \end{Bmatrix}$
> Or heedless of the storm or his abode
> Launches his paper boat across the road—
> Where the deep gullies which his father's cart
> Made in their progress to the mart
> Full to the brim, deluged by the rain,
> They prove to him a channel to the main.
> Guiding his vessel down the stream
> Even the pangs of hunger vanish like a dream.'

As poetry these lines have little to recommend them, but they give us a glimpse of the man himself, and they prove that he had something of the poet's comprehensive sympathies; that he was 'a man pleased with his own passions and volitions, and who rejoices more than other men in the spirit of life that is in him; delighting to contemplate similar volitions and passions in the goings-on of the universe, and habitually impelled to create them where he does not find them.'

CHAPTER VI

THE 'LIBER STUDIORUM'

The object of this chapter—The first 'Liber' drawings were made at
W. F. Wells's cottage at Knockholt, Kent—'Bridge and Cows'—
Development of the so-called 'Flint Castle'—Mrs. Wells—View of 'Basle'
—'Little Devil's Bridge' and 'London from Greenwich'—'Martello
Towers, Bexhill,' and 'Kirkstall Crypt'—Scene at Isleworth—The etching
of the 'Raglan Castle' and 'Source of the Arveron' plates—Suggestion
for the better exhibition of the 'Liber' drawings.

THE *Liber Studiorum* is an important aspect of Turner's
genius—so important that it seems to deserve a chapter
to itself, even in so summary an investigation as the
present. Yet from the point of view of its subject-matter, it is
evident that the 'Liber' does not throw into relief any side of
Turner's art not amply illustrated in his paintings. What light
the sequence of 'Pastoral' subjects throws upon the gradual
development of his conception of realistic art, has already been
touched upon in the previous chapter. But there remains one
point of view from which it seems to me the 'Liber' possesses a
special interest for our present study. In these designs we can
study the formal elements of Turner's art freed from the disturbing
influence of colour. Each plate is primarily an arrangement in line
and light and shade, and the requirements of what I may call melodic
invention are considered before those of mere representation; that
is to say, the emphasis is always on the subjective and constructive
side of art, as opposed to its power of reproduction of the elements
immediately given in ordinary perception.

Especially important from this point of view are those subjects,
generally amongst the earlier plates, in which considerable
alterations were made during the course of execution. An
examination of a few of the cases in which there are important

72

differences between the first preliminary drawing and the completed engraving is certainly well within the limits of our present inquiry; and such comparisons are worth making for their own sake, as they bring out very clearly certain characteristics of all pictorial art, and especially of Turner's, which are not easily grasped when our observations are complicated by the presence of colour.

The first drawings executed for the work were made in October 1806, when Turner was on a visit to Mr. Wells, at Knockholt, in Kent. One of Mr. Wells's daughters has told us that it was mainly on her father's advice that Turner decided to undertake the work. But he required 'much and long continued spurring' before he could be induced to make a beginning. 'At last,' we are told, 'after he had been well goaded, one morning, half in a pet he said, "Zounds, Gaffer, there will be no peace with you till I begin—well, give me a sheet of paper there, rule the size for me, tell me what I shall take."' The lady adds, 'I sat by Turner laughing and playing whilst he made the drawings,' 'and before he left us the first five subjects which form the first number were completed and arranged for publication greatly to my dear Father's delight.' (The letter is given *in extenso* in Mr. Rawlinson's *Liber Studiorum*, 2nd edition, pp. xii and xiii.)

One of the subjects executed at Knockholt was almost certainly the faded sepia drawing which hangs at present in the National Gallery, under the title of 'Bridge and Cows' (No. 504 N. G.); the engraving made from it was published (without a title) as the first 'Pastoral' subject in the first part of *Liber*.

This drawing is slightly faded, but the fading does not altogether account for its feeble and commonplace look. The design itself is feeble, the draughtsmanship petty, and the character of the figures and trees weak and amiable. These objects are not actually 'out of drawing'—that is to say, incorrect from a physiological or botanical point of view, but they are sadly lacking in intention. They have a listless air, and seem to take very little interest either in themselves or in each other. They seem, indeed, to be mildly wondering why they are there at all. In a word, it is just the sort of drawing that an artist would make when external circumstances induced him to sit down to 'do something,' while no strongly-felt subject-matter within him was urgently demanding expression.

This drawing (it is in reverse of the engraving) was traced on to the copper, and the etching was made from it by Turner himself. The etching is practically an accurate copy of the drawing: the objects represented are the same in each, and neither the actions nor positions of any of the figures have been altered. Yet in the etching there is a perceptible briskening-up of everything. It all hangs together better than in the drawing. In some way the whole now seems to have come to life in the artist's imagination. In the drawing we can see him laboriously bringing the parts together: in the etching he has infused the breath of life into them.

The change is due entirely to the execution. The line which defines the contours of the chief objects has lost its listlessness. It is now instinct with intention. Everywhere it hurries along, building up the design as a whole while defining the parts. The compulsion of the whole makes itself felt in every detail. It is certainly difficult to put into words the difference between the two versions, but I believe every one who will take the trouble to compare them carefully will be sure to feel it. In the two works there is an actual difference in the quality of the artist's stream of consciousness, and the difference makes itself felt in the workmanship, though, in all probability, he himself was quite unaware of the difference in his frame of mind, and regarded the etching as simply a mechanical process of transference from one medium to another. Yet from a psychological point of view, the impulsion of his mind was in each case in a contrary direction. In the drawing the scene as a whole was being laboriously invoked piecemeal, a collection of objects was being formed into a sum total; in the etching the subject as a whole is a real and living thing, guiding the artist's hand and moulding all the details into kinship with itself.

The whole now feels that certain of its parts require adjustment, *i.e.* demand to be brought into more intimate cohesion with the general purpose. The contrast between the rigidity of the dead branches of the willow on the right, and the springiness of the living branches nearer the foreground, calls out for clearer and

74

PLATE XXXVI

PLATE XXXVII

SCENE ON THE FRENCH COAST

GENERALLY KNOWN AS " FLINT CASTLE : SMUGGLERS "

ETCHING, WASHED WITH SEPIA. ABOUT 1807

more emphatic statement. The dance and sweep of the foliage, the bending bridge, the falling bank, require steadying by a bolder assertion of the straight horizontal line of the distant hills. The soft and rounded undulations of the tree-tops, running right across the upper part of the drawing, give a somewhat featureless though amiable character to it; in the etching, greater prominence is given to the harsher lines of the rigid white wall of the distant cottage and its sloping roof, as well as to the supports and planks of the rustic bridge. In this way, without altering the position of a single part of the design, or introducing any new matter, the whole is transformed; instead of a mere collection of parts, related to each other by a kind of chance or indifferent contiguity, we have now a definite whole, fused through and through into conceptual and emotional unity. The objects before our eyes have ceased to be merely indifferent and external facts; they have now become elements or members of a richly coloured whole of thought and feeling.

The careful and rather timid-looking drawing described as 'Flint Castle' (Plate XXXVI.), is certainly another of the designs made at the cheerful Knockholt cottage. On the margin of this drawing the artist has scribbled some verses, which I suppose one of the merry party had discovered in a book or magazine,[1] and which they were all delighted with. Probably the discoverer was Mrs. Wells, for the young ladies were too young to care much for books, and the only scrap of information we possess about their mother seems to suggest that she was something of a bluestocking, and what is now sometimes called a 'féministe.' Among the sketches in one of Turner's pocket-books there is the following jotting :—'There is not a quality or endowment, faculty or ability which is not in a superior degree possest by women.— *Vide* Mrs. Wells, Knockholt, Oct.' The poem itself is not strictly germane to our present study, but as there lingers about it a faint echo of those scenes of 'fun and merriment' which one of Turner's young playmates recalled in after years, I cannot deny myself the pleasure of transcribing it.

' A Row of Poplars in disgrace
Because they would not stop their pace

---

[1] It is, of course, possible that the verses were composed by Turner himself.

Or grew unnecessarily tall,
Their Master came and topped them all.

Some neighbourly poplars stood hard by
Beheld their growth with jealous eye,
Now saw—exulting—cried
"How near is pride to earth allied."

"Friends," said the poplars in disgrace,
"You see the fault of making haste,
Ambition's greatness caused our woe.
Ambition shun, mind how you grow,
For while you run you are bare below." '

The drawing, like the poem, is not a remarkable one. As a design it differs little from the average work of accomplished landscape draughtsmen like Westall, Arnald, Daniell, etc. But from a comparative point of view it is of singular interest, as the differences between this preliminary drawing and the published engraving are greater than those in any other *Liber* subject. It starts as a rather jejune and drawing-masterlike composition, and comes out finally as one of the most vigorous and impressive marine designs in the whole series.

The etching was made by Turner himself. As the spacing and arrangement of the etching differ considerably from those of the drawing, it is most likely that an intermediate study was made. The changes, however, might very well have been made on the tracing-paper used to transfer the original design to the copper, and this would naturally have been destroyed as soon as it had been used. When the design had been drawn on the copper and bitten in, a few proofs were taken of the etching, and over one of these Turner set to work again with washes of sepia to guide Charles Turner, the engraver, who was to mezzotint the plate. This second design is now in the National Gallery (No. 522) and has been reproduced here as Plate XXXVII.

Of course we cannot hope to grasp the whole difference that has taken place in this second version of the design. But here are two drawings made by the same hand, within a short space of time of each other, of the same size and the same subject, yet one is obviously a work of genius, and the other is as tame and lifeless as its companion is vivid, energetic, and full-blooded. The com-

76

parison is worth making, not, indeed, that there is the slightest hope that any of us may learn from it how to work such miracles, but because it will help to impress upon us the importance of the form or 'style' of a work of art, as opposed to the objects it represents —the importance of 'mere technique'; it will also give us some insight into the real nature of artistic expression —will show us how far removed the whole process is from that pious and passive reproduction of what is 'given' in sense-perception which plays such a large and dangerous part in current practice. Let us see therefore what we can discover.

In the first place it is evident that in the second version of the subject the design has been what artists call 'pulled together.' The foreground boat on the left (it is of course on the right in the plate) has been made, if not actually bigger, yet more important as a mass, by the addition of the sails of a second boat immediately behind it. The apparent height of the boat has been increased by dropping the height of the man standing in the cart in the water beside it, and by making the horses, carts and men relatively smaller. The castle in the distance has been shifted nearer to the boat, the height of the two masts of the boat in the middle distance which abut on to the castle have been reduced, so that the masts and sails of its neighbour on the right seem higher and bigger. More has been made of the men, boats, etc., at the foot of the low hills which appear on the right of the drawing, and the foreground group of men and horses has been shoved nearer to the figure of the man just entering the water, and, to make the connection firmer, the cask and grappling irons on the ground have been carefully added.

But it is useless merely cataloguing these changes, if we cannot discover the reasons for them. Is all this shuffling and rearrangement for the sake of balance and visual harmony? No doubt to some extent it is. But notice in the remodelled design the effect of that firm straight line of the distant sea in the centre, and the way the distant castle rises out of it. That is the nerve of the whole design. See how all the other lines and shapes fret the eye with their sharp and jagged forms, and yet lead it inevitably back to that one untroubled space. All this artfully calculated playing with lights and shadows, this complicated conspiracy of lines and forms, is assuredly something more than an aimless trifling with appearances. In that untroubled stretch of water we cannot but feel the steady, never-resting, inexorable march of the real powers of nature. It brings the whole mighty background of human life into the drawing; and this real spiritual presence sets the daily toil and hardship of everyday life in a new light, solemnising it, dwarfing it, yet not crushing it. It is as though we had heard the rustle of the wings of eternity in the passing moment. To do this, to produce this effect unerringly and with logical certainty upon every normally constituted Englishman who looks carefully at the drawing, cannot exactly be the chance result of a diligent shuffling and reshuffling of mere shapes and shadows. There is something of divinity in it. The shapes and shadows have meaning, and this timeless and spaceless meaning is the life-blood that animates and transfigures these bald signs and symbols. If art deals only with appearances, we must remember that appearance is also a form of reality, and that form and content can be so closely interwoven that the distinctions of our meddling understanding may become idle and misleading.

It is only from some such point of view as this that we can hope to grasp the full importance of what clever people call 'mere technique.'

Let us turn now to the 'Basle' design. Although this engraving was published in the first part of *Liber* I am inclined to doubt whether the preliminary drawing was made in the Wells's cottage. This design is based upon a sketch made at Basle in 1802, and it is hardly likely that Turner would have had this sketch-book with him when he went to spend a few days with his friends in Kent. Moreover, the first sepia drawing is not with the others in the National Gallery. Mr. Rawlinson believes that it passed into the hands of an American collector 'many years ago' (*Liber Studiorum*, p. 19). But we have Turner's etching of the subject, and if we compare this with the drawing made from nature, which certainly formed the ground-work of the subject, we see clearly what a great difference there really is between two processes which modern uncritical thought persistently confounds— between the process of 'drawing what you see' and 'copying nature faithfully,' and the process of artistic construction and invention.

PLATE XXXVIII

JUVENILE TRICKS

SEPIA. ABOUT 1808

PLATE XXXIX

BERRY POMEROY CASTLE

THE 'LIBER STUDIORUM'

Generally, with the really creative artists the two processes go on simultaneously or are fused into one, but here for once we find them separated. The pencil drawing was made as a simple record of facts; the etching was made some five or six years later, and it is curious to see what liberties Turner felt it was necessary and justifiable to take with his original record, before his notion of the requirements of a work of art could be satisfied.

In the drawing from nature the width of the river seems to dwarf the height of the buildings; in the engraving Turner seems to have felt that the height of the buildings ought to form the keynote of the whole design. First, therefore, the two towers of the Cathedral are carried well up above the house by the bridge, the gable of this building being reduced in size, so that it shall not compete in importance with the Cathedral towers. In the drawing, the buildings recede gradually and gently from the bridge, while in the etching, they are pushed into square step-shaped masses, thus emphasising the idea of weight and height. These impressions are further strengthened by deliberately making the supports of the bridge smaller and more fragile than they were in the drawing; in the engraving the straddling supports of the slender wooden bridge give it an air of weakness which makes the buildings at its side seem all the more firmly set by contrast.

These are only a few of the more obvious points of difference, but if the comparison were pursued further, we should find that every sweep of line and silhouette of the original material has been reconsidered and recast before it was allowed to form part of the new construction. I will not pretend that I regard the result obtained in this case as one of the great achievements of the series, but our observations are useful, I think, as showing the habitual thoroughness and earnestness which Turner brought to all his work. His attitude towards the matter in hand is always active and creative. His alterations are not always for the better—indeed, it is open to argument whether some of the changes made in this Basle subject were quite advantageous, but the fact remains that whatever he took up he threw himself heart and soul into, that he felt bound to recreate it from within, and that a mere cold and passive reproduction of the given would have seemed to him a cowardly shrinking from his artistic mission. He feels that he is responsible for the effect the shapes and arrangement of his subject make upon the spectator's imagination, and that to attempt to apologise for a tame and uninteresting subject by saying, ' It was so,'—' It is quite true,'—would have seemed to him an unworthy evasion of his work.

How incapable Turner was of copying even one of his own drawings accurately is clearly shown by the etching of the ' Little Devil's Bridge ' (R. 19). When we compare this with the original drawing (No. 476 N. G.) we find that almost every form in the design has been recast, not always to its individual advantage from the point of view of realisation, but with an invariable gain in the direction of greater general cohesion. Note, for example, how the straight tree trunk nearest the bridge in the drawing gets bent slightly to the left, just to make you feel the toughness and obstinacy of the tree itself. The fir-trees on the left, too, are more realistic in the drawing, but they are more forcible and dramatic in the engraving.

As we have been able to reproduce Turner's original pencil study from nature for the ' London from Greenwich ' plate, the reader will be able to make his own comparison with the published design. The preliminary sepia drawing for the engraving (No. 493 N. G.) forms an intermediate step between the two, a stage, as it were, in the process by which Turner's mind took complete possession of the subject. In the sepia drawing, the artist has not yet fully realised the exact rôle the main building has to play in the whole arrangement. When we turn to the engraving we find that the whole character of the mass formed by the hospital has been changed. In the drawing it forms a straggling mass, somewhat like a chance medley of wharves and warehouses, in the engraving this mass has been patted together into a solid and definite structure. The distant parts of the building have been raised, and they now tell as a rigid horizontal line. The gain to the hospital in dignity and in individuality is extraordinary, and its stiff straight lines are exactly what was wanted to throw emphasis on the subtlety and delicacy of the slow sweep of the distant river.

The drawing for the ' Martello Towers, Bexhill,' plate is a very tame affair, and the finished plate is only saved from comparative

PLATE XL

THE ALCOVE, ISLEWORTH

GENERALLY KNOWN AS "TWICKENHAM—POPE'S VILLA," ETC.

SEPIA. ABOUT 1816

PLATE XLI

SHEEP-WASHING, WINDSOR

failure by its fine sky. Yet it is worth comparing the two to trace out the subtle differences which spring up under Turner's hand in the etching. All the objects are forced into shapes that act more powerfully on the imagination, everywhere the tendency of the line is towards emphasis and distinctness.

In the 'Kirkstall Crypt' (R. 39), the design is also recast in the etching. The group of cows is altered, the foreground pillar is made thinner, the space between the two columns in the centre is widened out, and the aperture in the wall above the cows on the left is made light, instead of dark. These changes are all for the better. A careful study of these seemingly trivial alterations is valuable as an instance of the subtleties of design upon which all really fine art depends.

As these remarks indicate, I am in agreement with the general opinion that the engravings represent Turner's intentions more fully than his preliminary drawings. But though this is generally the case, there are exceptions, and the most notable is, I think, that of the plate sometimes known as 'Twickenham—Pope's Villa,' and sometimes as 'Garrick's Temple and Hampton Court,' but which really represents a scene at Isleworth. In this case the drawing (Plate XL.) is much finer than the plate, although Turner etched the subject himself. But somehow the spacing of the whole is much less felicitous in the engraving than in the drawing. The rendering of the trees, too, is more conventional, but this is a characteristic of nearly all the plates, and is due to the difficulties of the medium, it being impossible to get the same subtlety of tone and delicacy of form in etching and mezzotint that can be got with a pen and wash on paper.

This question of the comparative conventionality of the foliage in the engravings induces me to say a few words about one of the loveliest renderings of woodland scenery in the whole series—the so-called 'Raglan Castle' (R. 58).[1] This is one of the plates that Turner mezzotinted himself, yet because the etched lines are not so free and supple as those of the preliminary drawing (No. 865 N.G.), it has been assumed that Turner left the etching to be done by one of his engravers, probably Dawe. This assumption is one that I cannot accept. The lettering on the plate, 'Drawn and

---

[1] Plate XXXIX.

Engraved by J. M. W. Turner, etc.,' points to the conclusion that Turner was responsible both for the etching and the mezzotinting. And when we compare the etching with the drawing, a number of slight but successful differences emerge, which no engraver would either have attempted to make or could have made if he had desired to do so.

'The Source of the Arveron' (R. 60), another of the plates 'drawn and engraved' by Turner, has also had its etching condemned and attributed to Dawe. If the plate is really so fine as all the critics of this kind insist, it is curious that the etching can be so poor as they say and yet not affect the excellence of the whole. This is inconsistent with the proper appreciation of the important rôle the etched lines play in all these mezzotints. That Turner regarded the etching as far more important than the scraping is shown by the simple fact that he undertook (nominally at least) to do it all himself, but he had no hesitation in handing the scraping over to the engravers.

These general considerations are further strengthened when we compare the finished plate (I am speaking only of the etching in the published states, and not of the rare 'first state' of the etching in the late Mr. J. E. Taylor's collection) with the preliminary study made for it, now in the National Gallery (No. 879). The size and proportions of the plate differ from those of the drawing, so the etching could not have been traced from it, while the etching nowhere follows the drawing with the accuracy one would expect if it were merely an engraver's copy. There is no authority in this drawing for the shapes given to the crests of the distant mountains in the centre, nor for the shapes of the upper portions of the nearer mountains on the left. The lower parts of the design are also modified from the forms in the drawing in exactly the way Turner habitually recast all the drawings he etched. It is also hard to suppose that Dawe or anybody but Turner could have recast the vague shapes of the disappearing ridge of the glacier on the left in the masterly way this has been done in the etching, or that anybody but Turner could have invented, on the strength of the loose indications in the drawing, the masterly lines that give definition to the stretch of valley against which the ice of the glacier is relieved. The shapes of the

82

PLATE XLII

VIEW OF A RIVER, FROM A TERRACE
SOMETIMES CALLED "MACON"
SEPIA. ABOUT 1818

PLATE XLIII

CROWHURST, SUSSEX

THE 'LIBER STUDIORUM'

first two upright pines near the centre have also been recast by
the mind and hand of the master, not copied by another hand
from the indications given in the drawing. Alterations have also
been introduced in the character of the stems and their branches
which a professional engraver would not dare to make in an
ostensible copy; the same remark applies also to the tops of the
pines on the right. For these reasons, I think, those critics are
mistaken who deny that the workmanship of the whole plate is
Turner's. And the mistake has arisen to a large extent, I feel
inclined to add, through attaching too much importance to
a priori notions of technical mastery. As the late Mr. Arthur
Strong very justly said, we are inclined to start with an idea that
masters are always masterly and classical, and we often end by
finding that they have left nothing behind them quite worthy of
our preconceived ideas of what they ought to have done.

These are a few of the points suggested by a comparison of
the preliminary designs for the *Liber* plates with the finished
engravings. But to get any good out of it every student must
take the trouble to make these comparisons for himself. Should
my remarks succeed in inducing even a few adventurous spirits to
make such an experiment, I shall feel satisfied that I have done
something towards spreading an intelligent interest in the marvellous process of artistic creation. Perhaps, too, some day in the
future, the authorities of the National Gallery may see their way
towards the display of these drawings so that such a process of
intelligent study may be performed without the inconvenience
which the present arrangement entails. It is probably not necessary to have the whole series of drawings on exhibition at the
same time, but if those that are exhibited could be accompanied
by the finished engravings, and, where possible, by one or two
proofs of the unfinished states, I believe the gain to the public
would be considerable.

CHAPTER VII

THE SPLENDOUR OF SUCCESS, OR 'WHAT YOU WILL'—

1813—1830

A survey of the ground we have covered—The training of Turner's sympathies by the poets—The limits of artistic beauty—and of a merely 'musical' education—Turner unlike Wordsworth—the predominantly sensuous bent of his genius—The parting of the ways—The dependence of art upon society—Turner 'the fashion'—The influence of the Academy—The Italian visit in 1819—Turner's Italian sketches—Their beauty and uselessness—The Naturalistic fallacy—Turner's work for the engravers — The *Southern Coast* series—' Watchet ' and ' Boscastle '—Whitaker's *History of Richmondshire*—' Hornby Castle ' and ' Heysham '—Scott's *Provincial Antiquities* — ' Edinburgh, from the Calton Hill '—' Rochester,' in the *Rivers of England* series — *England and Wales*—' Bolton Abbey' and ' Colchester '—' Stamford '—'Tynemouth.'

WE have now followed the development of Turner's mind from boyhood to youth and well into manhood. We have watched the architectural and topographical draughtsman develop into an artist under the guidance of his admiration for Wilson. Then the mind of the painter of the sublime, of the picturesque in general, struck its unseen roots deeper into the interests and sympathies of the people amongst whom he lived. In the hour of national danger his heart beat high with courage and determination. His pictures of the sea are like war songs; they strike the Dorian note, they represent the tone of mind of a brave man who faces wounds and death and all contingencies with unflinching endurance. Then the mind of the laureate of a nation in arms takes a still wider sweep. It embraces humanity and animate and inanimate nature in one glance, and finds the soul of good in all things. The Dorian harmonies give place to the Phrygian.

In all this Turner's attitude seems entirely passive or receptive.

84

PLATE XLIV

KIRKBY LONSDALE BRIDGE
PENCIL. ABOUT 1816

PLATE XLV

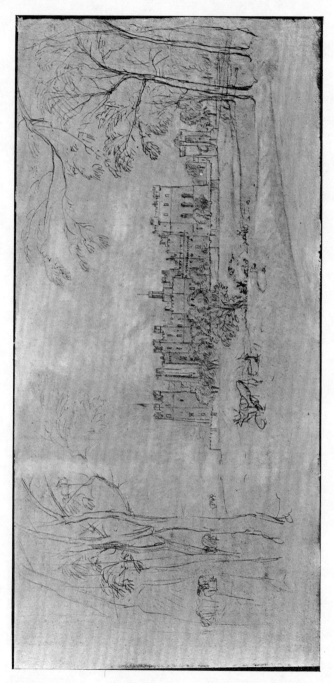

RABY CASTLE, CO. DURHAM

PENCIL. ABOUT 1817

THE SPLENDOUR OF SUCCESS

His amazingly rapid growth seems to be merely an effortless assimilation of the moral atmosphere of his time. All that was fairest and of good repute in the common spiritual heritage of the people seems to have passed insensibly into his thoughts and feelings. His art is a social or national phenomenon, so impersonal (or superpersonal) that it is difficult to point to traces of the mere individual in his work. The individual is lost in his universal function. The man himself is nothing but the voice or thought of what Hume has called 'a man in general.' Yet his work is as far removed as any work can be from the vagueness and coldness of the abstract universal. Behind every touch of his hand and every thought or idea in his mind beats the pulse of a full-blooded and passionate personality. Only, by some miracle, this man happens to be free from the local prejudices and limitations that deflect the judgment and sympathies of most men from the one true standard.

This education of Turner's sympathies and feelings was the work, we have seen reasons for concluding, of the poets and artists whom he loved and admired. In the light and warmth of their ideal creations his own high instincts were quickened into life and activity. Under their influence he had entered into the common spiritual world, and they had given the direction to his impulses and ideas regarding things human and divine. But education must be a lifelong process, and there comes a time in the growth of each individual when the need of something more clear-cut and permanent than his own impulses and desires, however wholesome they may be, declares itself. As Plato pointed out long ago, to secure the happiest results of the best 'musical' education, something more than a merely 'musical' education is needed. We have now reached that period in Turner's life when the lover of beautiful sights and thoughts and feelings must make a determined effort to unify these manifold beauties by an explicit principle, to exchange opinion for knowledge, if he is to preserve the advantages he has already won. In life there is no standing still, no resting upon our gains. We must go forward to higher victories, or find our arms tarnish and our gains dissipate themselves. But it may well be doubted whether art is capable of reaching a higher point of beauty than that which Turner had already reached. Forced to its extreme limits beauty insensibly passes into something which is at once more and less than beauty. Such pictures as the ' Frosty Morning,' ' Windsor,' and 'The Trout Stream' are, perhaps, the most beautiful that art is capable of producing. And the example of Wordsworth, who did strive upward to 'an intelligence which has greatness and the vision of all time and of all being,' is not on all points reassuring. His poetry, simply as poetry, did suffer from his philosophic studies. There may be something in the very nature of the human soul which sets bounds to the creation or expression of beauty.

But Turner was not like Wordsworth. He was for good and ill essentially and solely an artist. The play of shapes and colours was probably dearer to him than food or raiment. Having by sheer good fortune carried his art to its highest attainable pitch of beauty before he had reached his fortieth year, he was placed in an embarrassing position. The dialectical movement of beauty would now carry him outside his art, into regions where the individual man might reap rich gains, but where the artist could reap only sorrow and disappointment. The artist in Turner was stronger than the man. He loved the sensuous medium of art more than the spiritual beauty into which the current of traditional wisdom had carried him. The remainder of his life is therefore dedicated to the passionate and audacious development of the material beauties of his art.

We have now to trace in his works the gradual encroachments of the purely sensuous side of his art. For a time all seems well, perhaps more than well, for the gain in all the lower elements of his art is very striking. During the next twenty years his works gain constantly in the sensuous attractiveness of colour and in the formal beauties of rhythm and design. The loss of beauty is compensated by deep draughts of pleasantness. Yet amid the feverish intoxication of sensuous beauty a wild unrest and despair make themselves increasingly felt. The man has sacrificed himself to his art, and the starved human soul turns in bitterness from the ardently desired rewards of the most brilliantly triumphant artistic career that modern times have witnessed.

It is usual in treating mainly of Turner's oil paintings to fix upon the year 1815 as the great turning-point in his career. After

PLATE XLVI

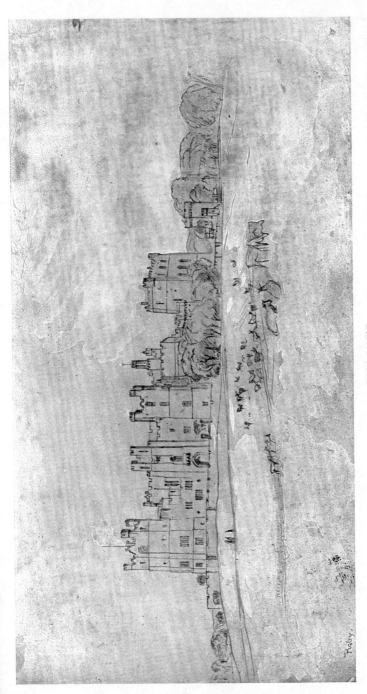

RABY CASTLE

PENCIL. ABOUT 1817

PLATE XLVII

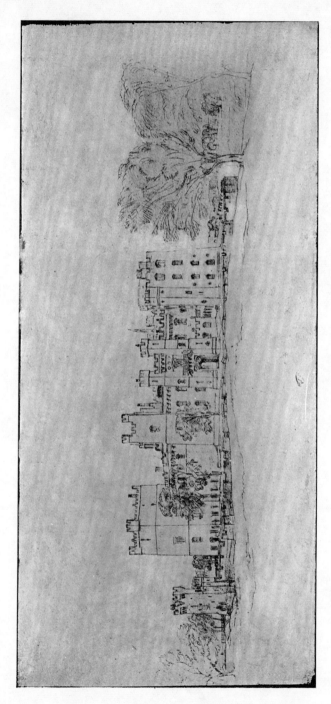

RABY CASTLE

PENCIL. ABOUT 1817

1815 there is a marked change in the aims and character of Turner's art, and it is convenient to date this change from the year that saw the end of the Napoleonic wars, and inaugurated a new era in the social and political condition of this country. From this date, too, the conditions of artistic production changed. The rapid development of industrial concerns brought a new class of patrons upon the scene. Before 1815, Turner's patrons had been mainly the landed aristocracy; after 1815, his chief patrons were the successful merchants of the great towns. From that time the men of commerce and the manufacturers ousted the aristocracy from the leading position which they had held in the councils of the country. With the change of men a change took place in the ideals, manners and taste of the country; and Turner, with his extraordinary sensibility, his ready powers of intuition and rapid assimilation, seemed bound to reflect the change in his work.

Yet if we look closer into Turner's career, we find that 1815 was rather the year that saw the brilliant public inauguration of the new era, than the actual beginning of the change. The 'Crossing the Brook,' exhibited in 1815, is often regarded as the impressive close of Turner's early manner, yet this beautiful picture already bears the impress of that *folie des grandeurs* to which we owe most of the excesses of the new manner. The 'Frosty Morning' of 1813 is really the last work in which the inspiration rings true throughout, in which the form and content are absolutely indissoluble. 'Dido and Æneas,' the only picture exhibited in 1814, is a frigid pseudo-classical pomposity, the due development of the strain of baser metal in Turner's genius, which had already betrayed itself in the 'Macon' of 1803, the 'Narcissus and Echo' of 1804, and the 'Schaffhausen' of 1806. In glancing rapidly over Turner's career we have been able to ignore these works; in the rush and splendour of his general development such pictures fall into insignificance, as casual indications that a busy professional man's industry may outrun his inspiration.

After 1813 it is impossible to ignore this side of Turner's production. It was just this regrettable side of his work that appealed most strongly to the middle-class public for whom he had now to cater. 'Dido Building Carthage' (1815) is a picture exactly to the taste of the admirers of the first instalment of

TURNER'S SKETCHES AND DRAWINGS

Childe Harold, *The Bride of Abydos*, *The Corsair*, and *Lara*. It has the historical remoteness, the vague and empty grandeur, the mysterious dreaminess, the warm, voluptuous atmosphere and intoxicating lyrical movement of the contemporary phase of Romantic poetry. In ' The Decline of the Carthaginian Empire ' (1817), 'The Field of Waterloo ' (1818), ' Richmond Hill, on the Prince Regent's Birthday ' (1819) and ' Rome from the Vatican ' (1820), we recognise the contemporary and fellow-worker of Byron, Moore, Southey, Chateaubriand and Lamartine. In 1822 Turner's only picture at the Royal Academy was entitled ' What you Will '! —an ominous but significant title. It seems to put into words the ruling motive of this new phase of his art ; to show that Turner is fully conscious that he is trimming his barque to catch the breath of popular applause. ' The Bay of Baiae ' (1823), the two ' Mortlakes ' (1826-27), ' Dido directing the Equipment of the Fleet' (1828) and 'Ulysses' (1829) indicate clearly the predominant bent of the artist's mind towards the grosser pleasures of his art.

These works brought and kept Turner prominently before the public eye. They made him the pride and glory of the Royal Academy, and put him on a level of celebrity with Sir Thomas Lawrence. They made him, in short, in Sir Walter Scott's words, ' the fashion,' yet it is these works that Turner's admirers of the present day regard with only moderate enthusiasm.

Compared with the work of the previous decade, such pictures cannot but strike us as unworthy of the artist's genius. Yet we have a tendency nowadays, I think, to overrate the independence of the artist. The modern artist, in so far as he is dependent upon the support of the society in which he works, is not an entirely free agent. The society that applauded them and for whose pleasure they were produced must therefore accept perhaps the main responsibility for the middle-class ideals stamped upon these pictures. In tracing the reaction of society upon art and art upon society, it is an extremely difficult matter to decide which factor is the more powerful, but I am inclined to think it is not art. But however this may be, it is certainly the duty of the individual to fortify himself as best he can against the contagion to which he is exposed. And it must be confessed that Turner was but ill-provided within himself with the means to resist the deadening influences of the atmosphere of bad taste into which he was now launched. It is true that Turner was not exactly what is called a 'society-man,' and he might therefore have more easily escaped the contagion of those drawing-room ideals to which men like Tom Moore succumbed. But Turner was a member of the Royal Academy. It was the recognised organisation of his profession, and he valued highly the honours it had to confer. His lack of general education made him an easy victim to the pretensions of officialism; like all uneducated people, he had a ridiculous reverence for the trappings and mummery of the learned world, for degrees, diplomas, titles. He was inordinately proud of the right to write 'R.A.,' 'P.P.,' after his name, and to alter these letters to *P.R.A.* was the height of his ambition. Under these circumstances he could not but identify himself with the immediate practical aims of the Royal Academy. Now this ill-starred institution is so unwisely and so unfortunately constituted, that its very existence, and all its powers of activity as a professional benevolent society, are made to depend almost entirely upon its popularity as an exhibition society. The Academy throve then as it thrives now, in proportion as it succeeds in catering for the taste of the fashionable and moneyed public; it could only lose ground if it made the slightest attempts to guide or educate the public sense of beauty. In this way it had become in Turner's time nothing more nor less than an organisation for stamping the ideals of the drawing-room upon English art.

In 1819 Turner made his first visit to Italy, the material for the pseudo-classical pictures painted before this having been derived from other artists' pictures and engravings. It is curious that he should have waited till his forty-fifth year before making this journey. The Continent, it is true, had to a great extent been closed to English travellers since the outbreak of the French Revolution; but in spite of political and other difficulties Turner had managed to see a good deal of France, Belgium, Savoy and Switzerland, and he had been down the Rhine. If he had been equally keen to see Italy he could certainly have gone there also, especially as Italy was more generally accessible to an Englishman than any of the other countries he had visited. This curious shrinking from Italy may very likely have been due to the promptings of his own nature. When we examine his art as a whole we clearly see that he found more delight in the wildness, irregularity and caprice of Switzerland and the Rhine valleys than in the more regular scenery of Italy. Even Mr. Ruskin admits that Turner got no good from Italian scenery; Naples, Rome and Florence only put him out and bewildered him; Venice is the only Italian city that lent itself at all gracefully to his genius, and Venice is the most northern in character of all the Italian cities.

But the requirements of his patrons and the peculiar Academic misunderstanding of the principles of landscape art conspired to send Turner to Italy. There the scenery is more beautiful in itself and richer in historical associations than elsewhere in Europe, therefore it is the duty of the ambitious landscape painter who happens to have had the misfortune to be born somewhere out of Italy to stop painting the mere scenes of his own country as soon as possible, and to set out at once for such spots as Tivoli, Narni and Lago Maggiore, the spots approved, stamped and consecrated by generations of the prosperous travellers of all the chief countries of Europe. The theoretical error at the root of this dangerous prejudice is the confusion of the materially pretty, agreeable, and pleasant, with artistic beauty, which is something essentially different from any of these things. But this confusion of the pleasant and the beautiful was a doctrine which the Academy of Turner's time was bent on inculcating by its teaching and exemplifying in its practice.

It happened that Sir Thomas Lawrence, one of the most brilliant exponents of the gospel of the pretty and pleasant, was spending the summer of 1819 in Rome. In the intervals of his labours and relaxations with the great and beautiful of society, he found time to notice the grandeur and beauties of the scenery around him. During this time 'his letters to England were full of entreaties addressed to their common friends to urge upon Turner the importance of visiting Rome while " his genius was in the flower." "It is injustice to his fame and his country," he writes on another occasion, " to let the finest period of his genius pass away . . . without visiting these scenes." '[1] Whether these

[1] Bell, Article on 'Turner and his Engravers,' in *The Genius of Turner* (Studio Extra), pp. 142-143.

PLATE XLVIII

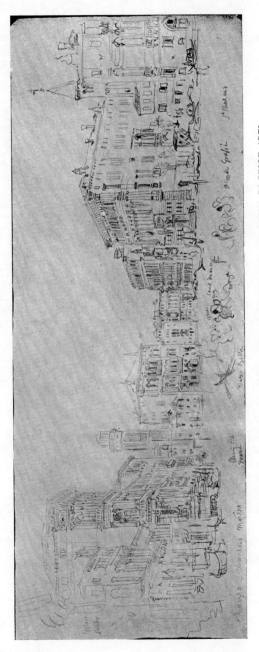

LOOKING UP THE GRAND CANAL, VENICE, FROM NEAR THE ACCADEMIA DI BELLE ARTI

PENCIL. 1819

PLATE XLIX

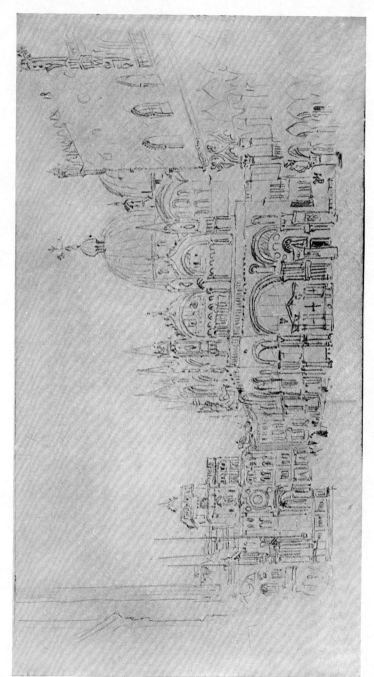

ST. MARK'S, VENICE, WITH PART OF THE DUCAL PALACE

PENCIL. 1819

appeals had any special weight with Turner we do not know, but he set out for Italy within a month or two of the writing of these letters.

He went from Calais to Paris, followed the usual coach-route to Turin, explored the Lakes of Como, Lugano and Maggiore, and reached Venice by way of Milan, Brescia and Desenzano. He must have spent some time at Venice to judge from the number of drawings made there, then went to Bologna, Cesena and Rimini, and continued along the coast of the Adriatic to Ancona. At Ancona he turned inland to Loreto and, following the high post road through Recanati and Macerata, entered the Via Flaminia at Foligno, and passing through Narni and Orticoli entered Rome by the Porta del Popolo, probably sometime in October. From Rome he explored Frascati, Tivoli and Albano, and made a tour to Naples, Baiae, Pozzuoli, Pompeii, Amalfi, Sorrento and Herculaneum. He was back in Rome by the 2nd December, then visited Florence, and, recrossing the Alps on the 24th January 1820, returned through Piedmont and France. On the 12th February we find him dining at Grosvenor Place, London, with his friends the Fawkeses.

To judge from the number of sketch-books filled on this journey Turner must have had the pencil in his hands practically the whole time he was away. Before starting he had 'got up' the subject carefully from books and engravings, and he knew exactly what buildings, antiquities and views he ought to look for at each place he went to. In this way he lost no time mooning about, like a modern artist, looking for unexpected beauties. He just went straight from one guide-book point of interest to another, sketched each methodically from every possible point of view and hurried on to the next. The sketch-books he used were generally about $7\frac{1}{2}$ by $4\frac{1}{2}$ inches in size, composed of ordinary white paper. His favourite medium was a hard-pointed pencil. His sketches are always made with a view to information, never for effect. In this way about a dozen books were filled, each of about a hundred pages, and most are drawn on on both sides of the pages. Our reproductions of the sketches of the Grand Canal, the Piazzetta at Venice, and Trajan's Column (Plates XLVIII., L., and LIII.) may stand as examples of the main body of work done by Turner during this visit.

TURNER'S SKETCHES AND DRAWINGS

In addition to these small sketch-books he also used some of larger size, with the paper prepared with a wash of grey. He used one of these books at Tivoli, and another at Rome and Naples. The grey tint was of such a nature that it lifted quite easily when rubbed with bread or india-rubber. In this way he was able to indicate the chiaroscuro of his sketches with ease and celerity. The more elaborate drawings of Rome were made in this way, among them those exquisite views from Monte Mario, which have long been among the most admired of the drawings exhibited in the Turner Water-Colour Rooms at the National Gallery. Where the subject was an interesting one he occasionally worked over it, or over parts of it, with water-colour, as in the ' View of Rome from Monte Mario' (No. 592) here reproduced (Plate LI.), and 'The Colosseum' (No. 596) among the exhibited drawings. But the number of drawings in which Turner had recourse to colour is extremely limited, quite nineteen-twentieths of them being simply in pencil.

The drawings made during this visit are, in Mr. Ruskin's opinion, the best Turner ever made from nature. ' All the artist's powers,' he wrote, ' were at this period in perfection ; none of his faults had developed themselves ; and his energies were taxed to the utmost to seize, both in immediate admiration, and for future service, the loveliest features of some of the most historically interesting scenery in the world.'[1] And again, ' They are, in all respects, the most true and the most beautiful ever made by the painter.'[2] And assuredly it would be difficult to praise these superb drawings too highly or too enthusiastically ; for sheer grace of pencilling, for skilful composition, for loving, unwearied rendering of architecture and natural scenery they are absolutely unrivalled.

But it is only as drawings, as works that contain their end within themselves, that they can be praised so highly. They are probably the most beautiful topographical drawings that have ever been made, but Turner did not regard himself as a topographical draughtsman, and from his point of view the results of this journey cannot have been completely satisfactory. If he had valued himself at all on his capacity for making beautiful topo-

[1] *Turner Catalogue*, written in 1881. National Gallery edition, 1899, p. 37.
[2] *Ibid.*

92

PLATE L

THE PIAZZETTA, VENICE, LOOKING TOWARDS ISOLA DI S. GIORGIO MAGGIORE

PENCIL. 1819

PLATE LI

ROME, FROM MONTE MARIO

PENCIL AND WATER COLOUR. 1819

graphical drawings, he would surely have taken some steps to bring these achievements to the notice of the public.[1] He did nothing of the kind. We have seen that it was his settled habit to regard his sketches and drawings from nature as merely the preliminary stages of his pictures. As Mr. Ruskin has pointed out, Turner, after his few years of apprenticeship, never drew from nature without altering and arranging what he saw. He never accepted the given momentary facts in a passive spirit. It is on record that once he said to the companion of one of his sketching tours who had got into a muddle with the drawing he was making, 'What are you in search of?' And this active spirit had been one of the chief characteristics of all the drawing from nature he had done before his visit to Italy : he had always been in search of something, he had always had a very clear and exact idea of what he wanted, and he had almost invariably managed to grasp just what he wanted, while encumbering himself with very little else.

This clearness of intention is absent from the Italian drawings. The scenery, the buildings, the people, the shipping and the effects of light are all new to him, and delightfully interesting. The novelty of his surroundings carries him out of himself. He becomes for a time a mere common tourist with a kind of accidental knack of making rapid and wonderfully beautiful pictorial memoranda. It is as though the creative artist had said to his familiar daemon, 'We are now in fair Italy. Sleep thou, and take a well-earned rest. The business of note-taking will go on automatically without thee ; and when we are once more back in dreary London thou shalt awake as a giant refreshed with slumber, and shalt knead with renewed vigour the material that has been accumulated.' But the results achieved were not as satisfactory as Turner might have expected. The best that could be made of these wonderful sketches was two or three charming water-colours for Mr. Fawkes, a weak and empty 'Forum Romanum' for Mr. Soane's Museum, and a large 'Bay of Baiae,' which, as Mr. Ruskin confesses, 'is encumbered with

[1] It is also worth remarking that the value of these drawings from a topographical point of view, *i.e.* as giving information pure and simple, is probably diminished by the fact that the material they contain is so skilfully selected and arranged.

TURNER'S SKETCHES AND DRAWINGS

material; it contains ten times as much as is necessary to a good picture, and yet is so crude in colour as to look unfinished.'[1]

It therefore depends very much upon what *we* are in search of, what conclusions we shall come to about these Italian drawings. If we are evangelists with a mission to preach the Gospel of Naturalism, we may accept them as the finest works of art Turner ever produced, in spite of the fact that he found them useless and worse than useless for his artistic purposes. From such a point of view it would be Turner's fault if these beautiful things threw him out and led him astray; or, as Mr. Ruskin puts it, 'the effect of Italy upon his [Turner's] mind is very puzzling . . . he seems never to have entered thoroughly into the spirit of Italy, and the materials he obtained there were afterwards but awkwardly introduced into his large compositions.'[2]

But if the processes of artistic creation are worth studying, we shall go on to ask ourselves how it is that the most elaborate, painstaking and thoroughly delightful drawings Turner ever made from nature were actually the least useful to him as a maker of pictures; and how it is that exquisitely deliberate and dainty drawings like those in the Roman and Neapolitan sketch-books lead actually to the production of frigid, hybrid, pseudo-classical pictures, while hurried and scarcely intelligible scribbles like those reproduced in Plates xxvii. and xxv. had been the means of bringing into existence such noble and impressive pictures as the 'Windmill and Lock,' and designs like the 'Hedging and Ditching'?

The answer to these questions is not far to seek. The state of mind necessary for the production of the two kinds of drawings is essentially different, and the one, which produces the exhaustive and accurate drawing, is antagonistic to the state of mind in which a strongly imaginative work of art is conceived, while the other, which produces a less immediately satisfying record, is actually the state of mind in which a passionately felt work of art comes to birth. In the drawing which we admire so much the emotional element is in abeyance, the cognitive or sense-perceptive is predominant; in the other the emotional element is predominant. But in the first case, while the immediate result, considered simply in itself, is more delightful, there has been

[1] *Modern Painters*, vol. i, p. 132.   [2] *Ibid.* p. 130.

PLATE LII

ROME, FROM THE VATICAN

PEN AND INK AND CHINESE WHITE ON GREY. 1819

PLATE LIII

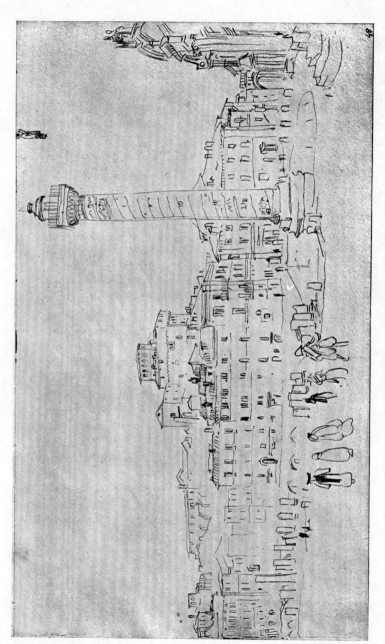

TRAJAN'S COLUMN, IN THE FORUM OF TRAJAN

PENCIL. 1819

no real quickening of the artist's spirit; in the second case, while the immediate result is deplorable for us, it is eloquent and glorious for the artist himself as the first stirring of his new-born spiritual progeny.

The object of these remarks is not to attempt to convince us that these charming Italian drawings are at all less charming than they seem; it is rather to combat the false deductions which Naturalism has succeeded in drawing from the fact that they are so genuinely delightful and so self-satisfying. It is inevitable that an artist shall constantly be making studies from nature, sharpening and exercising his powers of observation, and storing his note-books and memory with facts of natural appearances. But it does not follow that this business of observing and recording visual facts is the essential or even most important part of the artist's function. Naturalism assumes that it is. It therefore treats the power to copy natural objects faithfully and without alteration as the exact equivalent of the power of pictorial expression.[1] And so far as the system of art education pursued in this country has any rational foundation, it is based upon this doctrine of Naturalism. Hence the only kind of training that is provided for English art students is training in this capacity of reproducing objects of sight accurately. This has come to be the beginning and the end of modern art education, with what results we have only to walk into any summer exhibition of the Royal Academy to see. Under these circumstances, I think it is important that we should give its due weight to any evidence that tends to invalidate these generally received opinions. Of course the evidence of the practice and line of development of one artist, even an artist as great as Turner, is not by itself sufficient to settle such a question; but still, I submit, this evidence has a distinct bearing on the subject and should receive its due attention.

If the doctrine of Naturalism possessed the universal validity it is assumed to possess, the pictures based upon the truest and most elaborate drawings Turner ever made from nature—and that too of the most beautiful and the most historically interest-ing scenery in the world—should have been the best he had so

[1] *Elements of Drawing*, Preface, p. x.

far produced. They are admittedly among the worst. If the training acquired by making such drawings is essential to the development of the artist's powers of pictorial expression, how comes it that in Turner's case this training came after the production of his most perfect pictures —these Italian drawings being made in 1819, the 'Sheerness,' 'Windsor,' 'Abingdon,' and 'Frosty Morning' having been painted between 1809 and 1813, and he had never worked from nature like this before? This is the evidence. I can only beg the candid reader to give it the earnest consideration it seems to me to deserve.

Turner's oil paintings produced between 1815 and 1830 cannot but strike us as disappointing, especially when we compare them with the output of the years immediately preceding this period. It is only as a sea-painter that Turner reminds us of his former mastery, and with the exception of the 'Dort' (1818) 'Entrance of the Meuse' (1819), the Greenwich 'Battle of Trafalgar' (1823) and 'Now for the Painter' (1827), it would do Turner's reputation little harm if all his oil pictures produced during these years were destroyed. His real greatness is only shown in this period by the water-colours produced mainly for the engravers. In the work done for the *Southern Coast*, Scott's *Provincial Antiquities*, the *Rivers* and *Ports of England*, and the *England and Wales* series, Turner displayed all the genuine nobleness and sweetness of his nature. I propose therefore to occupy the remainder of this chapter with a rapid survey of these undertakings, singling out from each one or two representative designs for closer examination.

We have now seen what was the character of Turner's pictures which gained him most applause and favour in Academic circles and with the public of the Academy. It is no doubt regrettable that a man of his talents should have to waste his time—as it seems to us—in the manufacture of puerile and pretentious specimens of Academic 'high art,' but we can easily make too much of the matter. There is something altogether incommensurable about such a man ; he is like some great natural force, copious, abundant and unwearying. He must have drawn and painted with as little effort as ordinary mortals exert when they play cards or write letters to their friends. I have no doubt that

96

PLATE LIV

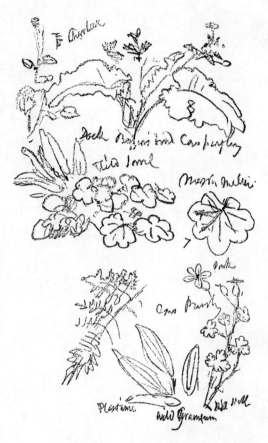

STUDY OF PLANTS, WEEDS, ETC.
PENCIL. ABOUT 1823

THE SPLENDOUR OF SUCCESS

the 'high art' concoctions bothered him much more than his better works, for it was all ratiocinative, conscious, all spun out of the understanding without any deep-struck roots in the unconscious life of his affections. But no doubt he felt prouder of the results, simply because he was more conscious of the efforts. We have no grounds for supposing that he did not enjoy the work, and in return it certainly gave him comparative independence, and encouraged him to produce. Printsellers and publishers were anxious to get the celebrated Academician to work for them, and the big middle-class public were eager to possess themselves of engravings from the great man's designs. It was certainly a clear gain that the designer of the *Southern Coast*, the *Richmondshire* drawings, Scott's *Provincial Antiquities*, the *Rivers* and *Ports of England*, and the *England and Wales* series could afford to keep publishers and editors at arm's length, that he was so strong in public favour that his work was influenced by none but artistic considerations.

It hardly comes within the scope of the present essay to study the drawings in detail which form the originals of Turner's engraved work, important as these drawings are as examples of the artist's genius. Each drawing is a perfect work of art in itself, the fact that an engraving was to be made from it counting practically as nothing with the artist. If the subject did not lend itself quite satisfactorily to the engraver's requirements, Turner introduced various modifications into the engraver's proofs, but he did not alter the drawings. In this way the original drawings were kept as independent creations. Into them the artist was free to pour all that spontaneous native side of his talent which could find no outlet in his ambitious 'high art' productions. As water-colours the originals of the engravings that were issued between 1814 and 1830 are among the most remarkable and consummate achievements of the medium. With hardly an exception they are worked entirely in transparent colour, and for sheer range of invention, variety of effect, and loveliness of colour they have no equals. But their place is among the artist's completed works, and as our immediate business is with the sketches and studies, we can only touch upon these exquisitely beautiful water-colours incidentally ; *i.e.* only in so far as they help us to grasp the significance of

TURNER'S SKETCHES AND DRAWINGS

the sketches and preliminary drawings which went to their production.

It is a curious sign how little conscious Turner was of the nature and limitations of his own capacities, that the plan of the *Southern Coast* series of engravings, as it first took form in his mind, included a long narrative poem from his own hand describing the history and local peculiarities of the places he proposed to illustrate. It is hardly probable that an individual with less capacity for verbal expression ever sat down to write a long poem. Yet it is easy to see how it was that Turner came to think himself competent to undertake such a task. The stamp of his mind was genuinely poetic. He had, and knew that he had, in a high measure 'the vision and the faculty divine.' The inspiration of his best works had been drawn from the poets, from Thomson, Akenside, and Milton. His pictures, so far as it is possible to distinguish content from form, are real poems. And the technical accomplishment of pictorial art had come to him so easily and naturally that it may well have seemed to flow inevitably from the innate strength of his emotions and the vivid hue of his imagination. He probably thought that he had only to take a pen in his hand to find the accomplishment of verse following with the same ease and inevitability.

The verses Turner did succeed in writing are pathetic failures; the mind so intimately versed in the subtleties of visible melody and harmony was dead to the witchery of verbal sound. It is true that his failure is not quite so abject as the extracts Thornbury has printed from the attempted *Southern Coast* epic would lead one to expect, but, when all due allowance is made for Thornbury's blunders of transcription, the result is still quite hopeless. But it is otherwise when we turn to the designs made from the same subject-matter, and, in spite of Lessing and a host of modern theorists, I must insist that in their heart and essence they are indeed poems.

The first number of the *Southern Coast* was published in January 1814, and the last number was not issued till May 1826, but with only one or two exceptions the whole of the Dorsetshire, Devon, Cornwall and Somersetshire subjects (and these form about three-quarters of the whole work) were made from sketches

98

taken during a single journey in the summer of 1811. These sketches are the kind of notes that a poet would take; from the point of view of the historian or topographer they are singularly incomplete. Occasionally we come across a tolerably elaborate drawing of a ruined castle or stretch of rocky coast, but even these are summary and hurried in comparison with the Italian drawings, and Turner seldom chose such sketches as the bases of his finished pictures. He certainly found them useful as the means of making a methodical analysis of the pictorial constituents of what he saw, and as storing his memory and giving matter and fulness to his own conceptions of natural phenomena. But there their usefulness ended. The actual embryo of the pictures he painted is generally a hurried scrawl about two square inches in size, made with a blunt pencil.

Among the *Southern Coast* sketch-books is a fat little volume bound in brown calf, having a brass clasp and lettered on the back, *British Itenary (sic)*. The title page runs as follows :—*The British Itinerary* | or | Travellers Pocket Companion | throughout | Great Britain | Exhibiting | the Direct Route to Every | Borough and Commercial Town | in the | Kingdom | with the principal | Cross Roads | Compiled from Actual Measurement | and the best Surveys and Authorities | By | Nathanl. Coltman ; | Surveyor. | Employed by the Post Office in Measuring the Roads of | Great Britain | London. | Printed and Published, by Wm. Dickie, No. 120 Strand ; and N. Coltman, Green Walk ; Black Friars Road. | Price 3s. Sewed.' It contains two hundred and fifty leaves, the printed matter only occupying about a third of the total number, the remainder having been left blank for notes. These are now filled with Turner's notes of expenses incurred, the draft of the poem he attempted to write, and a number of minute sketches. Among these it is possible to recognise the originals of several of the *Southern Coast* designs, including those of Combe Martin, Watchet, Boscastle and Clovelly, the 'Dartmouth' and 'Dartmouth Castle' of the *Rivers of England* series, and the sketch upon which the superb 'Stonehenge at Daybreak' (R. 81), in the unpublished 'Liber,' was probably founded. Two of these sketches have been reproduced on Plates LV. and LVI., together with the engravings of the completed designs. That the finished drawings could have been made from such slender material can hardly appear less than astonishing to those familiar with the methods of artists of the present day; but to the best of my belief, Turner had no other sketches or drawings of these places to assist him in his work, and it can only add to our amazement when we notice that in all probability the finished drawings were made, one nearly eight years, and the other nearly fourteen years, after the sketches were taken; the 'Watchet' plate having been published in April 1820, and the 'Boscastle' in March 1825.

When we examine carefully the sketch of Watchet we find that it gives us very little more than the general idea of a small fishing village, with a curved breakwater and a stretch of rocky coast running off into the distance. This general idea must have been all that the artist retained of his experiences of the place, *i.e.*, he cannot possibly have retained any bare unattached visual sensations of any of the particular objects comprised in the scene. The details of the construction of the breakwater in the engraving may, for all I know (I have never visited the place), be exactly like those of the actual one which Turner saw there, but what little I know of his ordinary methods of work inclines me to doubt it. It is probably true enough to the general facts of the case, but all those little local accidents of form which the conscientious realist of to-day would linger over so lovingly are certainly ignored. No doubt when Turner was on the spot he looked at the breakwater, as at everything, with keen and vigilant eyes, and his impression of the structure would have contributed to the building up in his mind of a definite and concrete idea of the laws and customs of breakwaters in general. And when he set to work to elaborate his sketch it was doubtless this general idea which came into play, and which turned those half-dozen rudely scratched lines in the sketch into a sharply defined mental picture, as vivid to Turner's imagination as a real scene, and infinitely more useful for his immediate purpose, for the task of selection and rejection was already done. In this way the whole subject came to life; the sketch, a fixed point in present perception, beckoning forth the stored essential riches of the artist's mind. Those three upright lines inside the breakwater turn into

PLATE LV

WATCHET, SOMERSETSHIRE
PENCIL. ABOUT 1811

WATCHET, SOMERSETSHIRE
ENGRAVING PUBLISHED IN "THE SOUTHERN COAST," 1 APRIL, 1820

PLATE LVI

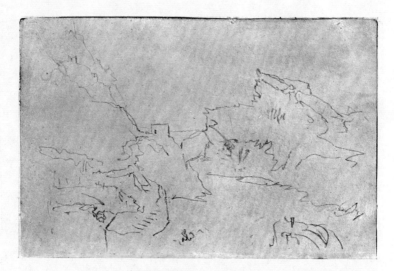

BOSCASTLE, CORNWALL
PENCIL. ABOUT 1811

BOSCASTLE, CORNWALL
ENGRAVING PUBLISHED IN "THE SOUTHERN COAST," 10 MARCH, 1825

an array of fishing boats, the sea ripples into the harbour and creeps up the shore, the village straightens itself out and grows into a collection of habitable houses, with gardens and parting walls, the women come out of the houses to spread their washing on the grass to dry, others gossip in the roadway, the men have a little business loading or unloading one of the boats, or else see to the nets, or stroll idly along the jetty, and a couple set off on important business along the road that leads over the hill and far away. The whole process, of course, is absurdly easy and familiar. Even the least imaginative of us is capable of some kind of success in this line of imaginative interpretation. The only point of difference between the least of us and the greatest in this kind of exercise is in the quality of the subjective filling-out with which we clothe our meagre data, in the wealth of experience stored and refined by thought, its coherence, and above all, its clear-cut precision and definition. The power to force all the floating imagery thus called up to what I think Blake called 'the seeing point'—to make the mental imagery as clear-cut and vivid as an actual object of sight, and then to use it as the material for the construction of a picture, these are exceptional capacities; but we can hardly doubt that the psychological processes which connect sketch and imaginative amplification, even in the mind of the most gifted artist, are the same as those which connect sign and interpretation in the minds of all normally constituted individuals.

To an artist trained in modern methods of literal transcription, it is curious to notice the liberties Turner allows himself to take with his own sketch. In it the main shapes of the mass of rock in the middle distance are pretty clearly marked, but instead of carefully retaining these and amplifying them, his busy mind sets to work and builds the whole structure up afresh. In the end it comes out very different from the sketch, but it is so well and truly put together, it is so thoroughly steeped in the profound knowledge garnered in years of the sharpest observation and study, that we accept it more gladly than an unintelligent transcript of any particular rock formation. Nay more, even if we had forced Turner himself to stay there on the spot, and elaborate his representation with the scene in front of his eyes, there would have been no gain to the drawing, for the result could not possibly have been more thoroughly penetrated with the laws of human thought and observation.

We notice the same freedom in dealing with the 'Boscastle' sketch. The general character only of the rocks on the right is there indicated, but in the engraving the whole mass is re-created from the stores of the artist's knowledge. In the sketch, too, there is no authority for the solid masonry on the rock to the left, immediately below the gang of men assisting the vessel into harbour. Note also the alteration in the profile of this rock, which slopes less abruptly in the sketch than in the engraving.

It is true that these two plates can hardly be ranked as among the finest of the *Southern Coast* subjects; the 'Watchet' is, I think, rather a poor design, and though the 'Boscastle' is finer, it can hardly be classed with such consummate achievements as the 'Plymouth Dock, from Mount Edgecumbe,' 'Poole,' or 'The Land's End.' In these designs the subjective synthesis has a more distinctly emotional setting, but there can be no doubt that the processes of imaginative construction are on exactly the same lines as those we have just indicated. In every case the active motive force is something within the artist's own soul; it is not given from without.

The next important publication with which Turner was con-nected after the commencement of the *Southern Coast*, was Whitaker's *History of Richmondshire*, to which he furnished a series of twenty illustrations. This set of drawings, often spoken of as 'the Yorkshire series,' has always been regarded with peculiar affection by all lovers of Turner's water-colour work. The originals are nearly all in private collections (where I hope they will be carefully guarded from the light, as the blues in them are of a fugitive nature), but there are two permanently accessible to the public in the Fitzwilliam Museum, Cambridge—thanks to Mr. Ruskin's generosity—and a third is in London, in the Victoria and Albert Museum. The Cambridge drawings, the 'Richmond, Yorks,' and the 'Mossdale Fall,' are already somewhat faded, especially the latter one, but the London drawing, of 'Hornby Castle,' thanks to Mr. Vaughan's wise

PLATE LVII

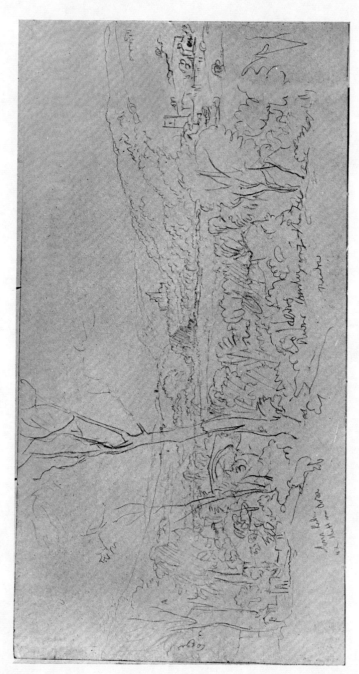

HORNBY CASTLE, FROM TATHAM CHURCH

PENCIL. ABOUT 1816

PLATE LVIII

HORNBY CASTLE, FROM TATHAM CHURCH

ENGRAVING PUBLISHED IN WHITAKER'S "RICHMONDSHIRE," JUNE, 1822

stipulation that it shall always be protected by a curtain when not being looked at, is still in fairly good condition. The engravings from the whole series were published between the years 1819 and 1823, but the sketches on which the drawings were based were all made during a tour in the summer of 1816.

So far as I know, Turner did not make a single colour sketch from nature during the whole of this tour. All the sketches are in pencil and the water-colours were all painted in the studio entirely from these pencil memoranda. The sketches are very similar to those made for the *Southern Coast* subjects, but they contain evidence that the artist was in a softer and gentler frame of mind. The conquering Napoleonic insolence has passed into an attitude of human and affectionate solicitude. The touch of the pencil point is everywhere light and graceful, yet it is as swift as ever, never lingering for a moment over details or particular facts. This is especially noticeable in the treatment of foliage; the pencil seeming always to caress the general idea of foliage, while holding the particular shapes and even positions of trees and bushes as of only slight importance. The work, one cannot but feel, is that of a happy and contented man, at peace with himself and pleased with his surroundings. When we remember the close proximity of Farnley Hall to these scenes, and that Mr. and Mrs. Fawkes and their family actually accompanied the artist over part of the ground, we can hardly be surprised at the sunniness of temper evinced by these sketches.

In nearly all the designs human figures and cattle play a prominent part. This is noticeably the case with the two subjects I have chosen for illustration. In the ' Hornby Castle ' the incident of the broken jug, the weeping maiden, the sympathetic bystanders, the picturesque passer-by on his donkey, the busy milk maid, and above all the cat, triumphantly lapping up the spilt milk, all this is at least as important an element in the picture as the Castle and view itself. In the ' Heysham ' the reapers, cattle, milkmaid, and passing waggon seem to form the keynote of the whole design. Yet there are no sketches or even the slightest indications of any of these things in the sketch-books. They were evolved, I firmly believe, entirely by the artist's creative imagination as each scene came to life under his hands in the studio. To some extent, no doubt, the decorative or mechanical requirements of the subject solicited their existence. In the 'Heysham,' for example, lines are wanted in the foreground to repeat with variations the horizontal undulations of the mountains in the distance and middle-distance; the cast shadows do this, and hence we have the presence of the cows and figures as pretexts for these shadows. And then we may as well make these objects useful in themselves; hence the turn of the foreground cow's neck placed just where it seems to complete the curve of the descending hills, and the sharp silhouette of the head catches the eye while the cast shadow swings it away in a new and happy direction. Exactly why the eye should find such exquisite enjoyment in the plunge down from the hill's profile to the head of the calf, rubbing her nose against the back of the seated white cow, and then on to the foreground beast, and then in springing off again at a sharp angle to the bottom of the large foreground stone in the corner just above the signature,—exactly why we take pleasure in this kind of visual melody, I do not know, but I know that the tracks laid for visible flights of this kind, crossing each other and interweaving in all directions, form a very large part of the enjoyment which Turner's drawings provide.

The pencil sketch of Heysham (Plate LIX. (a)) thus formed, as it were, the leading motive of the water-colour drawing, or rather it provided a series of shapes which could not be varied beyond certain limits, and these shapes formed the starting-point of the elaborate visual movement which Turner proceeded to invent and weave round it. I called just now this side of the work 'decorative or mechanical,' because I wished to distinguish it from a different but related aspect. This unmeaning and abstract play of lines is like the rhyme, assonance and rhythm of a poem ; a part, but an unconscious, and as it were dependent, part, of the whole effect. No sane person would read a poem expressly for the jingle of the sounds, unless for the purposes of analysis, and in the same way, no sane lover of pictures would look at this drawing of Heysham merely for the visible play of the lines and masses. Neither can the artist or poet abandon themselves to the

PLATE LIX

HEYSHAM, WITH BLACK COMBE, CONISTON OLD MAN, HELVELLYN, ETC., IN DISTANCE

PENCIL. ABOUT 1816

HEYSHAM AND CUMBERLAND MOUNTAINS

ENGRAVING PUBLISHED IN WHITAKER'S "RICHMONDSHIRE," 22 AUGUST, 1822

mere unmeaning play of sounds or lines in the process of composition. These external requirements must be subordinated to the requirements of the meaning. And so, though I said just now that these mechanical requirements may have had some share in calling the figures and incidents represented into being, we must be careful not to forget that that share is only of slight and subordinate importance. What is important is the essential congruity of the figures and incidents with the landscape itself; they must appear not as something arbitrarily added, but as a mere development or further determination of the meaning already implicit in the landscape. In the present case so intimate is what I may call the logical identity between the bare view, as represented by the initial sketch, and as a topographical fact, and the whole living and moving scene as represented by the finished design, that the development of the one from the other seems as inevitable as the march of the seasons or the processes of growth and decay to which we ourselves are subject.

From this point of view I think it is easy to see that such a result is attainable in no other way than that which Turner has followed. No actual scene could ever possess quite the same close-knit logical coherence, the same absolute absence of irrelevance, as we find in Turner's finished drawing; so that the most faithful and loving and skilful reproduction of the most carefully selected aspect of actuality would never give us the same kind of outer and inner unity that Turner has achieved by his method of amplifying, modifying, and interpreting his slight pencil sketches. Only in this way can the active forces of interpretation or assimilation, by which the artist as well as the meanest of us fills out the incoming suggestions of the given, achieve adequate expression. A psychologist might perhaps describe the difference between a faithful transcription of an actual scene and such an effort of the creative imagination as we have just been studying, by saying that the one is a representation of the incoming or given ideas or sensations, while Turner's picture represents these same ideas or sensations after they have been thoroughly 'apperceived' by the masses of ideas stored in the artist's mind. If we adopt such a description, we must not forget to add that Turner has used his knowledge of the mechanism of the pictorial language to set out his total idea for us in the clearest and pleasantest way.

As with the Heysham sketch, so with the Hornby.[1] I need perhaps hardly call attention to the deliberate heightening of Hornby Castle, and to the way the back of the nearer hill in front of it has been humped in the finished design. This deliberate falsification (as it must seem to the literalist) is paralleled by the treatment of the foreground tree, whose individuality is destroyed, and whose place is taken by a mere alien grown in the fertile climate of the artist's imagination. I have no doubt that if Turner could have got the same effect without making these alterations he would not have made them. But it is obvious that he could not. From his point of view such alterations are merely grammatical devices by which he throws the required emphasis on qualities which hills and trees do undeniably possess, but which were somewhat slurred over in nature's momentary presentment of the case. And if we think about the matter calmly, we see that we cannot expect any object to enter into new relations without undergoing some kind of modification ; I mean that we cannot expect physical facts to be taken up into the intelligible world and used as factors in the expression of ideas and emotions without requiring some kind of modification.

While Turner was producing these exquisite drawings for Whitaker's *History of Richmondshire*, he also executed a series of ten or eleven slightly smaller drawings to illustrate Sir Walter Scott's *Provincial Antiquities and Picturesque Scenery of Scotland*. Eight of these drawings were presented by the publishers to Scott, who had them framed from an oak felled on the Abbotsford estate during Turner's visit there in 1818. The effect of this frame on the drawings, it must be confessed, is atrocious. It might be guaranteed to kill the effect of any water-colour drawings but the radiantly immortal ones for which it was made. No doubt even these would look better out of it, but such as it is it hung in the breakfast-room at Abbotsford till after Scott's death, and as it then hung, so it hangs now in Mr. Thomas Brocklebank's hospitable mansion at Heswall, Chester.

When we draw the curtain, which has kept Turner's beautiful

[1] Plate LVII.

PLATE LX

EDINBURGH, FROM CALTON HILL

PENCIL. 1818

EDINBURGH, FROM CALTON HILL

ENGRAVING PUBLISHED IN SCOTT'S "PROVINCIAL ANTIQUITIES OF SCOTLAND," 1 NOVEMBER, 1820

PLATE LX

EDINBURGH FROM CALTON HILL

PENCIL. 1818

FIGURES ON CALTON HILL

PENCIL. 1818

PLATE LXI

BORTHWICK CASTLE
PENCIL. 1818

BORTHWICK CASTLE
ENGRAVING PUBLISHED IN SCOTT'S "PROVINCIAL ANTIQUITIES OF SCOTLAND," 2 APRIL, 1819

work as fresh as when it was first executed, and look at these drawings, it is difficult to single out any one of them for special attention. But after looking through the engravings made from them in Scott's book, the marvellous view of 'Edinburgh from the Calton Hill' leaves perhaps the most powerful impression on the imagination. I have, therefore, selected the drawing made from nature upon which this design was based as the subject of one of our illustrations (Plate LX.).

In this case we find that Turner has followed his sketch with great care, yet the whole material has been hammered this way and that by his powerful hand. We can see that the artist felt impatient with nature's calm and unhurried chronicle of facts, and was determined at all costs to make a more immediate and con-centrated attack on the spectator's powers of perception. Instead of stretching out calmly and indifferently on both hands, as in the sketch, the city in the finished design seems to soar upwards from the depths beneath our feet. The jail on our left has been squeezed together, making the line from the porch to the central turret much more oblique than it was. The perspective of nearly all the buildings has been modified, yet the artist has taken great care to preserve the character of the silhouettes of the leading planes. But it is in the invention of the play of light which animates the whole, and throws into such strong relief all the telling points of the design, that we find the clearest evidence of the artist's active intervention.

A curious instance of Turner's habit of using his notes rather as hints to his imagination than as providing ready-made material waiting for immediate incorporation, is afforded by the sketches of some figures made while he was standing on the Calton Hill. On the back of one of the pages on which our view of Edin-burgh is drawn, there is a rough sketch of the brow of the hill with groups of figures on it. Among these figures are three girls attending to the drying of the clothes they have washed. One of these is standing shaking out a cloth in the wind. But though Turner has introduced this incident into the foreground of his picture, the figure there is not a repetition of the graceful figure in the sketch. In the picture the action has been changed, and the figure presented in a different point of view. It is designed altogether afresh. In the same way none of the other figures is repeated in the finished drawing. The figures in the drawing are indeed the same sort of people as in the sketch, but each is designed specially for its place, and with reference to the movement of the whole picture. All this is eminently characteristic of the cast of Turner's mind, which seems to store scenes and incidents in complete independence of their momentary and particular appearance; he is thus able to set these invisible essences in motion before his mind's eye, and to wait till they arrange themselves to his complete satisfaction, and he has then no difficulty in clothing them with the attributes of time and space.

We will turn now to a sketch of a different kind. In the ' Edinburgh,' 'Heysham' and 'Hornby' sketches, as in most of those we have examined, we have seen Turner making a note of what we may call the chief items of the topographical data, leaving the problem of their arrangement, modification and amplification for future solution. In the two sketches of Rochester (Plates LXII. (*a*) and (*b*)) which I have had reproduced, we see the artist's mind moving on a different track. A few pages earlier in the sketch-book from which these two leaves are taken, he has indeed made his usual record of the facts about the church, bridge, etc., at Rochester, but apparently, as time did not press, he remained in his boat watching the scene and criticising, as one who understood such things, nature's own methods of design. His sketches now become not topographical records but swift and eloquent designs for pictures. The concrete particularity of the castle, church, bridge, etc., becomes abrogated or submerged. These objects are now taken up into a new kind of systematic unity, in which their relationship to the whole and to each other is of much more importance than their discrete individuality. Now, the important point is just how the Castle and the other topographical items drop into place with regard to the shipping on the river,—the kind of groups they all make, the way the one item affects the other, half hiding it or setting it off to advantage. In the sketch on page 18 of the sketch-book (Plate LXII. (*a*)) the exact position of the mast of the foreground vessel is the dominant factor —the way it unites the lines described by the silhouette of the castle and the trees sloping down to the bridge, bringing the

PLATE LXII

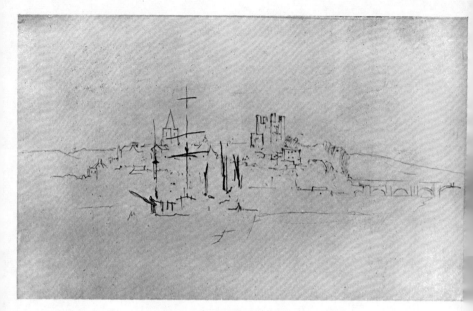

ROCHESTER

PENCIL. ABOUT 1821

ROCHESTER

PENCIL. ABOUT 1821

PLATE LXIII

ROCHESTER, ON THE RIVER MEDWAY

WATER COLOUR, ABOUT 1822

curves to a focus, as it were, and providing a rigid base for them to spring from again. In the other sketch (Plate LXII. (*b*)) Turner is trying a different arrangement of the material, or, to put it more accurately, nature is trying another effect, and Turner is watching and making notes of the experiment.

In this way, before Turner shut up his book he had made over a dozen skeleton designs, which he had only to clothe in colour and light and shade to develop into beautiful pictures. But when he got home and actually set to work to make the drawing of Rochester for the *Rivers of England* series, he deliberately ignored every one of nature's pregnant suggestions, and began to build up his own design in his own way. Perhaps he thought nature's designs wanted more space than he had at his command in a plate that was to be only a few inches square; perhaps it was the sheer delight in the exercise of his creative powers that was the main motive force, for though his sketchbooks teem with designs caught in this way on the wing, yet he never once, so far as I can discover, adopted one of them in his own pictures, without so modifying and recasting it as to make it into a quite new and independent construction.

I am not at all sure of the exact date when the sketch of Bolton Abbey (Plate LXIV.) was made. It is the sketch upon which the water-colour engraved in the *England and Wales* series was based. The engraving was published in 1827, so the water-colour must have been made a year or two earlier, but as the sketch occurs in a book which contains a number of the *Devonshire Rivers* subjects, it probably belongs to about the time of Turner's second visit to Devonshire. This visit took place in either 1812 or 1813, and the Wharfedale sketches, of which the 'Bolton' is one, cannot have been later than 1815. So it is probable that at least ten years elapsed between the making of the sketch and the water-colour drawing in which the sketch was elaborated.

The drawing itself is one of the most universally admired of all the *England and Wales* subjects. Mr. Ruskin alludes to it again and again in the various volumes of *Modern Painters*. In the fourth volume (chapter xvi.) he gives an admirable analysis of the imaginative conception, and in volume three (chapter ix.) he dwells with his usual eloquence on the knowledge displayed in the treatment of the foreground trees. With the general tenor of these remarks I am in entire agreement, and if the passages were not so long I should like to introduce them here, but unless the reader is very careful, I am inclined to think that Mr. Ruskin's constant appeal to 'the facts' is likely to mislead him into the belief that all the details of the design, and especially those of the foreground trees, are elaborately studied and accurately reproduced from the actual scene. Turner's sketch proves that this was not the case. Each individual tree, every curve in its trunk, the texture of its bark, the stains and hollows and flickering lights and shadows upon it, and the intricate play of the trees' upper branches, all these have been, not painstakingly studied from nature, but invented by the artist in his studio, and each detail has been invented not entirely for its own sake, but as a note, a chord, in the whole complex of visible harmony.

I do not think any more wonderful example could be given of the intense activity of creative genius than that which is furnished by a careful comparison of this drawing with the sketch upon which it was based. We look at the sketch, and all the subject seems there; as a synopsis of the finished picture it seems tolerably complete. Yet in the drawing we find almost every detail has been altered. Notice the way the foreground trees have been pushed nearer to each other. In the sketch one has to search for the abbey, and then one's eyes begin to wander about aimlessly. But in the drawing everything is brought into connection with everything else; it is all welded together. The abbey is the first thing one sees, then the eye goes easily and inevitably to the second couple of foreground trees, the seated angler and the distant river-bank. In passing from one object to the other the eye feels something of the same kind of pleasure that the ear takes in the rhythm of verse, so that one's gaze travels over the drawing not vagrantly and with effort, but gladly, and to the spectator all this visible melody and delight seem like the unconscious expression of the secret joy with which the artist's mind played round the scene, an echo of the mysterious music of his happy memories.

The effect of the 'Bolton' drawing is that of a bright summer's

PLATE LXIV

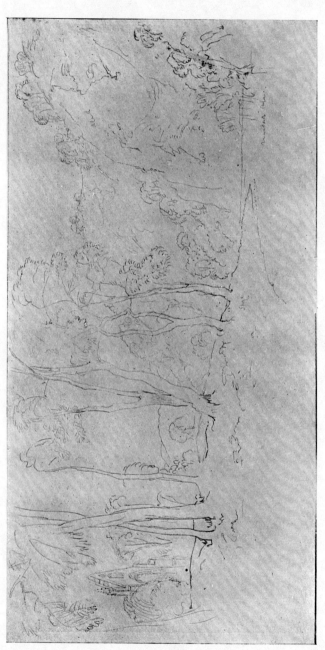

BOLTON ABBEY
PENCIL. ABOUT 1815

PLATE LXV

BOLTON ABBEY

ENGRAVING PUBLISHED IN "PICTURESQUE VIEWS IN ENGLAND AND WALES," 1827

PLATE LXVI

COLCHESTER

PENCIL   ABOUT 1824

COLCHESTER

PENCIL.   ABOUT 1824

PLATE LXVII

COLCHESTER, ESSEX

ENGRAVING PUBLISHED IN "PICTURESQUE VIEWS IN ENGLAND AND WALES," 1827

afternoon, an effect that does not change very rapidly ; the slightness of Turner's sketch was not, therefore, a necessary outcome of the transitory nature of his subject-matter. Had he been so minded he could easily have painted the whole subject out-of-doors. But with the 'Colchester' drawing, another of the *England and Wales* subjects, published about the same time as the 'Bolton,' the case was different. There the effect is a momentary one. It is evening, the shades of twilight have gathered, and the sun is on the point of disappearing. There was only time for a few hasty memoranda ; but while the modern artist would almost invariably make his memoranda in colour, Turner is quite satisfied with his usual hurried pencil notes. In the sketches here reproduced (Plate LXVI.) we have a kind of abstract of the whole scene. There is the miller's house beside the river at the foot of the hill, while the hill is crowned by a row of trees through which the abbey building and the roofs of the distant town can be seen. The position of the sun and of its reflection in the river are marked.

The general idea of the whole is certainly there in the sketches, but in a rudimentary or indeterminate condition. Note how deliberately vague and undefined the idea of the trees on the brow of the hill has been kept. A distant abbey-building set in the delicate tracery of gracefully branching trees, the whole framed in masses of feathery foliage, that was the general idea of this part of the design, and Turner knew that he was familiar enough with the nature and ways of trees to be able to carry out this idea with all the requisite wealth of detail whenever he should set himself seriously to the task. The exact shapes of the trees actually growing there on the hillside on the day and at the moment when he made this sketch were, apart from their general idea, a matter of indifference to him. If he had cared very much about them he could easily have gone there the next morning and drawn them carefully ; they would hardly have altered much in the night. But these shapes would have surely wanted revision, alteration and suppression, before they could have taken their places as a perfectly articulated limb in Turner's living, organic design. The result could not have been more satisfactory than the one reached without this labour.

111

TURNER'S SKETCHES AND DRAWINGS

As with the row of trees, so with the miller's house, the cottages creeping up the hillside and the distant town. The pencil hieroglyphs are enough to suggest the general idea of these objects, their appropriate particularities will unroll themselves from the stored treasures of Turner's mind so soon as he takes his pencil in hand again to carry forward his work; not the actual details of the cottages, etc., existing down there in Essex, but the details appropriate to the picture as an expression of an emotional experience.

The drawings in the *England and Wales* series produced in this way, in which a definite particular experience of the artist is enshrined as it were in a wealth of appropriate and beautifully arranged shapes and colours, are among the best of the series. But the pressure of professional engagements did not always permit the artist to wait for this kind of inspiration. On such occasions he appears to have fallen back on the material stored in his early sketch-books, and his rhetorical mastery of the elements of design was taxed to the uttermost to provide it with suitable clothing and ornament. An excellent example of this kind of work is provided by the drawing of Stamford, published in 1830. This was founded on one of the sketches made during Turner's first tour in the North of England, in 1797. This sketch (Plate LXVIII.) is no doubt a fairly accurate record of the place, its humdrum streets and houses, with its three triumphant bursts of idealism in the shape of its three unimaginative church towers.

In taking up this sketch thirty years after it was made, Turner seems to have asked himself, 'What am I to do to make this dull affair into something universally interesting?' that is to say, into something interesting and even amusing to those who care nothing for Stamford merely for its own sake. Of course the first thing for him to do was obviously to seize upon the three towers and make the most of them, setting them up against a gorgeous sky filled with rain and thunder and the darting rays of the thwarted sun, which, however, must so far triumph in its contest as to flood the towers with its light and transfigure them with its splendour. The street below remains dull and untractable, but yet something may be made of it. We can gain one point by insisting on the smallness and homeliness of the houses, intensifying their

PLATE LXVIII

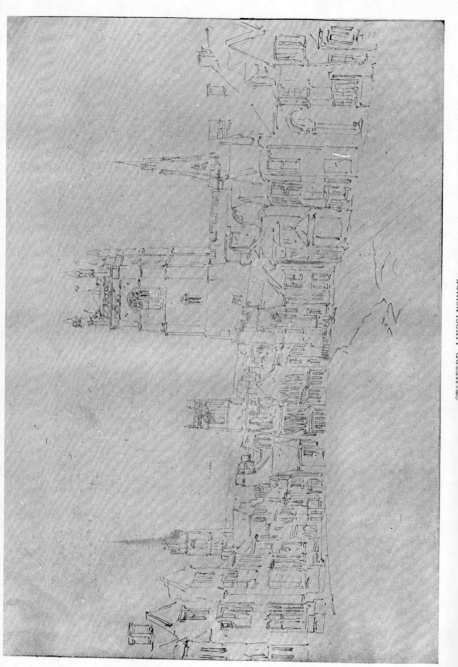

STAMFORD, LINCOLNSHIRE

PLATE LXIX

STAMFORD, LINCOLNSHIRE

ENGRAVING PUBLISHED IN "PICTURESQUE VIEWS IN ENGLAND AND WALES," 1830

PLATE LXX

TYNEMOUTH PRIORY
PENCIL, WITH PART IN WATER COLOUR. 1797

TYNEMOUTH, NORTHUMBERLAND
ENGRAVING PUBLISHED IN "PICTURESQUE VIEWS IN ENGLAND AND WALES," 1831

unimaginative character into something approaching the grotesque. Better the actively ugly, for that at least makes our dullest and largest church tower look almost beautiful by contrast, than the passively commonplace. And then, lest our modest efforts remain of small avail, we invent a couple of quaint old travellers hurrying across the road to their inn, accompanied by the barks and gambols of a lively little white dog; by good luck and our own skilful management they come just in front of our dull row of houses, so that what with one thing and another we find our eyes and thoughts very pleasantly diverted. As for the houses on the left we can shut off a great part of them by simply drawing up a lumbering stage-coach on that side of the road and heaping it with ample females in swelling draperies, with burgeoning umbrellas and bounteous baggage. And having got so far, we can now see exactly what it is we want to make our foreground and distance more immediately effective. In the sketch there is a hint that the road dips just a trifle down from the foreground to the church; we increase this slight inequality till we get a dip of something like forty or fifty feet between us and the church, a drop that gives uncommon height and dignity to our humble towers. And now, having got our street laid out to our liking, we want to make the most of its possibilities, so we set another stage-coach down at the foot of our little hill, load it with passengers impatient to be out of their wet clothes, and give it a couple of rearing, prancing, steaming horses to gallop it in hot haste up the declivity, so that now, as we look at the engraving, we can almost hear the ring of the horses' hooves on the stones and feel the rush of wind made by the coach as it dashes past us; all this merely by way of amplifying the artist's statement about his imaginary hill, and to drive the idea of his well-invented fiction home into the consciousness of even the dullest of his audience.

The 'Tynemouth' design, published in 1831, is on a higher plane of imaginative creation than the 'Stamford' subject, yet it was built up in just the same way from a sketch made at the same time on another leaf of the same sketch-book. The 'Stamford' design shows Turner struggling valiantly against the absence of any very pressing inspiration, and emerging with credit from the ordeal; the 'Tynemouth' drawing, on the other hand, shows that his youthful and thirty-year old topographical sketch had served to set his imagination aflame with all the urgency of a recent personal experience. The vision conjured up by what I can only call the potential or possible associations of a rocky coast had so much completeness, so much innate driving force, that Turner had no need to resort to the purely external and arbitrary tricks of composition which had proved such valuable auxiliaries in the ' Stamford' drawing. In the case of the 'Stamford' subject, we might almost say that the pictorial equivalent of the rhyme and metre had suggested the sense ; in the case of the 'Tynemouth' drawing the idea itself is so vivid that it creates its own lilt and harmony.

In looking through a number of Turner's drawings the hasty observer—especially should he be a professional student eager to pick up useful knowledge—is inclined to jump to the conclusion that the important thing about rocks and mountains is to be high, and that when the height of the most prominent buildings, especially if they happen to be in ruins, has been increased three or fourfold, all the duties of the imaginative designer have been attended to. In the 'Tynemouth' drawing we see how free Turner is from the constraint of any such ready-made and purely external rules of design. He has here deliberately lowered the apparent height of his buildings and cliffs, and, if we examine the matter carefully, we see that he has done this not at the dictates of a passing whim or fancy, but because the heart of the matter— the so-called 'subject,' that vague, intangible, elusive something which seems to sit in the centre of the dynamical idea and pump blood and life into every outlying portion of the organism, and tyrannises so beneficently over the structure and function of each part of the design—because this heart of the matter would clearly have it so.

In the sketch we have an item of brute fact waiting, as it were, pathetically to be taken up into the world of thought and feeling, asking, so to speak, to be made significant and human. The artist has granted the request in his finished design by making the physical facts the mere passive spectators of man's sorrow and suffering. In the sketch, the tall cliffs and ruined walls of the priory tower above the small fishing-boat struggling into port ; in the picture, the tall masts of the wrecked schooner dwarf the priory and the cliffs and drive them into subordination. The real centre of interest is the active, restless power of the sea for ill. The baneful little leaps of the waves that fill nearly all the lower part of the design tell their story of storm and wreck plainly enough. The wrecked barques under the cliffs are in a sad plight, but the pieces of floating mast and broken plank in the foreground tell of worse things. On the shore we have the thrifty gatherers of flotsam and jetsam, and a crowd of willing helpers. On all this moving scene the wreck of the priory looks down not without sympathy; it too, it seems to say, is a part of man's activity and ambition, it suffers also from the taint of mortality and from the merciless power of the wind and rain.

CHAPTER VIII

MENTAL AND PHYSICAL DECAY, AND THE ORIGIN OF IMPRESSIONISM—1830-1845

Mental characteristics of 1815-1830 period—Their influence on form—and colour—Colour enrichment a general characteristic of Romantic Art—What further development is required to give us the transition to Impressionism?—The first of Turner's so-called Impressionistic works—Vagueness or indistinctness as a means of expression—Two ways of painting one's impressions—Turner's earlier way—contrasted with the modern Impressionistic way—The change, after 1830, is it a change in terms of sight or of thought—visual or mental?—The content of Turner's later work—The relation of Turner's later work to Impressionism defined—The gradual development of Turner's later manner—The Petworth sketches (1830)—The discovery of the artistic value of the indeterminate—The Vignettes—'Rivers of France'—Venetian sketches (1834-1840)—Swiss and Rhine sketches (1841-1844)—The end.

WHEN we try to make clear to ourselves the inner characteristics of the period studied in the last chapter, we notice at once a change from the gloom, sternness and patient endurance of the earlier decade to a brighter and more cheerful frame of mind. Turner's predominant frame of mind is proud and happy. He seems to rejoice in the splendour of the world and exult over the richness and variety of its material. His attitude towards humanity is not so easily defined. In the best of his oil paintings, as in the 'Pas de Calais' ('Now for the Painter'), and in his water-colours, there is an abundance of close and sympathetic observation of the labours and sorrow of mankind. But in spite of the graces of a naturally kind heart Turner's attitude towards these labours and sufferings is not entirely free from traces of hardness and selfishness. His instinct for the picturesque side of this kind of subject-matter is so keen, and his insistence on this picturesqueness is so constant and so

116

emphatic, that it is hard to resist the suspicion that his interest is rather professional than personal. He does not seem to feel himself an actor and a fellow-sufferer. He was on the other side of the fence ; he was the artist, and labouring, suffering mankind his material. And so far as he himself was concerned he had every reason for exultation. The nature that could endow a humbly born youth with such gifts as he possessed, and the society that had rewarded these talents so generously, might be said to have fairly earned the young painter's gratitude. He gave it effusively, with none of the ulterior reserves an educated Greek would have felt in the presence of a great happiness or pre-eminent success.

Let us now turn to the outward and visible results of this exultant and somewhat heartless and selfish enjoyment. The movement of the design, the quality of the tone and colour, and the spirit of the handling of the pictures in which such a frame of mind is expressed, could not possibly be the same as in Turner's earlier pictures. The sober and restrained colouring of pictures like the ' Windsor,' the ' Frosty Morning ' and ' The Nore,' is in perfect harmony with the patient strength and sternness of the emotional colouring of their inspiration. The same mood could not be expressed in any other scheme of lighting and colour. But to treat what, for want of a better word, I may call a pictorial metre, as though it were equally admirable as a means of expression for all kinds and shades of emotion, would argue an extraordinary dulness or sheer absence of artistic capacity ; and Turner's shortcomings, if he had any, were moral rather than artistic.

Given then the mood of exultant enjoyment of the physical amenities of the world, a lighter and brighter colour scheme than that of Turner's earlier pictures was bound to be forthcoming, if that mood was to be fully expressed by pictorial art. And as a matter of history Turner was the first modern artist in the range of landscape art to give adequate expression to this sentiment of unrestrained enjoyment of the physical delights of nature, though we see the same swelling sense of the pride of life finding a similar form of expression in the works of contemporary figure-painters like Sir Thomas Lawrence, Shee and Hayter in England, and Delacroix, Isabey, and others in France.

TURNER'S SKETCHES AND DRAWINGS

In the present chapter I propose to deal with the closing phase of Turner's art. In the works of this period Turner has been said to have initiated a new kind of art, or at least to have invented or introduced certain important innovations in the region of colour and tone, which have had the effect of developing new possibilities in the art of landscape painting. It is from this point of view, and with reference to this aspect of Turner's work, that he has been hailed as the father of Impressionism. Before discussing the value of the innovations Turner introduced and their influence on subsequent developments of the art, it is important to study the immediate causes which brought them into existence. In other words, we must study this new phase of Turner's art in relation to its immediate antecedents ; in the first place, to see how far it can be regarded as a necessary development of what had gone before, and in the second place, to discover exactly what is new in it.

The two most striking characteristics of Turner's later work are the brightness and extended range of his colour schemes. But this formal characteristic is clearly taken over bodily from the previous period, and we have just seen that it was but the necessary outward expression of the spiritual content with which Turner was then preoccupied. In a picture like 'Ulysses deriding Polyphemus' (1829), for example, we have a colour scheme as bright and as extended as that of any of the later works, and yet it is emphatically a work of the Romantic period. It is all ablaze with the light and flame of human pride. Its gorgeous array of blues, its burnished gold and glowing crimson and scarlet and white are but the triumphant expression of the mood of unrestrained sensuous enjoyment which formed the key-note of the work we have just been examining.

But if the lightening of the colour scheme was simply an inheritance from the Romantic phase of art, what are we to regard as the special contribution of the later manner? A comparison of a few of Turner's later works with the 'Ulysses' will show us at once. The earliest example of Turner's later and so-called Impressionistic manner with which I am familiar is the 'Calais Sands, low water—Poissards collecting bait,' which was exhibited in 1830, and is now in the Bury Art Gallery. Its colour

118

BEMERSIDE TOWER

PENCIL. ABOUT 1831

PLATE LXXII

BEMERSIDE TOWER

ENGRAVING PUBLISHED IN SCOTT'S "POETICAL WORKS" (CADELL), 1834

scheme is actually more subdued than the 'Ulysses,' but the whole effect is more vaporous and the figures are less distinct. So far as I am able to judge, this is the chief *differentia* of Turner's later manner, and of all Impressionistic work on its formal side. As a second characteristic we may add the fact that it deals with a scene of contemporary life, something that Turner had actually seen with his eyes, not something that he had read about and imagined, as in the 'Ulysses.'

If we examine 'The Evening Star' and 'At Petworth' (both at the Tate Gallery), the 'Snowstorm' of 1842, the late Venetian pictures, and the 'Rain, Storm, Speed' of 1844, we find these works are all similarly distinguished by their general vagueness of definition and by the fact that they all represent scenes which had come within the range of the artist's own experience.

Yet it is evident that these two characteristics are not of equal importance. The vagueness of definition was a general characteristic of all Turner's later work, but a considerable number of these works were purely imaginary compositions, as for example the 'Agrippina landing with the Ashes of Germanicus' (1839), 'The Exile and the rock limpet' (1842), 'The Evening of the Deluge' (1843), 'Queen Mab's Cave' (1846), and the various 'Whaler' pictures (1845 and 1846). There is obviously, then, no necessary connection between Turner's vagueness of execution (his distinctively Impressionist manner) and his choice of subject of which he had been actually an eye-witness.

Besides, we must remember that Turner did not wait till his later years before beginning to paint his own impressions. He had been busy painting them ever since he had come to artistic maturity. His 'Calais Pier' (1803), the 'Spithead' (1809), 'Petworth—Dewy Morning' (1810), 'Teignmouth' and 'Hulks on the Tamar' (1811 and 1812), and 'Frosty Morning' (1813), —to name only a few—were certainly works of this kind; as were the 'Hedging and Ditching' of the *Liber* and the 'Colchester' of the *England and Wales* series. But there is no lack of determination in the execution of these works. The difference between Turner's later attempts to paint his impressions and his earlier must therefore be found in his attitude towards these impressions—the principle of selection, of suppression and adjustment upon which he dealt with the data of sense-perception ; and this brings us to the consideration of the *rationale* of that vagueness of execution which we have agreed to regard as the chief characteristic of Turner's later work.

An ingenious and at first somewhat plausible attempt has been made to explain the peculiarities of Turner's later style, on the ground that old age and failing health had brought about an actual organic change in the artist's powers of sight. But it seems to me that Dr. Liebreich's arguments [1] and conclusions are vitiated by his failure to discriminate between Turner's manner of expression and the action of his eyesight. These are two clearly distinct operations. Between the act of seeing and an artist's fully organised manner of expression, a whole host of considerations—among them the limitations and capacities of the material—interpose themselves. These considerations must all receive their due weight. I know several very short-sighted artists whose pictures are remarkable for their elaborate and sharply defined details, and there are others with strong and good eyesight, whose pictures are confused and indistinct. An artist puts into his pictures only what he chooses to put there. And when we work out in detail the reasons why Turner chose to make his drawings indistinct, we find that such considerations are quite sufficient by themselves to account for his change of style, without having recourse to any hypothetical alteration in his organs of sight.

The clue, then, to the nature of Turner's later manner of expression is to be found in the character not of his optical sensations but of his thought, or in other words, upon the mode in which his intelligent self reacted upon the immediate data of sense-perception. By the time he had reached the period with which we are now concerned, he had lost much of his interest in the material world. He cared no longer for the strength and weight, the toughness and tang of material ; that delight in the solidity of real objects which gives such a manly gusto to his early sea-pieces, is now altogether absent from his work. He cares no longer for the company of men, or for their avocations

---

[1] 'Turner and Mulready.—On the Effect of certain Faults of Vision, etc.' By R. Liebreich. *Macmillan's Magazine*, April 1872.

or joys and sorrows. He is now a lonely old man, with his thoughts mainly centred upon himself, upon his artistic genius, his artistic fame, and the visions of future pictures by which his genius was to continue to manifest itself, and by which his fame was to be increased or sustained.

We have then to think of Turner as a solitary dreamer of dreams, with a professional interest in the capacity of these dreams to startle a rather stupid public. If we want to enter intimately into the spiritual and emotional content of his dreams we have only to turn to the contemporary works of the poets. In pictures like 'The Fountain of Indolence,' the 'Agrippina' and those I have mentioned above, we see how deeply impressed his mind had become with the ideals of current Romantic poetry; the true Byronic disgust with himself and vague emotions of the infinite, the desire to

> 'steal
> From all I may be, or have been before,
> To mingle with the universe, and feel
> What I can ne'er express.'

There is no doubt that these obscure emotions and vague reveries can only be adequately expressed in one particular way. They defy embodiment in clear-cut determinate forms. They demand a style as indeterminate, as vaguely suggestive, as inarticulate as the loose-knit dreams which are calling for embodiment.

This, then, I take to be the proper explanation of the vagueness of Turner's later manner: It is not that he saw the world indistinctly, but that his ideas were incapable of definition; it is not that his eyes were newly opened to the vapours and mists of the physical world, but that his own thoughts were confused and his emotions, in spite of their strength, were incoherent and inarticulate.

We are now in a position to define the relation in which Turner's later works stand to modern Impressionism. The exact connotation of this term is not by any means easy to grasp, but so far as Impressionism has distinctive aims I think we are justified in describing them as the attempt to eliminate all those elements in art which are due to the reaction of the intelligent self upon the immediate data of sense-perception. The aim of Impressionism is to get rid of what one eminent psychologist has called the noëtic fringe in a state of consciousness, to abstract from memory and see objects as simple visual elements. The Impressionist wishes to see objects as though he was looking at them for the first time, as though they had no meaning for him. The theoretic justification of this procedure is that, in stripping off the formative and organising action of intelligence we isolate the pure element of objective reality; that pictures painted upon this principle give the real truth of nature and are free from all those errors and distortions which the action of thought is supposed to introduce into the irrefragably trustworthy elements of the given. These assumptions are, I need hardly add, untenable, but this is not the place to criticise them.

Now if Impressionism aims at getting rid of all the cognitive elements in concrete perception (recognition, classing, naming, etc.) as well as the later processes of interpretation and associative reflection, and would express only the bare sensational element of impression, it is clear that Turner cannot be properly described as an Impressionist. Turner's artistic aim was consistently lyrical, *i.e.* strongly subjective and emotional, while the chief aim of Impressionism is to eliminate all the merely subjective colouring from perception, with the single purpose of isolating and reproducing what is regarded as the objective element. So far, then, as Impressionism has adopted Turner's results, it seems open to the charge of having done so without understanding their real nature or significance.

Yet this result, however helpful it may prove to the student of present-day art, cannot be wholly satisfactory from another point of view. From the point of view of Turner's work our result is largely negative. We have endeavoured to make it clear that to regard his later work as a new and triumphant attempt to represent what is called the 'truths of nature' is pure misunderstanding; that Turner's aim is not to represent either truths of atmosphere, of lighting or of natural colour, or any kind or class of physical fact; that he is busied mainly with his own emotions and fancies, and that he is concerned with the objective

PLATE LXXIII

MEN CHATTING ROUND FIREPLACE : PETWORTH HOUSE

WATER COLOUR. ABOUT 1830

PLATE LXXIV

TEASING THE DONKEY: PETWORTH

WATER COLOUR ON BLUE.   ABOUT 1830

world only indirectly and only in so far as it furnishes or suggests the stuff out of which his pictorial symbols are woven. But we have still to search for the secret power of attraction which these symbols do unquestionably possess. Why is it, we must ask, that these signs and symbols have such power to move men, to delight and intoxicate some, to soothe and cheer others?

The answers to these questions may be conveniently grouped under two heads. In the first place we may consider what are the attractions which Turner's work shares with the Romantic poets whose works express the same kind of subject-matter, and in the second place we may attempt to indicate what are the qualities which are more intimately connected with his own individuality.

In the first place then, when we consider Turner as a fellow-worker with Byron, Shelley, and Lamartine, we see that like them he appeals constantly and unerringly to that illusion of the romantic temperament which lends a mysterious charm to all that is indefinite and indefinable. In a singularly acute analysis of this temperament Mr. George Santayana has traced one of the chief causes of the delight which this kind of art and poetry awakens to what he calls 'the illusion of infinite perfection.' There is, he says, a loose and helpless state of mind to which we all of us approximate when in a state of fatigue. In this state of mind we are not capable of concentrated and serious attention to one thing at a time, so we are apt to 'flounder in the vague, but at the same time we are full of yearnings, of half-thoughts and semi-visions, and the upward tendency and exaltation of our mood is emphatic and overpowering in proportion to our incapacity to think, speak, or imagine. The sum of our incoherencies has, however, an imposing volume and even, perhaps, a vague, general direction. We feel ourselves laden with an infinite burden; and what delights us most and seems to us to come nearest to the ideal, is not what embodies any one possible form, but that which, by embodying none, suggests many, and stirs the mass of our inarticulate imagination with a pervasive thrill. . . . That infinite perfection which cannot be realised, because it is self-contradictory, may be thus suggested, and on account of this suggestion an indeterminate effect may be regarded as higher, more significant, and more

123

beautiful than any determinate one.'[1]   These remarks help us to understand the positive qualities of Turner's indeterminate style; its power of evoking a fallacious sense of profundity and significance, just because of its indeterminateness, its power of suggesting and stimulating emotion, just because it is incoherent and variously interpretable.

Yet when we have pressed these considerations to their extreme limit, we have only drawn attention to certain qualities which Turner's later work shares with that of many indifferent artists and poets, and, far from exhausting the real and permanent elements of value in that work, they may be justly regarded as a searching and pitiless exposure of its weaknesses and defects. But we are on firmer ground when we turn to the purely personal qualities in this work, to the artist's delicacy of hand and fineness of sight.   It matters not what instrument Turner is working with, whether with the pencil, the pen, or the brush, or whether he is working hurriedly or at leisure, the movement of his hand is always graceful and delightful.   His powers of sight also seem to me to have been quite extraordinary; I do not mean that he had merely the power of seeing distant objects distinctly, not mere long-sightedness, though he seems to have had this faculty in an abundant measure, but a quite unusual power of discriminating beween minute shades of light and colour.   As the born musician is distinguished from other men by his capacity for detecting differences of sound which to others seem the same, so the evidence of Turner's work—and all who have attempted to copy even the slightest of his sketches will, I am sure, bear me out in this—shows that he possessed an abnormal power of visual discrimination.   No doubt his early training and especially the influence of Dayes had something to do with the development of this capacity, but the capacity itself was largely innate.   In addition to these two natural gifts, an abnormal delicacy of hand and eye, Turner had the priceless advantage of being passionately and unfalteringly in love with his art.   Some of the greatest artists give me the impression of loving their art less for its own sake than for the sake of the content which it enables

---

[1] *The Sense of Beauty*, by George Santayana.   A. & C. Black, 1896, p. 149 .

them to express — Rembrandt and Jean François Millet, for example, give me this impression, and I do not think that their greatness is imperilled in the least by it—but Turner seems to me to have loved his art, especially in his later years, entirely for its own sake.   This strong and deep affection threw a glamour over every detail of his work.   Nothing was too high or too low for him.   He brought the same inexhaustible patience and alertness of attention to the working out of a complicated problem of perspective as to the finishing of his most ambitious pictures.   Like Wordsworth's 'happy warrior' in the midst of danger, he had only to take a pencil into his hand to become 'attired with sudden brightness, like a Man inspired.'   This concentration, this master-bias, throws a fervour and an inimitable charm over what it seems almost ironical to speak of as the mechanical execution of his works.

It is difficult to define the exact relationship of Turner's love for his art, with his passionate and unwearying study of natural phenomena.   My own impression is that his love of nature was at best to some extent subordinate to his love of art; that he loved nature partly at least as a means to artistic expression, and not altogether for itself.   But however this may be, the extent of his knowledge of, and intimate familiarity with, nature's ways counts for much in the attractions of his pictures.   The evidence of his keen though intermittent study of natural phenomena is writ large in the collection of his sketch-books.   The very extent of his knowledge, no doubt, led at times to a certain overcrowding of his works, but it forms the secret of his supple and ample style, and the inexhaustible fecundity of his invention.

It is then to the magic of his style that Turner's later works owe a great deal of their strange power of compelling attention and extorting a sometimes unwilling admiration.   He had in a quite pre-eminent degree what Reynolds has called the genius of mechanical execution.   And this power is as remarkable in his earlier works as in his later.   But in his earlier works this power was used to give definite embodiment to a range of worthy and significant ideas and emotions, and the sheer beauty of their content is apt to divert our attention from the consummate skill implied in this rarest and highest artistic achievement.   But in the later work the very weakness and poverty of the content has the effect of keeping our attention fixed upon the suggestiveness and visual beauty of the material elements of expression. In the poetry of the French Symbolists we see a somewhat similar effect consciously aimed at. The poverty of thought is used as a foil to throw the greatest possible emphasis on the beauty of sounds and the faint suggestions of individual words. In this way the attenuation of significance in Turner's later works throws into startling prominence all the innate and intrinsic splendours of the painter's palette.

We shall have occasion to amplify and illustrate these observations as we trace the gradual development of Turner's later manner, the task to which we have now to address ourselves.

I have alluded above to what I regard as the first oil painting in which the change that took place in Turner's artistic aims about the year 1830 was clearly indicated. This was the ' Calais Sands, low water,' exhibited at the Royal Academy in May, 1830. But before painting this picture Turner had been experimenting in his new manner in a series of water-colour sketches. These sketches were made at Petworth, where Turner went to stay for a few weeks with Lord Egremont, probably in 1829, after his return from his second journey to Italy.

The two oil paintings of Petworth Park, still in the Petworth collection, as well as the brilliant unfinished sketch of ' Petworth Park' in the National Gallery (No. 559), were probably painted in the house during this visit ; at any rate, the sketches in water-colour upon which these canvases were based were made at this time. But when Turner was not busy at his easel or sketching in the park and neighbourhood, he seems to have felt the time hang heavily on his hands, so, to save himself from the ennui of small-talk and idleness, he began making colour sketches, first of the various rooms, then of the furniture and bric-à-brac, and finally of the people staying in the house. These sketches, which number about a hundred, indicate clearly a distinct change in Turner's outlook upon nature. Up to this time he had invariably employed form as the basis of his work. In these studies we see him turning his attention directly to colour as the chief element

PLATE LXXV

HONFLEUR

BODY COLOUR ON BLUE. ABOUT 1830

PLATE LXXVI

COUNTRY TOWN ON STREAM
BODY COLOUR ON BLUE. ABOUT 1830

MENTAL AND PHYSICAL DECAY

of representation. The difference is no doubt largely a matter of degree, for both elements are indispensable. Yet we have only to compare, say, a drawing like that of ' Rochester,' in the *Rivers of England* series, with any one of the *Rivers of France* subjects to see that the change of emphasis, upon colour instead of form, was fraught with important technical results. From a psychological point of view the change is also significant. It shows that Turner was dissatisfied with the language of form, which had served him so well all his life ; the vague unrest and conflicting emotions which now surged in his bosom demanded a less static, a more fluent and elusive medium of expression.

Let us examine one of these Petworth subjects, a sketch of people ' Waiting for Dinner.' The scene takes place in a large drawing-room. The fireplace comes in the centre of the design, and before it a corpulent and dignified figure in evening dress stands facing us. On either side there are groups of figures, also in evening dress, the white of the ladies' muslin frocks relieved with the yellow and black of an effulgent matron and the black suits and scarlet uniforms of the men. Examined in detail, the drawing of the figures is childish, but viewed at a proper distance, so that the eye can range freely over it all without bringing any one point into sharp focus, the effect is extraordinary. It is like catching a glimpse of the actual scene. The whole goes together, the room is filled with atmosphere, the sharp staccato touches sprinkled with such amazing cunning among the floating wreaths of colour give exactly that sense of relief which the eye experiences as it wanders over an actual scene —the sense of angles and sharp points of resistance which artists speak of as the ' lost and found ' of nature. The very slightness of the execution of the drawing and the reckless carelessness of the handling add to the feeling of immediate contact with reality, for the lack of definition is indissolubly associated in our minds with the experience of movement and change, and the figures whose precise forms elude us seem only to be moving before our eyes. Yet this effect would certainly not be produced were it not for the wonderful accuracy and subtlety with which the relative values of the masses of tone have been observed —the relation, for instance, between the exact

127

shade of grey of the shirt-front of the noble lord with his back to the fire and the exact tint of the firelight itself seen through his legs, or, in short, between every touch of colour and the whole which they constitute.

Yet when we compare this drawing with any of the more elaborately worked ones, we cannot but realise the enormous importance of slightness of definition as a means of expression. In the ' Spinnet Player,' for example, we find the same skill in the observation and rendering of tones as in ' Waiting for Dinner,' and the same extraordinary science of colour declension; yet the effect it produces is one of static unreality.

In this drawing a lady dressed in blue is seated in the foreground at a spinnet; on the left, there is another lady in white on a couch, and on the right, in the middle distance, a group of figures are seated round a table apparently playing cards, while a figure in a light-coloured dress stands behind the chair of one of the players. The objects on the wall of the room, the near furniture and figures are all considerably more defined than any of the objects in ' Waiting for Dinner,' but the definition of these parts sets up a standard which condemns the drawing as a whole. We feel disappointed, after getting so much definition, that we do not get more. The middle-distance figures are so well drawn, or rather are so vivaciously observed and full of individuality, that we cannot help complaining that the foreground lady's neck and shoulders are impossible, and that the lady on the couch is so much like a wooden doll. These observations suggest that each drawing sets up its own standard of definition. The comparative failure of such a drawing could not but help to impress on Turner the immense value for his purposes of a wise and consistent vagueness of statement.

In the vignettes made to illustrate the works of Rogers, Scott, Byron and Campbell we see the lesson of the Petworth experiments driven home. Though these drawings were made expressly with the object of being engraved in black and white, they are conceived entirely upon a colour basis, while their lack of definition must have made quite unwarrantable demands upon the skill and resources of the engravers. But it is evident that Turner had now firmly grasped the fact that the glamour and

PLATE LXXVII

SHEEP IN THE TRENCH

BODY COLOUR ON BLUE. ABOUT 1830

PLATE LXXVIII

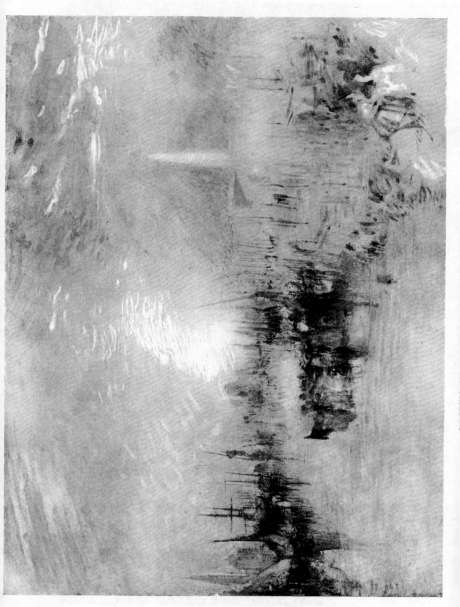

STORM IN THE RIVA DEGLI SCHIAVONI. VENICE

intoxication of colour had become the dominant and essential factor in his art, and that the vagueness of his ideas could only be adequately expressed by allusion and suggestion. These vignettes and the engravings made from them vary widely in value. One or two of them are worthy of the artist, for example the 'Datur hora quieti,' 'The Alps at Daybreak' and the 'Melrose,' but for the most part they owe the very great popular success they have enjoyed to the skill with which the artist has entered into the spirit of the second- and third-rate poetry he was called upon to illustrate, and to the admirable way in which his suggestions were engraved.

The designs for the *Rivers of France* are conceived in a somewhat similar strain of lyrical abandonment to the sensuous charm of colour. Translated into mere black and white they leave us but half convinced. It is rather like a prose translation into a foreign language of the poetry of Victor Hugo, Swinburne or Shelley. To feel their full effect we must turn to the original water-colours, with all their ravishing intoxication of colour. It is as though our reason must needs be lulled asleep by the dominant flood of purely sensuous delight, before we can feel about these drawings as the artist would have us feel.

We have seen, in the case of the 'Stamford' design in the *England and Wales* series, that Turner's interest in a place was specifically different from that of a resident or an historian. He cares little or nothing for local facts, merely as facts; his main concern is to skim off from the surface of observation a few telling points, a few heads of discourse as we might call them, which serve as a point of departure to his own abundant pictorial improvisation. The result may be more or less like the locality which furnishes the title of the drawing, but it is never in any strict sense of the word an accurate representation of the place. Yet the gulf that yawns between local fact and Turner's lyrical inspiration is never of quite the same character in the English drawings as in the French. In both the gulf is wide, but in the English subjects the artist's intimate knowledge of the general characteristics of the scenery gives such an air of plausibility to his improvisations that one might be tempted to explain his poetical licences as the result of an ardent striving after general and specific truth.[1]   With the French drawings it is impossible to make such a mistake.   Turner was not at all intimate with French scenery.   He got up the subject in a most perfunctory manner in a few short and hurried tours.   He merely paid a flying visit to the chief places mentioned in his guide-book and, instead of studying what he saw with a moderate degree of attention, was quite satisfied to look for mere hints of Turnerian phantasies; he did not want facts, but suggestions for pictorial inventions.   So that in spite of his voluminous note-taking we find scarcely an accurate detail in the whole of the sixty engravings.   The twin towers of Tancarville Castle are certainly the result of a misunderstanding of the hurried sketch made on the spot, and I have no doubt that the 'errors' and 'inaccuracies' so relentlessly ferreted out by Mr. Hamerton in the representations of the Castle of Amboise, the towers of Notre Dame and St. Jacques de la Boucherie, the old Hôtel de Ville and the Pump, were caused in the same way.   From the point of view of the topographer there can be no doubt that Hamerton's statement[2] that the engravings of this series contain only 'a sort of muddled reminiscence' of the objects and places Turner had seen is in the main correct.

The object of these remarks is far from that of suggesting that the presence of 'errors' and 'inaccuracies' of this kind interferes in any way with the purely artistic value of these drawings.   It is rather to emphasise the fact that it is only when we judge them from a totally irrelevant point of view, that we can begin to talk of errors and inaccuracies.   Rightly understood these so-called errors and inaccuracies are not only the justifiable licences of the artist, but the absolutely inevitable and proper and solely right means of expression which the artist had at his disposal.   His aim is to produce a state of consciousness in which feeling looms large, and thought-determination is reduced almost to the vanishing point. One might say, without exaggeration or unfairness, that mental confusion formed an important part of his artistic aim.   He had then to represent the objects he depicted not as they appear to a cool, level-headed, and accurate observer, but as they appear to a highly sensitive subject in a state of morbid excitement.

---

[1] This, I need hardly add, is Mr. Ruskin's explanation.
[2] Hamerton's *Turner*, p. 244.

MENTAL AND PHYSICAL DECAY

If we look at Turner's French drawings from this point of view, we cannot but admit that they are almost all highly successful. They are stamped with the impress of the genuinely romantic fervour, the lyrical movement of unbridled feeling. In them the joy of artistic creation has become triumphant, almost insolent. They are deep draughts of artistic intoxication, exultant with the rush of man's undying passion for pleasure, and of the resistless energy that moulds the world of matter into forms more harmonious with our own distinctly human cravings and aspirations; Châteaux Gaillards or 'Saucy Castles' of the imagination one might almost call them.

It was characteristic of Turner—I might almost say it was a necessity of his position as a landscape painter—that he felt compelled to search far and wide for material out of which to spin his web of visible phantasy. The need of novel shapes, glowing colours, striking and elaborate combinations was constantly felt. The rivers Meuse, Moselle and Rhine were diligently and repeatedly explored. The East—for his Bible illustrations—he was content to take at second hand, through the medium of other men's sketches, but he sailed down the Danube, as far as Vienna (or Buda-Pesth perhaps?), ransacked Germany, Italy, Switzerland, France, Holland and Belgium and part of Austria. But as the years moved on, his mental grip of the real world became always looser. His mind played only with the fugitive shades on the surface of appearances; but not with the elasticity, the free disinterestedness of youth and of the young-hearted. The professional bias became ever more pronounced, the point of view ever more abstract and one-sided.

One of his richest mines of pictorial imagery was Venice; not so much the actual city of the Adriatic, as the fragmentary ideas of an ideal Venice as they floated in the imagination of the ordinary Englishman — the unconscious crystallisation of the desires of the average middle-class tourist for Southern warmth, freedom, colour, variety, and bodily pleasure. With all the uncanny certainty of genius he gathered up the threads of these incoherent and fugitive desires and fixed them in the forms of immortality.

Let us look carefully at the two Venetian sketches here repro-

TURNER'S SKETCHES AND DRAWINGS

duced. In 'Shipping on the Riva degli Schiavone' (No. 55 N.G.) we see the Campanile and Ducal Palace on the right, a blaze of warm, palpitating light. In the centre there is a stretch of limpid green water, with a tangle of boats on it leading the eye to the opalescent Madonna della Salute in the extreme distance. There is a secondary group of shipping on the left, among whose masts the tower of San Giorgio Maggiore can be seen. No words can describe the intense blaze of light, the brilliance of the colours and their perfect harmony. The execution is breathlessly hurried and seemingly reckless, yet always perfectly under control ; the artist's hand is so audaciously swift because the full value of his colours can only be got in this way. Human skill can go no further in this direction, and no reproduction can do anything like justice to the wonderful original.

We find the same qualities in 'The Approach to Venice : Sunset' (51 N.G.), and 'Riva degli Schiavone, from near the Public Gardens' (56 N.G.).

In all these drawings Turner seems to be playing with his material medium, fondling and caressing his colours and the intrinsic beauties of water-colour. Yet it is not mere colour as colour that he gives us, not the cheap and arbitrary and mechanical splendour of merely decorative art. The colour is delicate and subtle, full of surprises, and as varied as nature herself; it is controlled and marshalled by the authority of the tone scheme ; it is nature grasped by human intelligence, and made obedient to its organising power. And a large part of the attractiveness of these drawings is due to the ease and grace with which the reign of purpose and intelligence is maintained.

After all it is the marvellous technical skill which they display which is the essence of the charm of these works. The subject-matter counts for less than the execution, the objects portrayed are less eloquent than the sense of freedom, mastery and real happiness evident in the artist's work. He wanted nothing beyond this ; the work to him was not a symbol of something higher —it did not point beyond itself. It was at once means and end, process and fulfilment, work and reward, the toil of life and its consummated bliss.

The intrinsic poverty of the subject-matter no doubt serves to

132

PLATE LXXIX

APPROACH TO VENICE: SUNSET
WATER COLOUR.   ABOUT 1839

PLATE LXXX

MENTAL AND PHYSICAL DECAY

intensify what I may call the material beauty of the workmanship. Yet we must beware of ranking this subject-matter too low. It is not mere sensuous feeling, it is not entirely devoid of the element of thought. The conscious action of thought is probably entirely absent. The scenes float before us in all the bareness of immediate sensation. They give us nothing more than a moment of immediate experience caught, as it were, on the wing, and pinned down all quivering with life. But the momentary experience is that of a man whose visual sensations have been organised by a life-time of strenuous intellectual control. The brain and the senses are but the organs of one function. There is not a single definite thought present, the artist has sunk himself in the flow of the merely animal life, yet his naked sentience is conditioned through and through and characterised by the pervasive activity of the mind.

To transfix a fleeting moment of immediate living experience is a very different thing from the deliberate analysis of the process of perception and the wilful abstraction of one of its elements. In other words, this work of Turner is essentially different in kind from the work of the modern Impressionists. The Impressionist adopts the methods of science. He operates on his perceptions, and cuts away this element and that, and in the end presents you with a dead and potted psychological abstraction, a diagram of the ' pure ' visual sensation, which delights us with its ingenuity and neatness, but which no one would take for a fragment of the living flow of thought and emotion which all concrete experience is. Impressionism is cold and heartless ; it is merely intellectual and ratiocinative, and therefore essentially inartistic. But the so-called impressionistic work of Turner, in spite of its other defects and shortcomings, remains ever in the flood of concrete living experience. It is never abstract ; it never loses its emotional contagion, though its emotional suggestiveness is somewhat vague and indefinite. Its power of evoking emotion is very strongly pronounced, but the emotions it calls up are sadly lacking in definition, and seem to lie very much at the mercy of chance associations.

The cause of this vagueness and emptiness is no doubt closely connected with Turner's triumphant grasp of the fleeting

133

momentary experience. His work is almost, though not quite, as empty and indeterminate as an isolated fragment of immediate sensation. A single steady look by a cool observer would grasp more of the character of a given scene than we find in these sketches. But the time occupied in a steady look at a scene is too long for Turner; though the look should last but half a minute the mind has time to grasp and organise the sensuous data. Turner's object is to catch these data of sense in their least organised condition. To do this, he must reduce the time of contact between the scene and his senses to its shortest possible extent. Some of the later Impressionists have found that merely to open and shut the eyes gives their senses and intelligence too long an exposure; they have therefore devised a mechanical instrument which they hold in front of their eyes, and which operates very much like a shutter used for taking instantaneous photographs. In this way they obtain a glimpse of a scene of shorter duration than the most rapid opening and shutting of the eyes can give. We have no reason for suspecting that Turner had recourse to any such mechanical aids, but he achieved similar results. He gives us the momentary bedazzlement of the sunlight, and, within this impression, a confused and fragmentary perception of objects. The objects seen are hardly recognisable, their attributes are reduced to a minimum, and the blur of living emotion which forms part of such rudimentary perception is reduced to its lowest terms. The control such sketches exercise over the thoughts and feelings of the spectator is therefore small and possesses very little individuality.

But even Venice soon palled upon Turner's imagination. He seemed desirous of getting away as far as possible from the disturbing influences of human association. Only among the lonely valleys and mountain tops of Switzerland could his perturbed and wearied spirit find something like the peace he sought so feverishly. Even here he shrank from the common light of ordinary day. He loved the solemn stillness of night, and would wait to surprise the first rosy hues of dawn upon Mount Pilatus or the Rigi. His sympathies are all with the silent and primary things of nature.

It is as though he were seeking to strip himself of the attri-

PLATE LXXXI

FREIBURG: THE DESCENT FROM THE HOTEL DE VILLE

WATER COLOUR, ABOUT 1841

PLATE LXXXII

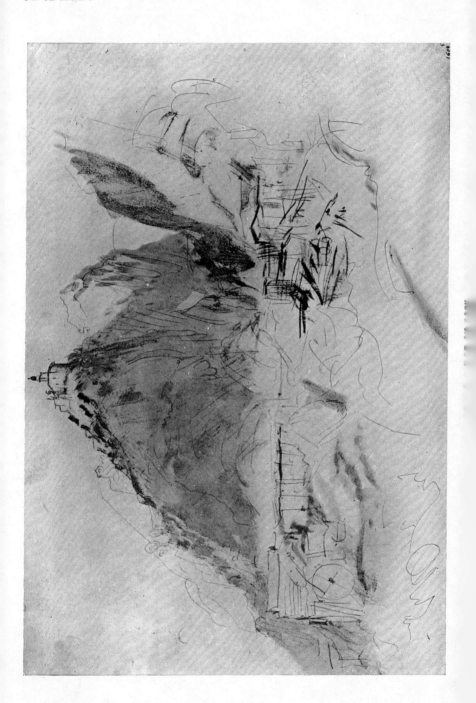

butes of humanity, to sink into the unconscious vegetative life of nature. Even when roused to activity his mind seems curiously dehumanised. When he draws for us the towers and churches of a place like Freiburg we seem to be looking at the work of a disembodied spirit. The city is divested of all its human associations. His eye seems now to classify and arrange what it sees in terms of space and motion, much as we should imagine an eagle to look down upon the welter and turmoil of our lives. I get the same impression from the 'Village and Castle on the Rhine' (82 N.G.) and 'The Via Mala' (73 N.G.).

In all this, in this gradual impoverishment of mind and feeling, it is difficult to discover anything more than the silent and inevitable ravages of old age. But it is not their poverty of content that makes these later drawings of Turner so remarkable. It is the virile and glorious artistic skill which only flames the brighter amid the decay of all Turner's other faculties. The man was dead before the incomparable master of tone and colour was exhausted. It is this curious combination of an unexhausted special aptitude with a moribund mentality that gives this later work of Turner its uniqueness, its lurid and uncanny fascination. In the whole history of pictorial art we have never had before quite the same display of senile apathy gilded and transfigured by the dying shafts of an incommensurable natural capacity.

By the time Turner was seventy years of age his bodily infirmities prevented him from visiting Switzerland. For a year or two we find him haunting the coast of Normandy, about Dieppe, Eu and Ambleteuse. Then he is unable to cross the Channel. For a short season he flits about Sussex and Kent— at Folkestone, Margate, Deal, and Sandwich—and then there is silence.

CHAPTER IX

CONCLUSION

The distinction between Art-Criticism and Aesthetic—The aim of this chapter—Art and physical fact—The 'common-sense' conception of landscape art as evidence of fact—The relation of Art and Nature—Mr. Ruskin's treatment of this subject—He distinguishes (a) physical fact and (b) the artist's thoughts and feelings about these facts, yet maintains that the representation of (a) is equivalent to the expression of (b)—His confusion of Nature and Mind exemplified in his remarks on the 'Pass of Faïdo'—Art as the organ of Beauty implies that the dualism of Nature and Mind is transcended—Nature is neither given nor immediate—Art therefore cannot copy nature—What does art represent?—An individualised psychical content present to the mind of the artist—Classification of Turner's sketches and studies from the point of view of their logical content—The difference between (1) Studies of particular objects, (2) Drawings from nature, and (3) Works of art proper—The logical reference of a work of art—The assertions in a work of art do not directly qualify the ordinary world of reality, but an imaginary world specially constructed for the artist's purpose—The ideal of complete definition—Yet the content must determine the form—Plea for a dynamic or physiological study of artistic forms.

WE have been engaged thus far upon a genuinely inductive investigation, upon a voyage of discovery, and not upon a dogmatic exposition of ultimate aesthetic principles. Our general aim has been to study the processes of artistic expression, but to study them as we find them in definite concrete instances. Moreover, the nature of our subject-matter rendered it necessary to keep faithful to the point of view of art-criticism. We were dealing with particular works of art, and to leave them while we plunged into general questions of aesthetic would hardly have been polite. But, as I have ventured to observe before, though art criticism and general aesthetic can be distinguished they cannot be rigidly separated. Aesthetic without close con-

CONCLUSION

versance with the concrete subject-matter of art - criticism is necessarily loose and empty, while art-criticism without a firm grasp of the broad principles of beauty easily degenerates into casuistry or a useless and rather despicable form of self-assertion. And however much we try to keep questions of principle apart from our estimation and study of particular works of art, we are bound inevitably to fail. We can begin as it were at either end of the scale, we can busy ourselves with the one or with the many, but before we have gone very far we are bound to realise that we are concerned with exactly the same problems. The distinction of art-criticism from aesthetic is merely one of convenience and degree.

In all that has gone before we have been concerned with the fundamental problems of aesthetic, though we have not treated them directly. In all that we have written a more or less definite and consistent answer to these problems has been implied. In this final chapter, therefore, I propose to draw out as well as I can some of the more general results of our observations and analyses, or rather to endeavour to state in a more general form the laws of artistic expression and action which we have discovered. The ultimate aim of art-criticism, as I understand it, is to grasp and render intelligible the whole region of artistic activity, and I cannot but think that it will facilitate our grasp of the wider laws of artistic phenomena, as well as help to consolidate or disprove the results of our detailed observations, if I make an attempt to render explicit what has only been implied in our remarks upon particular concrete instances.

I will begin by calling attention to a fact that has been repeatedly forced upon our notice. Though our attention has been mainly fixed upon Turner's studies and sketches from nature, we have never come into direct contact with the plain physical reality which, according to the invariable usage of common-sense, it is the mission of art to represent. Common-sense tells us that the ' subject' of every landscape painting is a group of physical realities—the fields, rivers, mountains, trees, houses, etc., in such and such a place, together with their invariable physical accompaniments, the air and any particular effect of light and weather that the artist may choose to select. Our analysis has invariably

137

shown us that the slightest sketch — much more then a fully organised work of art!—is something more than and something radically different from a mere representation of such physical constituents. The physical objects are indeed portrayed, but when we have recognised this touch of colour or that shape as the representation of this or that natural fact, we have not exhausted the meaning of the artist's work. This recognition is nothing more than what I may call the plain dictionary meaning of the words the artist has chosen to employ. It is not till we have gone on to grasp the special significance of the order in which these elements have been grouped, that we really begin to come into contact with the work of art itself. As we cannot interpret the meaning of the simplest sentence unless we give due weight to its grammatical construction, so with a picture we must take into consideration what I can only call the grammatical construction and distinctions proper to pictorial expression. When we penetrate in this way to the real significance of any of Turner's works we find we have been brought into contact with the artist's thoughts and emotions. We start, as it were, with trees and rocks and physical details, which, as such, are independent of man and indifferent if not actually hostile to human hopes and fears, joys and sorrows; and we end by finding that our so-called physical facts are but elements in a definitely organised whole of thought and feeling. We seem to start with natural facts, and they change under our hands into the symbols of mere ideas and emotions.

Our whole conception of the scope and possibilities of art turns upon the view we take of the artist's means of expression. Are we to regard pictorial art as a medium for imaging and recording the visible facts of the physical world, or as symbols of states of consciousness? And if we take the latter view, what is the exact relation of these symbols to the visible world, to the world of common perception?

So far as I know, only one English art-critic has attempted anything like an adequate discussion of these questions. It will help us, I think, if we glance for a moment at Mr. Ruskin's treatment of these subjects. In the first volume of *Modern Painters* we are told that the two great ends of landscape painting are (1) to induce in the spectator's mind the faithful conception of

138

CONCLUSION

any natural object whatsoever, and (2) to inform him of the thoughts and feelings with which these' (*i.e.* the natural objects) 'were regarded by the artist himself' (*Modern Painters*, Part II., Sec. 1, Ch. i, p. 44).

In attaining the first end, Mr. Ruskin adds, 'the painter only places the spectator where he stands himself; he sets him before the landscape and leaves him. . . . But he [the spectator] has nothing of thought given to him, no new ideas, no unknown feelings, forced on his attention or his heart.'

'But in attaining the second end, the artist not only *places* the spectator, but—makes him a sharer in his own strong feelings and quick thoughts ;—and leaves him . . . ennobled and instructed, under the sense of having not only beheld a new scene, but of having held communion with a new mind, and having been endowed for a time with the keen perception and the impetuous emotions of a nobler and more penetrating intelligence.'

It may seem at first sight that Mr. Ruskin is simply distinguishing two kinds of landscape painting, such as the simply topographical from the more imaginative kind. And he does say that 'it is possible to reach what I have stated to be the first end of art, the representation of facts, without reaching the second, the representation of thoughts.' But the point he is chiefly concerned to emphasise is the complete dependence of the second of these aims upon the representation of facts. An artist can give us physical facts, he says, without expressing his thoughts and feelings, but no artist can express thoughts and feelings without the accurate representation of facts. This is the point, he says, that he wishes at present 'especially to insist upon,' and this dependence of thought upon fact, or 'truth' as he generally prefers to call it, forms, as I understand it, the theoretical basis upon which a large part of Mr. Ruskin's art teaching rests.

All great art, he admits, gives us 'the thoughts and feelings of the artist,' but we have no standard by which we can test the value of mere thoughts and feelings ; but as there is a 'constant relation' between an artist's thoughts and feelings and his 'faithfulness in representing nature,' we have only to examine 'the botanical or geological details' in a landscape to 'form a right estimate as to the respective powers and attainments' of the artist.

TURNER'S SKETCHES AND DRAWINGS

It is from this point of view that he calls ' the representation of facts ' ' the foundation of all art,' and in the preface to *The Elements of Drawing*, the power ' to copy' natural objects ' faithfully, and without alteration,' is treated as equivalent to the power ' of pictorial expression of thought.'

Now there is a point of view from which these statements could be defended, and I will endeavour a little later to indicate that point of view, but as Mr. Ruskin expresses and applies these ideas, I think they lead to confusion. Much of the welter of confusion into which the reader of *Modern Painters* finds himself plunged seems to me caused by the author's persistent refusal to discriminate between physical reality and mind, between external nature and ideas. The mountains, trees, and clouds become human thoughts and feelings, not in a metaphysical sense, but as a matter of ordinary observation, and the artist is bidden to go out into the fields and draw, with the patience and precision of a geologist or land-surveyor, the visible shapes and hues of these materialised emotions and ideas.

Yet Mr. Ruskin is far too fearless and candid a thinker to attempt deliberately to falsify his evidence. He admits, when the point presents itself to him, that Turner ' never draws accurately on the spot'; and in the wonderful analysis of Turner's 'Pass of Faïdo,' in the fourth volume of *Modern Painters*, we are clearly shown that the artist's representation contains hardly a single accurate and faithful statement of the physical features of the place. Yet we are assured that in some inexplicable way the picture is truer to the facts of the place than the place itself.

The artist, we are told, made 'a few pencil scratches on a bit of thin paper' during a momentary stoppage of the diligence in the pass. Afterwards he put a few blots of colour to these pencil scratches, possibly ' at Bellinzona the same evening' but ' certainly *not* upon the spot.' In the course of a few months he showed this sketch to Mr. Ruskin, who commissioned the artist to make a finished water-colour from it. (The sketch is reproduced as the frontispiece of the present volume, so the curious reader may compare it at his leisure with the reproduction of the completed drawing and Mr. Ruskin's topographical drawing made on the spot in *Modern Painters*.)

140

VILLAGE AND CASTLE ON THE RHINE

WATER COLOUR. ABOUT 1844

PLATE LXXXIII

PLATE LXXXIV

CONCLUSION

The first sketch is certainly sufficiently inaccurate as a representation of the physical facts of the scene, but in the finished drawing Turner permitted himself further liberties. In it 'the whole place is altered in scale.' The rocks on the left which should be four or five hundred feet high are made to look 'about a thousand feet.' 'Next, he raises, in a still greater degree, all the mountains beyond, putting three or four ranges instead of one.' In this way all the parts of the scene are modified, important features are eliminated at will, and facts that the artist had seen elsewhere are freely introduced. This is what we find Mr. Ruskin means when he talks about receiving ' a true impression from the place itself, and the accurate and faithful representation of physical facts' (*Modern Painters*, vol iv, p. 21).

Now I am far from denying that Turner's procedure was thoroughly justified, but from the ordinary standpoint of common-sense it does stand in need of justification, and it seems to me that it is not a proper way to justify it by passionately declaring that the imaginative vision of the artist does indeed give us 'the real facts of the world's outside aspect,' or a faithful and unaltered copy of a portion of physical reality. Indeed I feel very strongly that this playing fast and loose with Nature and Mind (with physical fact and mental interpretation) is no gain to the cause Mr. Ruskin has at heart. In spite of all his passionate eloquence and transparent earnestness and good faith, the ordinary reader continues to regard nature as the hypostatised world of the physical sciences and as that part of the world which falls outside of mind. And when we regard nature in this way as a mechanical and external system, and declare that it is 'God's work,' we can go on, as Mr. Ruskin does, to attack 'idealisation,' and heap contumely on such painters as Claude and Poussin, for daring to modify God's works and for casting the shadow of their puny selves on the works of their Creator (*Modern Painters*, vol. i. Preface to second ed., p. xxvi). But if we do this we must at least go on to admit that Turner and all the other great artists sinned in exactly the same way.

There is only one way, I am convinced, of working our way to a firmer and more consistent point of view, and that is to get above this naïve dualism of human and physical nature. I may even say that before we can understand the nucleus of truth in

141

TURNER'S SKETCHES AND DRAWINGS

Mr. Ruskin's own work, we must get above the unreflective realism in which the theoretical parts of his writings are steeped. Again and again, in passages of the noblest wisdom and insight, he transcends the limitations of his own thought and language, but always to sink back into the confusion inevitable to all adherents of the psychological philosophy when they come to deal with mental and moral questions.

The influence of Locke and Hume upon the form of Mr. Ruskin's theories is obvious and avowed. He believes that 'fact,' 'nature,' and 'truth' are only given in sense-perception, and that therefore sensation gives us the truest and fullest knowledge of reality; his distrust of ideas is due to the belief that they distort and obscure the revelations of this unerring mirror of reality. But these assumptions do justice neither to the real independence of the physical world, nor to the claims of the mind to discover and possess absolutely reliable knowledge. And when we are dealing with such a concrete reality as pictorial art we cannot afford to do less than the fullest justice to both nature and mind. We cannot, like the practical man or the students of the physical sciences, rule out the unseen world of human feeling as irrelevant to our immediate purposes, any more than we can neglect the concrete course of phenomena, like the student of the *a priori* forms of knowledge. In art we have to do with nature and mind in active co-operation. We are therefore bound to treat them as two factors in a common process. We cannot have two aims in art, and we cannot separate (*a*) physical objects from (*b*) an artist's thoughts and feelings; if we make the attempt we are inevitably driven, as we have seen Mr. Ruskin driven, to maintain that (*a*) is (*b*), and (*b*) (*a*), and then the point of our distinction seems lost. In art-criticism the problem is not to separate mind from nature, but to unite them—to bring out the permanent and universal relation which binds them together. And the only way to do this is to treat them both as elements or members in the formed world of the self-conscious subject.

It is not the special business of art-criticism to show that the conception of nature as what is 'given' in sense-perception, and as 'God's work' as distinguished from the action of human intelligence, is contradictory and untenable. The work is already

CONCLUSION

done. The theory of the perceptive judgment, upon which all modern philosophies, realist as well as idealist, are based, is too firmly established to render necessary any further discussion of Locke's and Hume's imperfect analysis of perception. All that art-criticism has to do is to realise that its own point of view is essentially identical with the point of view of logic and metaphysic, and to adopt and use any of the established truths of these sciences which are relevant to its purposes.

In insisting that the philosophical point of view is the only possible platform from which the facts which art-criticism deals with can be adequately correlated, I am aware that I am advancing a somewhat novel proposition. It is also one which I do not think it advisable to defend in detail on the present occasion. The present volume is the outcome of an attempt to apply this point of view. So far as all that has gone before is in harmony with my intentions, it is an exemplification of the practical usefulness of such a working hypothesis, but the subject seems to me to call for full and free discussion, and I hope on a suitable occasion to revert to it. At present I hope it will be sufficient if I say that art-criticism, if it is to be regarded as a form of knowledge, can have only one consistent aim, and that is intellectual satisfaction. And the subject-matter of art-criticism is essentially a form of communication, and therefore is concerned only with certain aspects of the formed world of human experience. And in dealing with any aspects of the ' world of discourse ' with a view to the satisfaction of our intellectual requirements of coherency and consistency of thought, the terms and ideas used in our non-systematised everyday thought and language are certainly inadequate, and those in use in all the special sciences, though valid enough when confined within the limits prescribed by their initial assumptions, are no less unsatisfactory for our purpose.

For the artist to regard nature as anything but an existing reality independent of individual experience and given ready-made in immediate perception must, no doubt, be exceedingly difficult. Both the original bent of his mind and the whole course of his professional training and practice have tended to consolidate his spatial intuitions into something apparently primary and instinctive. But an artist, as an artist, is not called upon to undertake the business of art-criticism. The difficulty, however, remains nearly as great for the art-critic, for he also is necessarily one whose visual faculties have received early and special development. When even an art-critic looks at the familiar objects with which he is surrounded and notices their sharply defined forms and colours, he finds it hard to believe that the very distinctness of these perceptions is the result of a long process of education which his own faculties have undergone. The clearness seems so unmistakably to belong to the objects. Yet however difficult the step, it must be taken. We are bound to admit that animals and infants cannot have the same ordered visual image of space definitely stretching away all round them which we are apt to regard as one of the primary and fixed constituents of the external world. But if the spatial system into which objects of perception fall so easily has to be constructed in some way by each human being for himself, it follows that pictorial art, which as a means of expression and communication is based entirely upon that system, cannot by any possibility present us with bare physical fact, with a nucleus of solid, ready-made reality—of 'God's work,' in Mr. Ruskin's sense of these terms. So that when we talk of art as representing nature, it is evident that we must be careful to distinguish exactly what we mean by such an expression. If we take it to mean that art does or can or ought to give us a copy of the given actual world as it exists apart from what Mr. Ruskin calls the meddling action of man's intelligence, then it is obvious that we have fallen into a very serious error. Apart from the action of his intellect, an artist could not possibly make the external world an object of his thought ; he could not, therefore, represent it on paper or canvas ; and even if we suppose these difficulties overcome, and the copy of bare unadulterated reality fixed on the canvas, nobody could possibly recognise it or know that it was there.

If this is so, I think it is clear that art cannot portray or represent or imitate or copy nature, at least in the sense in which nature is taken at the unreflective level of thought. What art portrays must be some part of the ideal construction present to the mind of the artist. Perhaps the simplest way of putting this is to say that the artist can operate only with ideas, and not with

CONCLUSION

any directly given elements of reality; with idea, in short, in the sense of 'meaning,' 'significance,' or 'logical content,' and not with idea as physical fact or immediate experience. But as ideas in this sense—which we must be careful to remember includes emotion—are not gifted with the property of visibility, it seems on the whole better not to say that a work of art imitates or portrays them. Strictly speaking, a work of art is a symbol, and a symbol is not a copy or imitation of the meaning it stands for. The meaning of pictorial art is then always some connected circle of psychical states with their presentative and emotional contents. These contents may refer to the common physical world of ordinary experience, or they may refer to a dream-world that has no existence except as an element of human consciousness; and this reference is determined in each case by the nature of the contents themselves.

In reducing nature in this way to an element within the consciousness of the artist and spectator, I may seem to have destroyed at a blow all the pure unsullied beauty of the external world as it exists in apparent independence of human experience. I have done nothing of the kind. I have insisted that nature, as an existent independent of individual experience, is an unreal abstraction; that the very fulness and reality and splendour of nature exist for each of us nowhere but in the world of our own consciousness, and that within that world of consciousness nature does exist as a system of objects acting and reacting on one another, and is therefore independent of the presence or absence of the consciousness which presents them.

Such a conception of nature seems to me an inevitable corollary from the general conception of the purpose and mode of action of art forced upon us by our previous investigations. From this point of view I will define a work of pictorial art as an arrangement of spatial symbols embodying an individualised psychical content present to the mind of the artist, and intended to call up always the same ideas and emotions in the minds of others. I will make no attempt to conceal my opinion that such a theory is valid of all pictorial art, and I will add that I am also disposed to think that such a point of view is a peculiarly fruitful one from which the whole field of art-criticism could be reconstituted. And as criticism, as at present understood and practised, is declared on all hands—even by its most accomplished exponents—to be bankrupt,[1] I might urge that the revolutionary character of any general theory was a strong argument in its favour. But the present occasion is not a suitable one for dwelling upon the general and far-reaching character of this theory. Here I am only justified in insisting upon its validity as a working hypothesis for the proper understanding of our immediate subject-matter. Only on such an hypothesis, it seems to me, can we give an intelligible explanation of the essential character of Turner's studies and sketches and drawings from nature, and of their connection with his completed works.

Whether this assertion is justified at all, and if so how far, depends, of course, upon the whole of the foregoing study of Turner's works, but I will add a few cursory remarks, partly of a recapitulatory nature, but treating our subject-matter from the point of view of its logical content or meaning. In these remarks I will try to deal with some of the difficulties that stand in the way of such a treatment.

We will deal first with Turner's studies of separate objects, such as those of an arm-chair (No. 563 N. G.), of fishes (373, 374 N. G.), and birds (375, 415 N. G.) among the exhibited drawings.[2] Here the artist works directly from an external object, and seems to be aiming not at the expression or representation of his own ideas, but at the reproduction of the attributes or qualities *given* in sense perception and belonging to an independent reality. The object was there before the artist began to draw it, and the artist's drawing only reproduces the visible qualities (form and colour) of the object itself. But the object is much more than its visible qualities, and even its visible qualities are far from exhausted by the one aspect of them which is all that the artist can represent. He therefore takes one aspect of an object and uses that as a sign or symbol of all the other possible aspects and sense qualities which we may suppose the object to possess. So that even if we insist on regarding the image on the paper as a particular image, it is clear

---

[1] See, for example, Professor C. J. Holmes's *Notes on the Science of Picture-Making*. Introduction.   [2] Two of these studies are reproduced in *The Genius of Turner*.

146

CONCLUSION

that it must be used as a universal sign, if it is to be understood. The profile view of a face, for instance, means or implies not only the whole head, but also the whole concrete individuality of the person to whom the profile belongs.

So far, then, as a particular visual image is used as a rallying point for calling up the whole range of ideas which constitute the thing as an object of thought, so far have we to do with a logical idea, with an element in our world of knowledge, with what is strictly an universal or an identity. A sharply defined sensuous image of a thing forms, no doubt, a more easily and generally recognisable vehicle of reference than a name, but its function as a means of communication is the same. And as in speaking and writing it is not a matter of indifference what words we use to designate the objects about which we are thinking, so in pictorial communication, the particular sensuous image employed has considerable importance in directing attention to certain constituents of the total idea called up. In this way pictorial signs certainly have a general tendency to focus attention upon the corporeity of objects, but it is, I believe, a grave error of principle not to acknowledge that all the properly associated elements of the subject referred to are more or less involved. Some elements are kept more in the background of consciousness than others, but they are very far from being non-existent.

It is important, certainly, to think of pictorial signs as endlessly supple and fluid. Even the rigidity of the meanings of words has been absurdly overstated. Poetry is only possible because the powers of evocation possessed by words are much less limited and defined than certain theorists would have us believe. But pictorial signs are more delicate agents than words. They vary in ways that words cannot. They are made *de novo* on every occasion of their use, and therefore they can adapt themselves more adroitly to each new context. And every shade of variation in the constitution of the sign has its influence in determining the constitution of the mental presentation which it calls up.

But even when we make all due allowance for the artist's power of emphasis and discrimination with regard to the elements which make up the total thought-content of his object, we must confess that the range of expression centred round any single

material object is limited. A study of such an object points to
the object it was made from—it assures us that this particular
object was bodily present to the eyes of the artist when he made
the study, but it does not tell us in what ideal context we are to
take the object. A study as such is not a work of art, or perhaps
it would be better to say that it is a mere fragment of a possible
work of art. A study is simply a pictorial name, and a name has
meaning only in a sentence or by suggesting a sentence.[1] If we
look at a study from the same point of view from which we regard
a work of art, we should go on to ask ourselves, ' Well, what of it,
what is the artist's purpose in painting or drawing this?' It
would start us upon an objectless and endless intellectual exercise,
in which we should miss the purpose which every work of art
implies.

This indeterminateness and incompleteness of meaning forms, I
believe, the essential characteristic of a study, as distinguished
from a work of art. One result, then, of our insistence upon the
content of pictorial art is the re-emergence of an old traditional
usage or term which recent theorising has done its best to discard.
Apart from the question of content, I believe there is nothing to
distinguish a study or a sketch from a complete picture.

Let us now turn from the elaborate studies of individual
objects to the pure outline drawings of places and buildings which
Turner made at the beginning of his career. The drawings of
' Ripon ' and ' Lincoln Cathedral ' here reproduced may stand as
typical of this class of work. Such drawings are defective in the
same way as the studies. Their meaning is incomplete. We do
not know exactly how to take them. They are very much on the
footing of perceptive judgments, that is to say, they are not cut
loose from the artist's personal focus of presentation. This is
what he saw at a certain moment; but why did he draw it? As a
mere record of fact, or as material which would or might be useful
in a subsequent imaginative construction? The drawings themselves do not answer these questions, but their defects of meaning
point beyond themselves.

Such drawings are also defective in another way. Being

---

[1] See Dr. Bosanquet's *Essentials of Logic*, p. 91 *sq.*

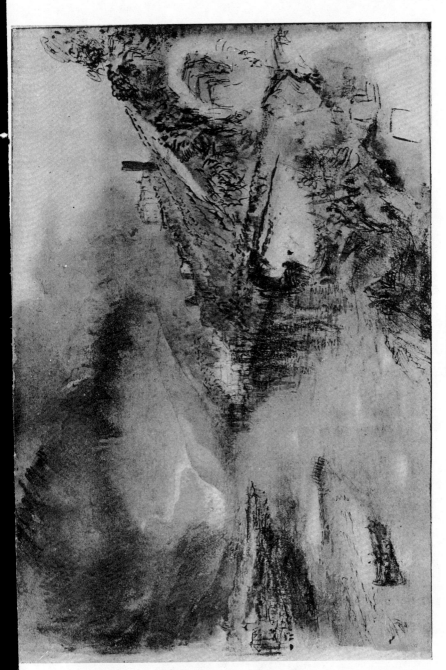

PLATE LXXXV

ON THE RHINE

WATER COLOUR. 1844

PLATE LXXXVI

BADEN, LOOKING NORTH

WATER COLOUR. 1844

CONCLUSION

entirely in outline they make abstraction of the tone, colour, and light and shade. If we are to take them as topographical illustrations they demand further visual determination, if, as having an imaginative purpose, the emotional setting of the facts calls for specification.

So far, then, we have been dealing with operations preliminary or subservient to the genuine processes of artistic expression. In studies and sketches made in the presence of the object or model the personal focus of presentation, and therefore time reference, remains clearly in evidence. It is not, I am inclined to think, till the drawing or painting cuts itself loose from the demonstrative of immediate perception that we find ourselves on the threshold of free artistic expression.

Such a sketch as that of the 'Hedging and Ditching' subject (Plate xxv.) may serve as a connecting link between the two categories. Like the drawings of Lincoln and Ripon Cathedrals, it is probably only a record of a scene actually witnessed, and as a record of the objects constituting such a scene and their relations to one another it is considerably less complete than they are. But somehow I find it hard to take it simply as a record of fact, perhaps simply because of its very incompleteness. As a symbol of a determinate complex of feeling present to the mind of the artist, it demands to be placed in a different category from those drawings which only aim at the accumulation of the raw material of artistic invention; and this in spite of its defects and insufficiencies which make it, it must be admitted, quite unintelligible as such a symbol to everybody but the artist himself. Yet here, it seems to me, we have crossed the threshold which divides a study from a work of art proper. The reference to reality is no longer direct. The artist is no longer giving evidence about matters of fact. He has cut himself free from the demonstrative of immediate perception and is groping his way towards a definitory judgment.[1] We have here an operative identity cut loose from its context, though in a singularly inarticulate form. But if so, the sketch must be taken as an incipient work of art, which possesses the capacity of growth or development.

[1] The transition is from the singular to the universal judgment. See Dr. Bosanquet's *Logic*, vol. i, chap. v ; and *Essentials of Logic*, p. 64 *sq.*

149

In the sepia drawing of this subject, reproduced in Plate XXVI., we come to a later stage of this development. Here the whole subject has become defined, not indeed to the point of realisation that would satisfy a modern artist, but sufficiently to evoke and control the ideas and emotions present to the mind of the artist. We can say if we like that such a drawing is or may be a more or less accurate realisation of an actual scene, and though such an assertion would require qualification, I do not think we could reject it altogether. But if we said that it was nothing more than such a realisation we should certainly be wrong. It is a great deal more. The connection between any fact or series of facts and the emotional standpoint from which we regard them is at times a matter of chance. But in Turner's design the connection between subjective feeling and the objects upon which our attention is focussed is not left to the caprice of chance or to the accidents of individual initiative; the connection is necessary, and objective and universal. Indeed if we examine the matter carefully we find that the whole *raison d'être* of the drawing turns upon its power of evoking and qualifying ideally a definite range of emotion. The objects selected and the manner of their presentation are such that a normal mind, so far as it understands the artist's symbols, is bound to feel about the presented scene in exactly the way that the artist felt.

Now, so long as the scene which the artist evokes exists only for the sake of suggesting and limiting a certain range of emotion, the relation of this scene to fact is entirely irrelevant. The artist is not bearing witness to what he has seen, he is defining a definite complex of thought and emotion; and as an artist, his work is complete when he has worked out this definition. When he has done this his work is complete within itself, and all direct reference to a particular time and place in the world of fact is wiped out. What we have before us is a hypothetical connection of ideal and universal meanings. We are now in the region of the hypothetical judgment. The hypothetical form is adopted not because there is any uncertainty in the matter, but because the artist wishes to concentrate attention on the attributes themselves, and not on any particular embodiment of them. The subject is taken, not given, and taken not for its own sake but for the sake of that which is to follow from it —in this case, the whole emotional complex which is to be called up.

We might, if our space were not limited, attempt to work this out more in detail. We might exhibit others of Turner's studies and designs as steps or stages in the process which aims at the complete analysis or definition of its content. But the main conception will, I hope, have been made evident. If the work of art as operative is nothing but a connection of content, it can rely upon no other driving force than that of systematic rationality. The assertions made in a work of art are made on the strength of rational grounds, and not on the strength of testimony. If the artist uses fact, he does not use it as fact, and the most outrageous fiction may be truer than fact within the four walls of his special construction. In interpreting pictures, as in following fiction, we are engaged in an act of comprehensive abstraction ; the conjunction of objects or events is all within a judgment that we are dealing with abstractions used for a certain purpose. Colonel Newcome and Turner's trees and mountains are as much abstractions and as unreal as the abstractions of the physical sciences, as matter, force, atoms, etc. —as unreal, but also quite as real, and probably in the same way. They are provisional conceptions employed for certain purposes. And all the details and secondary judgments used in interpreting a picture must be recognised as *transformed* by the system to which they belong.[1]

But each work of art though rational is nevertheless a unique individual, and though all works of art as forms of communication must necessarily aspire to the ideal of complete definition, yet it does not follow that some of the stages short of absolute determination may not very well possess considerable aesthetic interest of their own. Conversation among people who understand each other tends to become elliptical. A hint of one's meaning is generally sufficient for a friend ; indeed, when we are thoroughly assured of the good will of our auditor, a hint often conveys our meaning better than a more laboured form of expression. It is the same in pictorial art. To those who understand the language and are on terms of intimacy with the artist's usual modes of

[1] The best discussion of these points with which I am acquainted is contained in Dr. Bosanquet's *Knowledge and Reality*, pp. 140-155.

TURNER'S SKETCHES AND DRAWINGS

expression and habitual range of thought and feeling, a few hurried scribbles or washes are as delightfully suggestive and full of significance as a completed painting; and at the same time, from the very fact that we have gone more than half-way to meet the artist, we enjoy the additional pleasure of intimate intercourse. The sympathetic and imaginative and well-informed spectator is therefore apt to resent the suggestion that such delightfully eloquent sketches as the 'Pass of Faïdo,' 'Lucerne,' 'Zurich,' and a hundred others equally eloquent and suggestive, are in any way short of perfection. And no doubt from the strictly aesthetic point of view they are right. 'The best of this kind are but shadows, and the worst are no worse if imagination amend them.' But I think it is clear that considerable experience of the completed works of an artist is necessary before even the privileged spectators can feel perfect confidence in their own interpretation of the artist's slighter work. When dealing, for example, with some of the sketches and studies for marine subjects, as 'Fishermen launching a Boat in a rough Sea' (Plate XIX.), or with the marine and pastoral subjects in the *Liber*, we can interpret them with perfect confidence because, in pictures like 'The Guard Ship at the Nore,' 'Windsor,' and 'Frosty Morning,' the artist has shown us exactly the kind of completion his sketches point to. But with the latest sketches (Faïdo, Lucerne, etc.), we are on a different footing. A few only of these sketches were carried farther, and I believe I am right in saying that according to the consensus of educated opinion the subjects lost rather than gained by elaboration. I believe this opinion to be correct, and I would suggest that the explanation is not entirely to be found in the waning powers of the artist. Some mental and emotional contents are incapable of definite embodiment. The vague yearning and enigmatical unrest which form the most prominent elements in these designs are probably of that kind. Contents of such a nature that they are only partially amenable to artistic treatment are therefore more adequately treated in the less explicit forms of art. Such cases as these impress on us the importance of not confusing that mechanical kind of realisation which is known in artistic circles as 'finishing' or 'high finishing' with the demands for ideal determination. The ideal towards which all works of art

152

PLATE LXXXVII

LUCERNE: EVENING

WATER COLOUR. 1844

CONCLUSION

aspire is that of making the connection universally valid between the sign and the state of consciousness which is its meaning, *i.e.* to exclude all kinds of accidental and not strictly necessary emotional effects. But this demand is only a formal one. Where a certain ambiguity of interpretation forms a necessary factor in the meaning of the work, the demand for definition is obviously limited. The form, on a final analysis, must be determined by the content, and not *vice versa*.

In conclusion, I will only say that I am well aware of the inadequacy of these remarks, but that I cannot regard this as the proper place to amplify or develop them. I have said enough, I hope, to draw attention to the point of view which the novel character of our subject-matter has forced upon us. In dealing with the completed work of art, as art-criticism mainly does, it is comparatively easy to rest satisfied with a mere analysis of external shape, or a simple description of the machinery or anatomy of pictorial art; to treat works of art, in short, as the dried specimens of the botanist's herbarium. But when we come to study the rudimentary forms of artistic expression,—an artist's sketches and studies—we begin to discover the shortcomings of the merely statical or morphological point of view. Works of art, we find, are something more than the fossil remains or dead bodies of artistic activity. They are factors in the living process by which the artist's thought and emotion are kindled afresh in the bosom of the spectator. Instead, therefore, of merely describing the anatomy of the dead specimen, we have had to address ourselves to the much harder task of attempting to comprehend the living activity of art. The old static or morphological point of view had to give place to a dynamic or physiological system of interpretation. The emphasis was placed on function rather than on structure. The new ideal of art-criticism which has thus been forced upon me is a synthetic view of function and form, the interpretation of function in relation to structure. Art-criticism would thus become a science which treats of the mode of action of works of art and of the function of their parts. It would be concerned entirely with the positive facts of art as an active method of communication, and it would

TURNER'S SKETCHES AND DRAWINGS

seek only for verifiable generalisations—for a classified and unified account of the phenomena of artistic activity.

The present volume, with all its shortcomings and defects, is, I hope, at least a feeble and hesitating step in this direction.

154

INDEX

THE names of Turner's oil paintings and water-colours are printed in italics. Oil paintings in the National Gallery have the gallery numbers immediately after the names, thus (N.G. 523); water-colours and drawings in the National Gallery have their reference numbers in the official Inventory of the Turner Bequest, thus (T.B. CCLXXX. 184). Where I have been able to do so I have added references to the books where reproductions of the paintings, etc., have been published. These are placed at the end of the entries, in square brackets, thus [Turner Gallery, Pl. 4].

List of Volumes referred to

'The Turner Gallery.' With Memoir, etc., by R. N. Wornum.
London : James S. Virtue, . . *Referred to as* Turner Gallery

'Turner and Ruskin.' Edited by Fredk. Wedmore.
London : George Allen, 1900, . . . ,, Turner and Ruskin

'Turner.' By Sir Walter Armstrong. London : T.
Agnew and Sons, 1902, ... ,, Armstrong

'The Genius of J. M. W. Turner, R.A. Edited by
Charles Holme. Offices of 'The Studio,' 1903, . ,, Genius

'Hidden Treasures at the National Gallery.' 'Pall
Mall' Press. Holborn, 1905, . . . ,, Hidden Treasures

'The Life of J. M. W. Turner, R.A.' By P. G.
Hamerton. London : Seeley and Co., Ltd., 1895, ,, Hamerton

'J. M. W. Turner, R.A.' By W. L. Wyllie, A.R.A.
London : G. Bell & Sons, 1905, . . . ,, Wyllie

'The Water-Colours of J. M. W. Turner.' Offices
of 'The Studio,' 1909, ... ,, Water-Colours of Turner

'J. M. W. Turner, R.A.' By Robert Chignell.
London : Walter Scott Publishing Co., 1902, . ,, Chignell

'Ruskin on Pictures.' Edited by E. T. Cook,
London : George Allen, 1902, . . . ,, Ruskin on Pictures

'James Orrock, R.I. Painter, etc.' By Byron Webber.
London, 1903, ... ,, Byron Webber

TURNER'S SKETCHES AND DRAWINGS

ABBOTSFORD, 106.
Aberdulâs, Mill at, 27.
Abingdon, 11.
Abingdon, Berkshire, with a View of the Thames : Morning (N.G. 485), 5, 55, 96. [Turner Gallery, Pl. 12 ; Ruskin on Pictures, p. 24 ; Chignell, p. 24.]
' Aesthetic, History of' (B. Bosanquet's), 31.
Agnew, Messrs., 20.
Agrippina landing with the Ashes of Germanicus. Ancient Rome (N.G. 523), 119, 121. [Genius, 0-17.]
Aitken, Dr., 19.
Akenside, M., 69, 98.
Albert Memorial Museum, Exeter, 35.
Alps at Daybreak, The (T.B. CCLXXX. 184), 129.
Ambleteuse, 42, 135.
Anchorage, Ships bearing up for (Petworth House Collection), 44.
Anderdon Catalogues (Print Room, B.M.), 17.
Anselm's Chapel, with part of Thomas à Becket's Crown, St. (Whitworth Institute), 18, 19.
Antinoüs, The Belvedere, 14.
Antique Class, R.A. Schools, 14.
Apollo and Python (N.G. 121), 5. [Turner and Ruskin, vol. i, p. 42.]
Apollo, The Belvedere, 14.
Arm Chair, Study of an (T.B. XCV.(a) F.), 146.
Arnald, G., 76.
Art-Criticism and Aesthetic, separation of, 3, 136.
Arveron, Source of the (Farnley Hall Collection), 82. [Study for, Genius, MW-10.]
Avon, R., 15.

Baiae, Bay of, with Apollo and the Sibyl (N.G. 505), 88, 93. [Genius, 0-11 ; Wyllie, p. 68 ; Chignell, p. 64.]
Bamborough Castle, 34.
Barnard Castle, 34.
Basire, J., 9.
Basle (R. 5), 78, 79.
Bass Rock, the, 48.
Bath Abbey from the North-East (T.B. VII. F.), 14, 15.
Bell, Mr. C. F., 90.
Bellinzona, 140.
Bembridge Mill (T.B. XXIV. 49), 25.

156

Bernard, Dr. J. H., 32.
Berry Pomeroy Castle (R. 58), 81.
Berwick, 48.
Birds, Studies of (T.B. CCLXIII. 340 and 341), 146. [Genius, w-7.]
' Birmingham,' 20.
Blair's Hut, Mer de Glace (Farnley Hall Collection), 39. [Turner and Ruskin, vol. ii, p. 198.]
Blaze Castle (T.B. VI. 20 a), 15.
' Bolton Abbey,' 109, 110, 111.
Borrowdale, 34.
Bosanquet, Dr. B., ' Essentials of Logic,' 148, 149.
—— ' History of Aesthetic,' 31.
—— ' Knowledge and Reality,' 151.
—— ' Logic,' 149.
Boscastle, 99, 100, 102.
Boulogne, 42.
Boydell, John, 36.
Brading, Isle of Wight, 25.
Bridge and Cows (R. 2), 57, 73.
Bridgenorth, 20.
Bridgewater Sea-Piece, The, 43, 44, 45, 46. [Turner Gallery, Pl. 2.]
Bristol, 14, 15.
' British Itinerary, The,' 99.
Brocklebank, Mr. Ralph, 45.
—— Mr. Thomas, 106.
Burke, Edmund, 31.
Bury Art Gallery, 118.
Buttermere, 34.
Buttermere Lake (T.B. XXXV. 84), 35.
Buttermere Lake, with part of Cromack-water, Cumberland ; a Shower (N.G. 460), 35.
Byronism, 121, 123.
Byron, Lord, 128.
Byron's ' Childe Harold,' 88.

Caernarvon Castle, North Wales (T.B. LXX. M), 45.
Calais, 43.
Calais, Pas de. See *Now for the Painter.*
Calais Pier, with French Poissards preparing for Sea : an English Packet arriving (N.G. 472), 23, 47, 119. [Hamerton, p. 92 ; Turner Gallery, Pl. 3.]
Calais Sands, Low Water : Poissards collecting Bait (Bury Art Gallery), 118, 126. [Illus. Cat. Bury Art Gallery, p. 72.]
Callcott, Sir A. W., 4.

INDEX

Cambridge, 20.

Campbell, T., 128.

Canning, 58.

Canterbury Cathedral, St. Anselm's Chapel, with part of Thomas à Becket's Crown (Whitworth Inst.), 18, 19.

Cardiff Art Gallery, 29.

Carew Castle, 26.

Carisbrook Castle, 25.

Carlisle, 34.

Carthaginian Empire, Decline of the (N.G. 499), 88. [Turner Gallery, Pl. 21.]

'Castle of Otranto' (Walpole's), 31.

Chamounix, Mer de Glace (Farnley Hall Collection), 39. [Genius, MW-24; Turner and Ruskin, vol. ii, 196.]

Chateaubriand, 88.

Chepstow, 24.

Chester, 20.

Chinese Art, 22.

Christchurch Gate, Canterbury, 17.

Clifton Nuneham, 11.

Clydach, R., 27.

Clovelly, 99.

Cobham, 51.

Colchester, 111, 119.

Coltman, N., 99.

Combe Martin, 99.

Coniston, 34.

Content, Form and, 3.

Conway Castle, 37.

Cook's Folly, Bristol, 15.

Cook, Sir Frederick, 55.

Copper Plate Magazine, 20.

Cottage, Interior of a (T.B. XXIX. x.), 23, 24, 28. [Genius, MW-5.]

Cox, David, 4.

Crossing the Brook (N.G. 497), 87. [Turner Gallery, Pl. 18; Armstrong, Pl. 58; Genius, 0-10; Wyllie, p. 60.]

Crowle, Mr., 6.

Cumberland, 34.

Cyfarthfa Sketch Book (T.B. XLI.), 44.

Dacre Castle, Cumberland (T.B. I. D.), 9.

Daniell, Thomas, 76.

Danish Ships seized at Copenhagen entering Portsmouth Harbour. See *Spithead; Boat's Crew*, etc.

Dartmouth, 99.

Dartmouth Castle, 99.

Datur hora Quieti, 129.

Dawe, H., 81, 82.

Dayes, E. 18, 19, 124.

Deal, 135.

Decline of the Carthaginian Empire (N.G. 499), 88. [Turner Gallery, Pl. 21.]

Delacroix, 117.

De Loutherbourg, 18, 19, 31, 32, 43.

Deluge, The (N.G. 493), 45.

Derby, 20.

Derwentwater, 34.

Derwentwater, The Head of (T.B. XXXV.82),35.

Devil's Bridge, Cardiganshire, 17.

Devil's Bridge, The Little (R. 19), 80.

'Devonshire Rivers, The,' 109.

Dewick, Rev. E. S., 29.

De Wint, P., 4.

Dido and Aeneas (N.G. 494), 5, 87. [Turner Gallery, Pl. 16.]

—— *building Carthage* (N.G. 498), 87. [Genius, 0-9; Wyllie, p. 62; Turner Gallery, Pl. 19.]

—— *directing the Equipment of the Fleet* (N.G. 506), 88. [Hamerton, p. 216].

Diskobolos, The, 14.

Dolbadern Castle (Diploma Gallery, R.A.), 45. [Genius 0-1.]

Dort (Farnley Hall Collection), 96. [Mag. of Art, July, 1887, p. 300.]

Dover, 43.

Dunbar Castle, 48.

Dunbar Sketch Book (T.B. LIV.), 48.

Dunstanborough Castle, 34.

Durdham Downs, Bristol, 15.

Durham, 34.

Durham Castle, 34.

Durham Cathedral, 34.

Dutch Boats in a Gale (The Bridgewater Sea-piece), 43. [Turner Gallery, Pl. 2.]

Dying Gaul, the, 14.

EDINBURGH, 48.

Edinburgh from the Calton Hill (T.B. LX. H.), 107, 108.

Egremont, Lord, 126.

'Elegy,' Gray's, 31.

Ely Minster, Transept and Choir of, 23,

'Ely Minster, View of' (Girtin's), 19.

'England and Wales' Series, 4, 26, 96, 97, 109, 111, 112, 119, 129.

'Environs of Manchester,' Dr. Aitken's, 19,

157

Evening of the Deluge, The (N.G. 531), 119.

Evening Star The (N.G. 1991), 119. [Cassell's Illustrated Catalogue, N.G. of B. Art., p. 33.]

Ewenny Priory, Transept of, 28, 29, 30, 31.

Exile and the Rock Limpet, The (N.G. 529), 119. [Cassell's Cat., p. 136.]

FABRIS, 7.

Faïdo, Pass of (T.B. CCCLXIV. 209), 140, 152. [See 'Mod. Painters,' 1st ed.,vol. iv, pl. 20; Turner and Ruskin, vol. ii, p. 168.]

Farington, Joseph, 36.

Farm-Yard with the Cock (R. 17), 57.

Farnley Hall Collection, The, 39, 52.

Fast Castle, 49.

Fawkes, Mr. F. H., 52.

Fawkes, Walter, 91, 93, 103.

Fishermen at Sea, 23, 42.

—— *becalmed previous to a Storm — Twilight,* 42.

—— *coming Ashore at Sunset,* 42.

—— *launching a Boat,* etc. (LXVIII. 3), 152.

—— *upon a Lee-shore* (Lord Iveagh), 23, 43, 48. [Armstrong, p. 50.]

Fitzwilliam Museum, Cambridge, 18, 102.

Flint, 20.

Flint Castle. See *French Coast, Scene on the.*

Flushing, 51.

Folkestone, 135.

Folly Bridge and Bacon's Tower (T.B. I. A.), 9. [Genius, MW-1].

Form and Content, 3.

Forum Romanum (N.G. 504), 93.

Fouché's 'Memoirs,' 59.

Fowler, Captain, 15.

Franco-British Exhibition, The, 48.

Freedom and Necessity, Reconciliation of, 68.

French Coast, Scene on the (R. 4), 57, 75-78.

Frosty Morning, A (N.G. 492), 4, 5, 55, 61, 63, 64, 66, 68, 86, 87, 96, 117, 119, 152. [Hamerton, p. 148; Wyllie, p. 56; Armstrong, p. 112].

GAINSBOROUGH, T., 57.

Garrick's Temple and Hampton Court (R. 63). See *Isleworth, Scene at.*

'Genius of mechanical excellence,' 10.

Gessner, 57.

Gilpin's 'Northern Tour,' 9.

Girtin, Thomas, 19.

Glaramara, Hills of (T.B. XXXV. 83), 35.

Goodrich Castle, 26.

Gould, Mr. G. J., 52.

Goyen, Van, 28.

Gravesend, 50, 51.

Gray's 'Elegy,' 31.

Greenwich, 51.

Greenwich Park, London from (N.G. 483), 63, 80. [Genius, 0-14.]

Grose's 'Antiquities,' 9.

Guisborough Shore Sketch-Book (T.B. LII.), 48.

HAMERTON'S 'Turner,' 130.

Hannibal Crossing the Alps (N.G. 490), 5. [Turner Gallery, Pl. XIV.]

Harding, J. D., 12.

Hardwick, P. C., 10, 11, 14.

Hastings, 51.

Hayter, G., 117.

Hearne, Thomas, 18, 19.

Hedging and Ditching (R. 47), 61, 94, 119, 149.

Hereford, 15.

Herne Bay, 51,

Heysham, 103-106, 108.

High Force of Tees, 27.

Hind Head Hill (R. 25), 58, 61.

Hoare, Sir R. C., 25.

Holmes, Mr. C. J., 146.

Holt, Collection of the late Mr. R. F., 23.

Hornby Castle, 102, 103, 106, 108.

Hotwells, Bristol, The, 15.

Hugo, Victor, 129.

Hulks on the Tamar (Petworth House), 119. [Armstrong, p. 74.]

Hume, David, 85, 142, 143.

Indolence, The Fountain of, 121.

Interior of a Cottage (T.B. XXIX. X.), 23, 24, 28. [Genius, MW-5.]

Isabey, 117.

Isle of Wight, 24, 25, 26.

Isleworth Old Church, 11, 12.

Isleworth, Scene at (R. 63), 81.

Italy, 6.

Iveagh, Lord, 23, 43, 48.

JAPANESE ART, 22.

INDEX

Jason (N.G. 471), 38.
Jeffrey, F., 67.
Johnson, Dr., 33, 35.
'Judgement, Kritik of' (Kant), 31, 32.
Juvenile Tricks (R. 22), 57.

KANT'S 'KRITIK OF JUDGEMENT,' 31, 32.
Kershaw, Mr., 25.
Keswick, 34.
'—— Lake, View of' (Dayes), 19.
Kidwelly Castle, 26.
Kilgarran Castle, 41. [Armstrong, p. 40.]
King's College, Cambridge, 20.
Kingston Bank (N.G. 491), 55.
Kirkstall Abbey, 34.
Kirkstall Crypt (Soane Museum), 91.
Korin, 51.

LAMARTINE, 88, 123.
Lambert, Mr., 25.
'Landscape with Bathers' (R. Wilson), 36.
Landseer, Mr. C., 25.
Land's End, 102.
Langhorne, Dr., 69.
Laugharne Castle, 26.
Laurie, Mr., 25.
Lawrence, Sir T., 88, 90, 117.
Lee-Shore, Fishermen on a (Lord Iveagh), 23, 43, 48. [Armstrong, p. 50.]
Liebreich, Dr., 120.
Lessing, 98.
'Liber Studiorum,' 4, 48, 56, 57, 58, 61, 64, 72-83, 99, 119.
Lichfield, 20.
Life Class, R.A. Schools, 14.
Lincoln, 20.
Lincoln, Cathedral Church at (Print Room, B.M.), 20, 21, 22, 29, 31, 148, 149. [Genius, MW-4].
Lindisfarne, 34.
Lippincott, Sir H., 15.
Llandaff Cathedral (T.B. XXVIII. A), 23, 29, 31.
Llanstephen Castle, 26.
Locke, 142, 143.
London from Greenwich Park (N.G. 483), 63, 80. [Genius, 0-14.]
Loutherbourg, De, 18, 19, 31, 32, 43.
Lucerne (T.B. CCCLXIV. 324), 152.
Lysons' 'Environs of London,' 10.

Macon (Lord Yarborough), 87.
Macpherson, James, 31.
Maiden Lane, 6.
Malden, Viscount, 25.
Mallet, David, 69.
Malmesbury Abbey, 15.
Malvern Abbey, Porch of Great (Man. Whitworth Inst.) 17, 18.
Manchester, Whitworth Institute, 18, 20.
Margate, 51, 135.
Marshall, J. M. W., 11, 14.
Martello Towers, Bexhill (R. 34), 80.
Martineau, H., 59.
Matthews, Dr., 25.
Matlock, 20.
'Mechanical Excellence, Genius of,' 10, 125.
Meleager, the Vatican, 14.
Melincourt, Fall of (T.B. XXXVI. 8), 27.
Melrose, 129.
Melrose Abbey, 34.
Mer de Glace, Chamounix (Farnley Hall), 39. [Turner and Ruskin, vol. ii, 196; Genius, MW-24.]
Meuse, Entrance of the (N.G. 501), 96. [Armstrong, p. 84; Hamerton, p. 170.]
Millbank, Study at (N.G. 459), 28.
Miller, Mrs. Pitt, 45.
Millet, J. F., 67.
Milton, 31, 53, 69, 98.
Mitchell, Mr., 25.
'Modern Painters' (Ruskin), 2.
Monmouthshire, 15.
Monro, Dr., 19.
Moonlight Study at Millbank (N.G. 459), 28.
Moore, T., 88, 89.
Morland George, 43, 57.
'Morning' (Wilson), 36.
Mortlake, Early (*Summer's*) *Morning*, 88. [Armstrong, p. 118.]
—— *Terrace: Summer's Evening*, 88. [Armstrong, p. 120.]
Mossdale Fall, 102.
'Musical' Education, Defects of, 85.

NAPLES, Part of, with the Ruin'd Tower of St. Vincent, 7.
Napoleon, 42, 58, 59.
Narcissus and Echo (Petworth House), 87.
Narraways, The, 14.
Naturalism, Wordsworthian, 4.
Nature and Art, 3, 4, 8, 11, 15.

159

Needles, The, 25.

Neer, Van der, 28.

Nelson, The Death of (N.G. 480), 53, 54. [Genius, 0-5 ; Turner Gallery, Pl. 9.]

Newcome, Col. 151.

Newport, Isle of Wight, 25.

'Night Thoughts' (Young), 31.

Nile, The Battle of the, 42, 43.

Nore, Guardship at the. See *Sheerness.*

Norham Castle, 34.

Norham Castle on the Tweed, Summer's Morn, 36, 41. [Armstrong, p. 34.]

Northampton, 20.

Northumberland, 34.

Norwich School, the, 4.

Nottingham, 20.

Now for the Painter (J. M. Naylor), 96, 116. [Turner Gallery, Pl. 27.]

Nuneham Courtenay, 11.

ORROCK, Mr. J., 55.

'Ossian,' 31, 69.

Oxford, 11, 15.

—— Almanack,' 9.

—— Loan Collection, 27.

—— Sketch-Book, The (T.B. II.), 14.

—— University Galleries, 46.

Oxford, View of High Street (Wantage Coll.), 5. [Illus. Cat. of Wantage Coll.]

Oxford, View of the City of (T.B. III. B), 13.

'Pastoral' and 'Elegant Pastoral,' 56.

Paterson's 'Road Book,' 34.

Patterdale, 34.

Pembroke Bay, 24.

Pembroke Castle: Clearing up of a Thunderstorm (R. Brocklebank), 45. [Turner and Ruskin, vol. ii, p. 158 ; Armstrong, p. 50.]

Pembroke Castle: Thunderstorm approaching (Mrs. W. Pitt Miller), 45. [Genius, w-1.]

Pembury Mill (R. 12), 57.

Percy's 'Reliques,' 31.

Peterborough, 20.

—— *Cathedral: West Entrance*, 20.

Petworth, Interior at (N.G. 1988), 119.

—— *Dewy Morning* (Petworth House Coll.), 119.

—— House Collection, 44, 126.

—— *Park* (Petworth House Coll.), 126.

Petworth Park (N.G. 559), 126. [Wyllie, p. 48.]

Pilot hailing a Whitstable Hoy (Farnley Coll.), 52. [Turner and Ruskin, vol. i, p. 132 ; Genius, 0-7.]

Plato, 85.

Pleasant and Beautiful, The, 90.

Plymouth Dock, from Mount Edgecumbe, 102.

' Pocket Magazine,' 20.

' Poetry, History of English ' (Warton), 31.

Poetry, Turner's, 69, 70.

Poole, 102.

Pope's Tower, Stanton Harcourt, 11.

Portrayal and Portrayed, Problem of, 3.

'Ports of England ' Series, 4, 96, 97.

Portugal, Prince Regent of, 58.

' Prelude, The' (Wordsworth), 65.

Print Room, British Museum, 6, 17, 20.

'Provincial Antiquities,' Scott's, 4, 96, 97, 106.

Purfleet, 54.

Purley, nr. Pangbourne, 70.

Pyke-Thompson Bequest, 29.

Queen Mab's Cave (N.G. 548), 119.

Radley Hall, near Abingdon, 11, 12, 13.

Raglan Castle. See *Berry Pomeroy Castle.*

Rain, Storm, and Speed, (N.G. 538), 119. [Turner and Ruskin, vol. i, p. 270 ; Genius, 0-23 ; Wyllie, p. 132.]

Raleigh's (Professor), ' Wordsworth,' 67.

Rawlinson's ' Liber Studiorum,' 73, 78.

Reichenbach, Falls of the (Farnley Hall Collection), 39. [Genius, M.W.—19.]

' Reliques,' Percy's, 31.

Rembrandt, 67, 125.

' Review of Publications of Art,' 60.

Reynolds, Sir Joshua, 10, 125.

Richmond Castle, Yorkshire, 34.

Richmond Hill on the Prince Regent's Birthday (N.G. 502), 88.

' Richmondshire, The History of,' 4, 97, 102, 106.

Richmond, Yorks, 102.

' Rimini, Bridge of Augustus at ' (Wilson), 36.

Ripon Cathedral (T.B. XXXV. 6), 34, 148, 149.

INDEX

'Rivers of England' Series, 4, 96, 97, 99, 109, 127.
'Rivers of France' Series, 127, 129.
'Rochester Castle' (Sandby), 19.
Rochester on the Medway (T.B. ccviii. w.), 109, 127.
Rogers, Samuel, 128.
Romantic Art, Inauguration of, 31.
Rome, from Monte Mario (T.B. clxxxix. 33), 92.
Rome from the Vatican (T.B. clxxxix. 41), 88.
Rooker, M. A., 18, 19.
Roslin Castle, 48.
Rowlandson, T., 43.
Royal Academy Schools, 14.
Royal Academy, Winter Exhibition, 11.
Ruskin Bequest, Cambridge, 102.
Ruskin, Mr. John, 8, 27, 49, 90, 92, 93, 94, 110, 130.
'Ruskin on Pictures,' 50.
Ruskin's 'Elements of Drawing,' 95, 140.
—— 'Modern Painters,' 109, 138 *sq.*

St. Abb's Head, 49.
St. Anselm's Chapel, etc. — Canterbury Cathedral' (Man. Whit. Inst.), 18, 19.
St. Catherine's Hill, near Guildford (R. 33), 61.
St. Gothard, Pass of (Farnley Hall Collection), 39.
St. Vincent's Tower, Naples (T.B. i. e.), 6, 9.
Salisbury, 25.
Sandbank with Gipsies (N.G. 467), 55.
Sandby, Paul, 7, 13, 18.
Sandwich, 135.
Santayana, Mr. George, 123, 124.
Schaffhausen, Fall of the Rhine at (Tabley House), 87.
Scott, Sir Walter, 49, 88, 106, 128.
Scott's 'Provincial Antiquities,' 4.
Shee, Sir Martin A., 117.
Sheerness (Wantage Collection), 52, 53, 54, 96, 117, 152. [Armstrong, p. 52; and Illus. Cat., Wantage Collection.]
Shelley, P. B., 123, 129.
Ships bearing up for Anchorage (Petworth House Collection), 44.
Shipwreck, Studies of a (T.B. lxxxviii. 1-8), 49. [Wyllie, pp. 19-22.]

Shipwreck, The (N.G. 476), 23, 49, 50. [Genius, 0-3; Monkhouse, p. 50; Wyllie, p. 36.]
Shrewsbury, 20.
'Simple Nature,' 4, 5.
Snowstorm, The (N.G. 530), 119. [Wyllie, p. 126; Turner and Ruskin, vol. ii, p. 220.]
Soane Museum, The, 93.
Southampton, 25.
Southend, 51.
'Southern Coast, The,' 4, 96-102, 103.
Southey, R., 88.
Spinnet Player, The (T.B. ccxliv. 37), 128.
Spithead: Boat's Crew recovering an Anchor (N.G. 481), 53, 54, 60, 119. [Armstrong, p. 66; Turner and Ruskin, vol. i, p. 154.]
Spithead Sketch-Book (T.B. c.), 59, 60.
Stamford, Linc., 112, 113, 114, 129.
Stanton Harcourt, 11.
'Stanton Harcourt, The Old Kitchen at,' 9.
Stoke, near Bristol (Mrs. A. Thomas), 15.
Stonehenge at Daybreak (R. 81), 99.
Straw-Yard, The (R. 7), 57.
Strong, The late Mr. Arthur, 83.
Subject and Treatment, 3.
'Sublime and Beautiful, Essay on the' (Burke), 31.
Sunningwell, 14.
—— Church, 11, 12.
Symbolists, The French, 126.
Swinburne, A. C., 129.

Tantallon Castle, 48.
Taylor, The late Mr. J. E., 82.
Tees, High Force of, 27.
Teignmouth, 119.
Téméraire, The Fighting (N.G. 524), 5, 54. [Armstrong, p. 116; Genius, 0-19; Hamerton, p. 282; Wyllie, p. 118.]
Teniers, 57.
Thames and Medway, The Meeting of the (N.G. 813), 46. [Wyllie, p. 142.]
—— —— —— (Mr. Widener's), 52. [Armstrong, p. 54.]
Thomas, Mrs., 15.
Thomson, 57, 98.
Thomson's Lyre (Basildon House), 5.
Thornbury, Walter, 6.
Tilsit, Treaty of, 58.

TURNER'S SKETCHES AND DRAWINGS

Tintern Abbey (V. and A. Museum), 18 [Genius, MW-3].

Topographical Art, limitations of, 22.

Trafalgar, Battle of, (Greenwich Hospital), 96 [Turner and Ruskin, vol. i, p. 4; 'Hidden Treasures,' p. 91.]

Treatment and Subject, 3.

Trossachs, The, 41.

Trout Stream, The, 55, 86. [Armstrong, p. 58.]

Truth, 3.

Turner, Charles, 76.

Twickenham — Pope's Villa. See *Isleworth, Scene at.*

Tynemouth, 113-115.

ULLSWATER, 34.

Ulysses deriding Polyphemus (N.G. 508), 88, 118, 199. [Armstrong, p. 114; Turner and Ruskin, vol. i, p. 54; Genius, 0-12; Hamerton, p. 224; Wyllie, p. 80.]

Union of the Thames and Isis (N.G. 487), 55.

Usk, R., 44.

VAN DER NEER, 28.

Van Goyen, 28.

Vatican Meleager, The, 14.

Vaughan Bequest, 102.

Venice, Riva degli Schiavone, from near the Public Gardens (T.B. CCCXVI. 21), 132.

Venice, Shipping on the Riva degli Schiavone (T.B. CCCXVI. 20), 132.

Venice, The Approach to (T.B. CCCXVI. 16), 132.

Ventnor, 25.

Venus de' Medici, 14.

Via Mala, The (T.B. CCCLXIV. 362), 135.

Victoria and Albert Museum, 18, 19, 102.

Village and Castle on the Rhine (T.B. CCCLXIX. 22), 135.

Waiting for Dinner (T.B. CCCXLIV. 31), 127, 128.

Wallis Wall, Bristol, 15.

Walpole, Horace, 31.

Walton Bridges, 51.

Walton Bridges (Wantage Collection), 55. [Armstrong, p. 58.]

—— (Mr. J. Orrock), 55. [Byron Webber, vol. i, 94].

Wanstead, New Church at, 10.

Wantage, The Lady, 52, 55, 63.

Warkworth Castle, 34.

Warton, Joseph, 4, 31.

Watchet, 99, 100, 101, 102.

Waterloo, Field of (N.G. 500), 88.

Water Mill, The (R. 37), 61.

Wells, 26.

Wells, Mrs., 75.

—— W. F., 73.

Welsh Bridge, Shrewsbury (Man. Whit. Inst.), 20.

Welsh Coast, A View of the, from Cook's Folly, (T.B. VI. 9), 15.

Westall, William, 76.

Whalers (N.G. 546, 547), 119.

Whalley Bridge and Abbey (Wantage Collection), 63. [Illus. Cat. Wantage Collection.]

'Whatman's Turkey Mills,' View of (Sandby), 19.

What You Will, 88.

Wheatley, F., 18, 19, 57.

Wheeler, Mrs., 75.

Whitstable Hoy, Pilot hailing a (Farnley Hall Collection), 52. [Turner and Ruskin, vol. i, p. 132; Genius, 0-7.]

Widener, Mr. P. A. B., 52.

Wight, Isle of, 24, 25, 26.

Wilson, R., 4, 31, 32, 33, 36, 37, 39, 84.

Winchester, 25.

Windermere, 34.

Windmill and Lock (R. 27), 57, 58, 61, 94.

—— (Sir Frederick Cook), 55.[Genius 0-8]

Windsor, 15.

Windsor (N.G. 486), 4, 55, 63, 64, 67, 68, 86, 96, 117, 152.

Wint, De, 4.

Worcester, 15.

Wordsworth, 4, 65, 86, 125.

—— Dorothy, 64.

'Wordsworth' (Prof. Raleigh), 67.

Wordsworthian Naturalism, 4.

Wordsworth's ' Excursion,' 67.

162

INDEX

Wordsworth's 'Lines, composed a few miles above Tintern Abbey,' 66.
—— 'Lyrical Ballads,' 58.
—— 'Prelude,' 65.

Wrexham, 20.

YORKSHIRE, 34.

Yorkshire, Coast of, near Whitby (R. 24), 48.
'Yorkshire Series, The.' See 'Richmondshire, History of.'
Young, Edward, 4, 31.
Zurich (T.B. CCCLXIV. 289), 152. [Water-Colours of Turner, Pl. XXVII.]